THE

UNITED STATES

GOVERNED

BY

SIX HUNDRED

THOUSAND

DESPOTS

A True Story of Slavery

———————

A REDISCOVERED NARRATI
WITH A FULL BIOGRAPHY

———————

T0049139

JOHN SWANSON JACOBS

Edited by Jonathan D. S. Schroeder

The University of Chicago Press CHICAGO AND LONDON

The University of Chicago Press, Chicago 60637
The University of Chicago Press, Ltd., London
© 2024 by The University of Chicago
Published 2024
Printed in the United States of America

33 32 31 30 29 28 27 26 25 24   1 2 3 4 5

ISBN-13: 978-0-226-83280-7 (cloth)
ISBN-13: 978-0-226-68430-7 (paper)
ISBN-13: 978-0-226-83281-4 (e-book)
DOI: https://doi.org/10.7208/chicago/9780226832814.001.0001

Library of Congress Cataloging-in-Publication Data

Names: Jacobs, John S., 1815–1875, author. | Schroeder, Jonathan (D. S.),
    1981– editor.
Title: The United States governed by six hundred thousand despots : a true
    story of slavery : a rediscovered narrative, with a full biography / John
    Swanson Jacobs ; edited by Jonathan D. S. Schroeder.
Other titles: United States governed by 600,000 despots
Description: Chicago : The University of Chicago Press, 2024. | Includes
    bibliographical references and index.
Identifiers: LCCN 2023039961 | ISBN 9780226832807 (cloth) |
    ISBN 9780226684307 (paperback) | ISBN 9780226832814 (ebook)
Subjects: LCSH: Jacobs, John S., 1815–1875. | Jacobs, Harriet A. (Harriet
    Ann), 1813–1897. | African Americans—North Carolina—Biography. |
    Fugitive slaves—North Carolina—Biography. | Enslaved persons—
    North Carolina—Biography. | Enslaved persons—United States—
    Biography. | Slavery—North Carolina. | Slavery—United States.
Classification: LCC E450 .J33 2024 | DDC 973/.049607300922 [B]—dc23/
    eng/20230919
LC record available at https://lccn.loc.gov/2023039961

♾ This paper meets the requirements of ANSI/NISO Z39.48-1992
(Permanence of Paper).

THE
UNITED STATES
GOVERNED
by
SIX HUNDRED
THOUSAND
DESPOTS

Joseph Whiting Stock, *A Portrait of John Swanson Jacobs*
(currently known as *The Man Holding the Liberator*).
Courtesy of the African American Museum in Philadelphia.

to SHEIDA,
who betters worlds

CONTENTS

THE UNITED STATES GOVERNED BY

SIX HUNDRED THOUSAND DESPOTS:

A TRUE STORY OF SLAVERY

John Swanson Jacobs

ONE

The Death of Mrs. Hanablue, and the

TWO

THREE

NO LONGER YOURS:

THE LIVES OF JOHN SWANSON JACOBS

Jonathan D. S. Schroeder

75

INTRODUCTION

A Global Slave Narrative

Since I cannot forget that I was a slave, I will not forget those that are slaves. What I would have done for my liberty I am willing to do for theirs, whenever I can see them ready to fill a freeman's grave, rather than wear a tyrant's chain. The day must come; it will come. Human nature will be human nature; crush it as you may, it changes not; but woe to that country where the sun of liberty has to rise up out of a sea of blood.

JOHN SWANSON JACOBS, *The United States Governed by Six Hundred Thousand Despots: A True Story of Slavery* (1855)

No outside tongue, however gifted with eloquence, can tell their story; no outside eye, however penetrating, can see their wants; no outside organization, however benevolently intended, nor however cunningly contrived, can develope the energies and aspirations which make up their mission.

THOMAS HAMILTON, "Apology (Introductory)," *Anglo-African Magazine* (1859)

In the spring of 1855, a man walked into the office of a newspaper called the *Empire* in Sydney, Australia, with an unusual request: he wanted to borrow a "correct copy" of the United States Constitution and Richard Hildreth's recently completed *History of the United States*. In "a style of speech decidedly American," the "respectably dressed" person gave a "modestly expressed apology," presumably for causing any inconvenience. The office buzzed, work stopped, and the daily routine of getting out the paper was broken as all eyes turned to the greater "novelty" unfolding before them. For the person, one editor wrote, was not simply an American but an American "man of colour"—though his "complexion would be hardly noticeable among the average specimens of the English face." In admitting that the man could pass as white, the editor inadvertently revealed that it was only by noting other details that they were able to read him as Black. Invisible to the eye, these details pressed upon other senses, above all the ear. Something in his "manner" led them to read him as Black, but, more important, as a man not to be taken lightly.[1]

By jamming their ordinary modes of knowing the world, the stranger was making an example of himself. And in so doing, he was artfully training them to dignify his Blackness. He drew his audience's attention to his cultivation, evident in his clothes and the way he wore them, the way he moved, expressed emotion, modulated his voice, chose his words. For these white Australians, as for the white audiences he had performed before in New England, New York, and aboard ships and in goldfields around the world, his sophistication made him mysterious. What could explain how this man had come to seem "intelligent on almost any subject," "appear at ease in any society," and speak with a "fluency and depth of interest scarcely excelled by any of his predecessors—even by [Frederick] Douglass himself?"[2] And how had this American come to Australia, of all places?

With "bright intelligent eyes" and a "gentle firm voice," he patiently answered their questions, gaining respect and drawing them in, until they found themselves listening with "abiding interest," hungry for more information. How he had attained his powers was not their chief concern, for these were newspapermen, on the lookout not for narratives of education and uplift but for a story that sold. And this man was just that: a story. Staying one step ahead of them and knowing from long experience how it would play, he revealed that he was a capital *F*, capital *S*, "Fugitive Slave," who had come to Australia and succeeded in the gold rush that had followed California's and who was now about to go to sea. For almost all his remaining life, from 1856, when he sailed for England, until 1872, when he returned to America at the end of his life, he would be in constant motion, sailing to every corner of the world, spending three hundred-plus days a year on the water, touching solid ground only briefly at far-flung ports like Elsinore and St. Petersburg, Constantinople and Odessa, Bangkok and St. Kitts, even working in India for part of 1867. At that precise moment, in 1855, however, he was "engaged in writing out his experiences of American slavery."[3]

And so, in a matter of minutes, a Black man with no country walked into the office of the leading newspaper in Sydney and not only disarmed the editorial staff but so intrigued them by performing his self-fashioning that they were persuaded to do something much more than lend out a few books. They agreed to publish his life story.

———

We don't know whether John Swanson Jacobs mentioned that he called Frederick Douglass a friend and ally and had five years before lectured alongside him as a rising star in the antislavery movement. And we can only assume that he didn't mention his sister, Harriet Ann Jacobs, who was still five years away from finding a publisher for her landmark autobiography, *Incidents in the Life of a Slave Girl*, as she had been unable to find a suitably famous white abolition-ist to edit, introduce, and legitimize her book, a virtual prerequisite for Black authors to publish in the transatlantic abolitionist world (she would be rejected at least three times before summoning up the courage to approach Lydia Maria Child). But we can be sure about one thing: the *Empire* editors were not ready for what was coming to them.

Two weeks later, John Jacobs returned with a manuscript with a truly awesome title: *The United States Governed by Six Hundred Thousand Despots: A True Story of Slavery*. By citing the six hun-dred thousand slave-owning Americans in his title, instead of the three million enslaved people more commonly mentioned by abolitionists, Jacobs announces from the start that his will be no standard slave narrative. Rather than make himself into an example of the horrors of slavery, John Jacobs turns his life into an arc of refusal.[4] And what he refuses is America itself. Not only does his autobiography zero in on the stark injustice of owning humans, concentrating his dazzling intellectual and emotional powers into casting his Blackness against this sharpest of white backgrounds, but it does so for a higher end: to prove that slavery and white supremacy are written into the conceptual bedrock of the American republic, starting with the Constitution, the "bulwark of American slavery." "The slave's life is a lingering death," he writes, and not simply because "six hundred thousand legalised robbers" operate a violent, abusive system of labor exploitation but because American law permits them to do so. And since the "law" is "the will of the people—a mirror to reflect a nation's character," Jacobs holds all American citizens, South and North, accountable for writing despotism—absolute rule over an unfree people—into a democratic charter. "That devil in sheepskin called the Constitution of the United States," which "contains and tolerates the blackest code of laws in existence," represents "the great chain that binds the north and south together, a union to rob and plunder the sons of Africa, a union cemented with human blood, and blackened with the guilt of 68 years."[5] Taking John Jacobs at his word requires taking seriously political theorist Judith Shklar's claim that, in 1776, the American nation "embarked upon two experiments simultaneously: one in democracy, the other in tyranny."[6]

Reading such rhetorically gifted, unapologetically defiant prose, it becomes clear that John's performance for the Australian editors had been an act, an effort to ease open the doors to publication so that he could write with the righteous fury that his condition as a fugitive slave after 1850 demanded—but that no transatlantic antislavery publisher permitted. Although he was a stateless refugee and migrant laborer, Jacobs was able to find a forum to print his narrative that did not come with the usual strings attached. He did not have to accept the indignity of giving a white ghostwriter free rein over his words as a condition of publication. Neither did he have to festoon his narrative with certificates of good character solicited from notable white abolitionists, nor pay the psychic tax levied on Black Americans when forced to choose between expressing righteous anger over the injustices of the world or remaining silent in the hopes of improving their lot.[7] In choosing to make a forthright profession of his hatred of slavery, in a style that dissolves the false but widely held opposition between rage and reason, John turned an unenviable situation to his advantage, using it to demonstrate that his own unfiltered, unedited words could stand as proof of his self-worth.

It is to the editors' credit that they "scarcely altered a word" of John Jacobs's manuscript other than correcting spelling and adding punctuation. Consequently, the recovery of *Despots* gives us an unprecedented chance to understand how, outside American law and humanitarian authority, African Americans reconfigured the relationship between liberty and truth. While the promise of gaining direct access to the "mind of a slave" through unedited texts has made handwritten manuscripts of autobiographical slave narratives into a holy grail for some scholars, *Despots* reveals that there is something more precious still: an *unfiltered* text. The rediscovery and republication of this lost autobiography represents the first opportunity to reckon with John Swanson Jacobs. Beyond American power, Jacobs speaks truth to American power, in a life story built on the conviction that words can ring so true as to build new worlds, a conviction that Jacobs and Douglass shared: "Yours for the truth," he writes to his friend.[8]

And yet even as John Jacobs found that he enjoyed greater freedom of speech in Australia than in the US or UK, his story was forgotten. In 1860, he would try to find an audience once again, submitting a copy of *Despots* to a London magazine called the *Leisure Hour* before leaving on a voyage to Rio de Janeiro, where an epidemic of yellow fever swept through the ship's crew, killing two, hospitalizing John. On returning to London, how crestfallen must he have been to find his once powerful narrative chopped in half, censored and rewritten, and published under a sanitized title, *A True Tale of Slavery*? At about half the word count, the 1861 version contains about sixty paragraphs in common; of these, a handful are identical, while the rest are censored, rearranged, and reworded. The entire legal critique is eliminated, and the text is recomposed as a relatively conventional autobiographical slave narrative. Until now, that declawed version has been the primary means by which the public has come to know John Jacobs.

The Discovery

The United States Governed by Six Hundred Thousand Despots has been utterly lost since 1855—surviving only in libraries, attics, and old stacks of unread newspapers. Since writing his autobiography, John Swanson Jacobs has become a footnote in his sister's life, even though he once stood side by side with some of the most important and daring transatlantic abolitionists: not only his sister and Douglass but also F. W. Chesson, William and Ellen Craft, Martin Robison Delany, William Lloyd Garrison, William Cooper Nell, Sarah Parker Remond, and George Thompson. I discovered John Jacobs's autobiography on the night of October 26, 2016, while researching the fate of Harriet Jacobs's son, Joseph Jacobs, who had followed John to the Australian mines and supposedly killed himself in Melbourne in 1860. This is arguably the most important recovery of an autobiographical slave narrative on record, with the only notable exception his sister's *Incidents*, which was believed to have been written by Lydia Maria Child and passed off as the fictionalized autobiography of Linda Brent until the 1980s, when Jean Fagan Yellin proved that "Linda Brent" was Harriet Jacobs's pseudonym and that Jacobs had written her own autobiography. Almost all other pre-1863 narratives were published as stand-alone hardbound volumes and were never lost so much as no longer read. When renewed interest in the slave narrative "gained a place in the 1940s," in Marion Starling's words, proclamations that these narratives were lost, made in service of promoting a new field of study, tended to equate "loss" with "out of print," and indeed by the 1940s all known slave narratives, with the exception of *The Life and Times of Frederick Douglass*, were out of print.[9] Until recently, however, no genuinely lost narratives have been rediscovered, and none so significant as *Despots*.[10] If no other narrative had so little impact at the time, had no afterlife, and was so completely forgotten as *Despots*, no narrative has so much to offer now. When viewed as an African American autobiographical slave narrative, published outside American borders by a Black citizen of the world and written by a person with intimate ties to Harriet Jacobs and Douglass, this work now stands to open up new routes for the study of race, ethnicity, and migration.

More than ten million African-descended people lived and died in American slavery between 1619 and 1863. Yet fewer than one hundred firsthand accounts survive.[11] Since the early 1970s, as part of a sweeping effort to confront the legacy of slavery head-on and combat the evasions of an earlier historiography, scholars have restored the African American autobiographical slave narrative to its rightful place at the heart of American history. The slave narrative constitutes the most direct form of testimony about slavery and the most important document for understanding both the history of slavery and the literature of the Black diaspora. Exemplary works such as the *Narrative of the Life of Frederick Douglass, an American Slave* (1845) and Harriet Ann Jacobs's *Incidents in the Life of a Slave Girl* (1861) have emerged as radiant objects for understanding men's and women's lives under slavery, the problems awaiting African Americans afterward, and the potential of Black lives to thrive against the odds.

Despots is a major contribution to the tradition of Black protest that runs from David Walker's *Appeal* (1829) through Black Lives Matter. The uncompromising antislavery politics and apocalyptic intelligence of John Jacobs's narrative, so reminiscent of Douglass, hint at the closeness between the two men. At the same time, John's story allows us to establish a series of connections between Douglass and Harriet Jacobs that have been obscured ever since *Incidents* was rewritten and rearranged by Child, who famously removed a final chapter on the revolutionary martyr John Brown. It now seems likely that what Child sought to eliminate was the frank truth-to-power language that the Jacobs siblings had developed in conjunction with Douglass in Rochester, New York, in the late 1840s, when John traversed the Northeast on lecture tours with Douglass and others, and Harriet ran the Anti-Slavery Reading Room above the *North Star* office.[12] It was in Rochester that the Jacobs siblings began writing their life's stories. Given how much their autobiographies converge around shared life experience, narrate common events, and connect thematically—the sentimental and unsentimental, personal and impersonal, Black femininity and masculinity, and the sensational and legal constraints of citizenship—it is quite possible that Harriet and John intended for their stories to be read together, as two sides of the coin of slavery and abolition.[13] These texts certainly should be read together today.

Yet if *Despots* provides new opportunities for closing the gap between the Jacobses and Douglass, it also demonstrates what sets John Jacobs apart from his sister, his friend, and all other authors in the genre. For his narrative is not the work of a full-time abolitionist, clergyman, prisoner awaiting the gallows, or fugitive slave whose case was taken up by white publishers. Indeed, it is the only known slave narrative written by a revolutionary Black sailor.[14] It is likewise the only known slave narrative printed outside the abolitionist network that linked the United States, Canada, and Great Britain. *Despots* is a text that stands for the untold lives of millions of individuals who left their homes fleeing slavery, persecution, genocide, war, authoritarianism, and other catastrophes.

By 1855, when *Despots* was printed in Sydney, John Jacobs had given up his promising career as an abolitionist. The Fugitive Slave Act of 1850 had confronted him with a terrible choice: either betray William Lloyd Garrison's credo—*No Union with Slaveholders!*—by letting others purchase his freedom, or continue to speak in public as a fugitive and risk reenslavement. He instead found a third way, falling back on the one trade that he knew would take men of color like him and allow him to leave American slavery behind: the sea. Unlike Douglass, who permitted two Scottish antislavery women to buy his freedom and thereafter began to abandon Garrison's belief that the Constitution was a proslavery document—"a covenant with death, an agreement with hell"—Jacobs remained true to the Garrisonian position that the transformation of the United States from a slave state into a free society could not be "achieved through politics within the Union" because the Constitution represented an "insurmountable impediment."[15] Thus, far from a retreat from political action, John's turn to the sea can be viewed as a more extreme commitment to the core tenets of radical abolition. "If the American flag is to be planted on the altar of freedom, then I am ready to be offered on that altar, if I am wanted," Jacobs wrote from London at the outbreak of the Civil War, but "if it must wave over the slave, with his chains and fetters clanking, let me breathe the free air of another land, and die a man and not a chattel."[16] It is the sheer force of this commitment that unites him with the many-headed hydra of pirates, slaves, servants, and outcasts who devised and disseminated radical ideas about freedom and equality in the age of sail and steam.[17]

When *Despots* was published, Harriet was on the other side of the world writing out her own story at Idlewild, the Hudson River Valley estate where she worked as a nurse for the children of her employers, Cornelia Grinnell Willis and Nathaniel Parker Willis. The rediscovery of *Despots* prompts us to wonder how Harriet would have written *Incidents* had she gone to California in 1850 with John, as she had talked about.[18] What would *Incidents* look like if she had shed the layers of obligation the Willises had put her under? If they had not secretly purchased her freedom in the spring of 1853 and she had become not a fugitive slave in America but an ex-American, a Black citizen of the world like John? If she had published her manuscript without the editorial intervention of Lydia Maria Child? To appreciate what was, what might have been, and what can still be, we turn to John Jacobs's autobiography itself.

The Narrative

Printed in the *Empire* in two installments, on back-to-back days in April 1855, on elephant folio paper twice the size of a page of today's *New York Times*, *Despots* strains against the conventions of the slave narrative genre, ultimately turning them inside out (see figure 0.1). Signally, the narrative refuses the sentimental objectification of Black life in favor of a go-for-broke denunciation of slavery and the state—a style that radically rewrites the humanitarian contract between reader and text. The first seven chapters, which make up the first installment, are devoted to life in slavery, and cover the period from John's birth in Edenton, North Carolina, in 1815 until his escape in New York in 1839. The second installment's four chapters begin with an account of John's 1839–43 whaling voyage to the Pacific, his reunion with his sister in New York, and the renewed attempts of the Norcom family to recapture her. In the last three chapters, *Despots* departs from slave narrative convention and autobiography altogether, no longer interweaving vignettes of Jacobs's own life as a slave and the slave lives of others in North Carolina. Instead, Jacobs directly critiques the Constitution, the Declaration of Independence, and the Fugitive Slave Act of 1850. Throughout, the narrative uses personal experience and eyewitness accounts to speak to structural oppression and serve as occasions for denunciation; through this potent combination, readers come to recognize broader logics at work in slavery and the state, as well as the narrative itself. As critique, these moments connect the cruelty of slavery to unregulated economic self-interest, proslavery Christianity, a corrupt legal system, and a morally bankrupt nation. As narrative, they constitute a symbolic journey through a fallen world, in which Jacobs's exposure to the laws, customs, and institutions of the nation leads not to the walls of Jericho tumbling down but to his growing conviction that the only true escape from slavery is to leave America altogether.

Yet even as the first installment adopts the opening phrase, "I was born," and standard time line—from birth until escape—that characterize the genre of the slave narrative, there is very little that is autobiographical in it, if by autobiography one means the creative and active use of memory to give "patterned significance" to a narrated sequence of events called a life.[19] Remarkably, the second installment abandons any attempt to narrate individual experience in favor of delivering readings of America's founding documents.[20] Jacobs calls these readings "interlineations." By borrowing this term from the law, he instructs readers to recognize that he is writing *between the lines* of American law and that he is doing so as a *stranger*, a person who does not benefit from these laws, because they were not written for him and because, as an exile, they no longer apply to him—not that they ever did when he was enslaved.[21] It becomes apparent that this section is not merely "tacked on at the end to demonstrate post-narrative activities of the narrator" but is integral to the narrative, the logical conclusion to a sustained argument about the law, Black life in the absence of personhood, and the moral imperative to disobey and otherwise evade unjust laws.[22] In fact, in these chapters, Jacobs's narrative suggests that the essays and speeches that often close slave narratives may be the best places to discover—by reading between the lines—what is most intrinsically autobiographical about an author.

This is because ex-slave authors were typically precluded from writing traditional autobiography. In particular, they were unable to use memory creatively and deliberately because they were expected to portray "American slavery as it is." To do so, and to earn audiences' trust and dissolve suspicions of their bona fides, they had to create the impression that they were *not* giving their own meanings to events in their lives by acting as if their memory were neither creative nor faulty but an objective, neutral record of experience. As if in a courtroom, they were supposed to provide testimony that faithfully and truthfully transmitted their experiences and could be easily corroborated. Ex-slave narrators thus found that white abolitionists placed the highest value on events that were public, depicted the social and institutional aspects of slavery, and contributed to abolitionism.[23] All other events in their lives—particularly

THE UNITED STATES GOVERNED BY SIX HUNDRED THOUSAND DESPOTS.

A TRUE STORY OF SLAVERY.

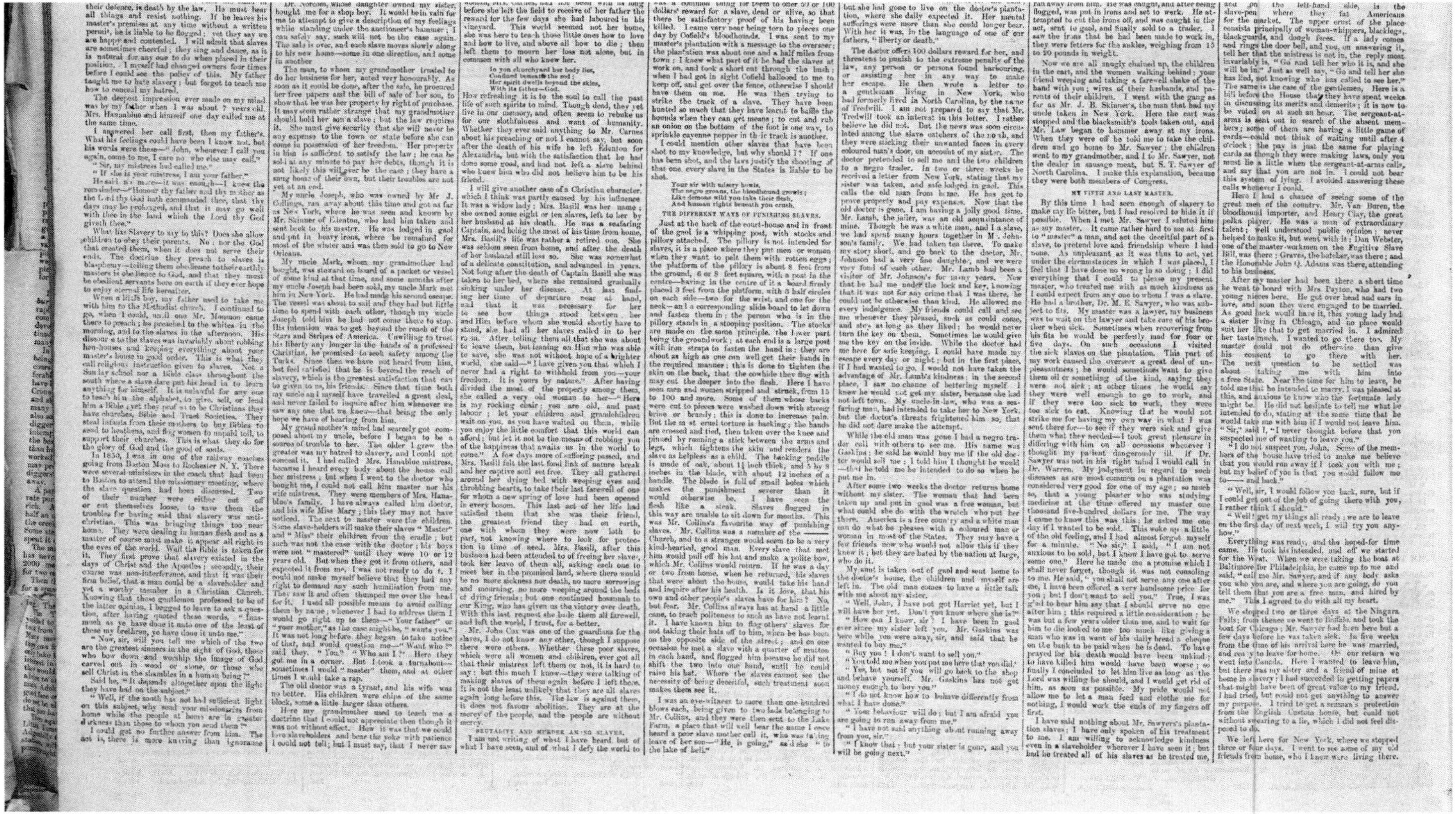

FIGURE 0.1. *Despots* in the *Empire*, April 25, 1855, Sydney, Australia. Courtesy of the State Library of New South Wales.

the intimacies of private life and Black communal life, including extended family, friends, and ancestors—were considered irrelevant if they did not contribute to "the cause."

Despots refuses to play this game. Paradoxically, by reducing the account of his autobiographical experience to a minimum, John creates more space to critique slavery *and* more space to narrate his own life on his own terms. *Despots* directs readers' attention to the numerous ways that the law actively creates openings for acts of violence by slaveowners. At the same time, it does not tell a story of how slavery made the narrator abject. In contrast to *Incidents*, which narrates how the master-slave relationship traps Harriet in a vicious cycle of spiritual anguish and bodily pain, John's *Despots* is unsentimental to its core. This is not to say that the narrative refuses emotion, tears, and calls to humanity altogether. Rather, it refuses a sentimental mode that is hardwired into the liberal contradictions of American national fantasy and that makes scenes of pain serve as both the embodiment of Black *inhumanity* and proof of Black humanity. For Jacobs, this effort "to produce political worlds and citizen-subjects who are regulated by the natural justice" gener-ated by consuming this pain is a major problem.[24] Not only does it privatize feeling, but it also turns the body in pain into a machine for translating the complexity of individual Black experience into general claims of structural injustices. This is why for James Bald-win, "sentimentality" is no mark of true feeling, but its opposite, "the mark of dishonesty, the inability to feel; the wet eyes of the sentimentalist betray his aversion to experience, his fear of life, his arid heart; and it is always, therefore, the signal of secret and vio-lent inhumanity, the mask of cruelty."[25] Jacobs belongs within this tradition of Black radical antisentimentalism.

The problem that he confronts in *Despots* is how to prevent his story from becoming enmeshed within sentimental conventions of narrative suffering while also remaining true to the facts and feelings of his subordination. He therefore devises a new auto-biographical style focused on the actors who are most responsible for structural injustice. His body does not appear at all, and he refrains from making spectacles of the suffering of other Black bodies too. And this is not simply a result of gender difference. Of his sister Harriet, who suffered from chronic pain and physical disability from her nearly seven-year confinement in their grandmother's garret, he simply says that "the change that it had made in her, was enough to make one's soul cry out against this curse of curses, that has so long trampled humanity in the dust."[26] And in comparison with Douglass's infamously voyeuristic scene of the whipping of his aunt Hester, through which a young Frederick Bailey crossed the "blood-stained gate, the entrance to hell of slavery," consider Jacobs's account of the whipping of the pregnant Agnes. His description is neither sentimental nor pornographic, for he does not depict an entire scene at all.[27] In fact, he represents himself not as a spectator but as a caretaker, who comes to Agnes to dress her back and apply the oils and salves he had learned to make for Dr. James A. Norcom. Crucially, Agnes's back is the only part of her body described. If slaveowners enacted their violence in the marketplace by breaking the bodies of the enslaved down into parts (field *hands*, long *fingers* for picking cotton, and so on), and if sentimental texts both humanize and dehumanize the enslaved in order to develop a sense of social obligation among the privileged, John reverses these operations by turning Agnes's back to the reader.[28]

Instead of reproducing trauma without consent, Jacobs's carefully delimited description serves as an act of repair, a response to violent fragmentation that does not further objectify Agnes, that does not use her wounding to galvanize white sympathy (as in the "scourged back" photo of ex-slave Peter published in *Harper's* in 1863).[29] Rather, Jacobs draws attention away from her body toward the people who kill and the state and federal laws that license the killing of the Black body. It is perhaps for such reasons that he does not mention his sister's sexual domination by Norcom and Samuel Tredwell Sawyer. "When I have thought of all that would pain the eye, sicken the heart, and make us turn our *backs* to the scene and weep," he concludes, expanding our vision, "I then think of the oppressed struggling with their oppressors, and have a scene more horrible still."[30] In this and other passages, Jacobs anticipates Saidiya Hartman's claim that the only thing "more obscene than the brutality unleashed at the whipping post is the demand that this suffering be materialized and evidenced by the display of the tortured body or endless recitations of the ghastly and the terrible." One must turn away from such "routinized violence" toward areas where terror and violence are diffused and distributed. Whereas Hartman turns to scenes "of pleasure, paternalism, and property," Jacobs turns to the domain of the law.[31] It is the law that not only makes such violence possible but also disenfranchises Jacobs of his own emotions and sensations by rendering them politically meaningless. "I would be ashamed of myself to offer these acts of wanton cruelty as a reason why slavery should be abolished," he writes, for "if they can be considered an evil, they are a necessary evil, and you can only remove the evil by removing the cause."

Therefore, rather than direct attention to the wrong place by painting the slave with the brushstrokes of abjection, he points a finger squarely at slaveowners, politicians, and proslavery institutions and holds them responsible. This is why he calls out America's despots by their names. They include wealthy North Carolina planters such as Stephen Cabarrus, Josiah and James Coffield, and John Beasley, and Washington politicians such as John Calhoun, Henry Clay, Martin Van Buren, and Daniel Webster, all of whom played leading roles in the proslavery compromises of 1820, 1833, and 1850. And sometimes, as in the case of Sawyer—John's former master, father of Harriet's two children, and a congressman who becomes less willing to free the Jacobses the closer he gets to national power—his reasons go far beyond the law. *Despots* challenges readers to form not a sentimental relationship that focuses on the pain of the enslaved but a revolutionary one that traces bodily and psychic pain to its sources: the master and the state.

In drawing this new contract, Jacobs abandons the humanitarian injunction for ex-slave authors to prove their worthiness as humans on a scale that implicitly defined the human as white. And in doing so, he fashions himself as an alternative to Enlightenment conceptions of the human and humanity. As a prophet of justice, he harangues: "Do you ever expect to see the day when the stranger and sojourner with you will not be dragged from your doors? Do you believe that God holds you guiltless of the blood of the three million slaves?" Yet this is no American jeremiad, no call for the nation to recommit to its founding promise and divinely ordained mission, but a condemnation from a stranger outside the state.[32] "The blood of your coloured countrymen cries out against you— the laws of God condemn you."

This is precisely the kind of writing that led slaveowners to hang sailors found with David Walker's *Appeal* in their possession. And this is precisely the kind of "philosophy" that white abolitionists steered Douglass away from. "Give us the facts," one American Anti-Slavery Society member notoriously said, "we will take care of the philosophy."[33] Like Douglass, who found it unsatisfying simply to "repeat the same old story" of his life over and over "to *narrate* wrongs," Jacobs "felt like *denouncing* them." And faced with the fact that those who govern in America refused to give him his right to govern himself, Jacobs decided, like Martin Delany, that "emigration beyond the United States is a necessary condition for any and every colored individual currently inhabiting the United States to obtain political liberty."[34] In exile, it became possible for him not to show how slavery formed him but to state the opinions *he* had formed about slavery. Beyond the state, beyond fear, beyond unequal compromises, the very opinions that Black narrators were not supposed to profess because they were supposed to be too subjective and too radical become the very best evidence of Black resilience, brilliance, and individuality. As a fugitive from America, but no longer a fugitive slave, he could represent himself, expressing the intrinsic and sincere worth of his life through the creative performance of his own words.

The language of *Despots* constitutes a spectacular performance of autobiographical freedom. It is the account of a remarkable man committing his life to paper in each turn of phrase, change of tone, inside joke, and argument. He startles with presence: "Here I am!

looking through the grates of your prison." He is revolutionary with a chiasmus: "Give me liberty with a cannibal, rather than slavery with a professed Christian." He has timing: "I believe Henry Clay is as good an authority as I can find for the introduction of slavery into the United States, which was at that time one of the British colonies. At least, he has said as much against slavery and done as little for liberty as any man." He is rebellious: "I am not writing of what I have heard, but of what I have seen, and of what I defy the world to prove false." He is a poet: "Like demons wild you take their flesh / And human rights beneath you crush." And he is everyone and no one: an American slave in a foreign land.

Framing *Despots* as a radical truth-telling text draws out over-looked aspects of Harriet's *Incidents*, beginning with its represen-tation of "America as a negative space, a massive space of darkness, ghosts, shame, and barbarism." In a remarkable twist on the trope of the pilgrimage to Washington, DC, and particularly Elizabeth Keckley's *Behind the Scenes; or, Thirty Years a Slave, and Four Years in the White House* (1868), John Jacobs relates traveling to the nation's capital with Sawyer in 1837. In this "place that I so much wanted to see," a naïve Jacobs discovers that visible from the windows of the White House, "where they make laws for a nation of freemen," are the nation's slave pens, "where they fat Americans for the mar-ket." Yet Jacobs is no innocent, but puts on a parade of public vio-lations of democratic principle, in the process turning the format of national spectacle inside out; like Harriet, he experiences "a psy-chic rage at America for not even trying to live up to the condi-tions of citizenship it promises in law and spirit."[35] When Harriet writes that "if the secret memoirs of many members of Congress should be published, curious details would be unfolded," she refers to the sexual morality of men like Sawyer and Charles Johnson, fellow Edentonians and North Carolina congressmen. When John describes the secret history that unfolds before him as he works the Washington hotels and boardinghouses where politicians lodge and socialize, he says that he "could not bear" perpetuating "this system of lying" by lying on behalf of politicians who would rather gamble than vote on a bill in the House.

Yet for both siblings, pulling back the curtains on private life does not lead to any scandalous revelations of why the nation is the way it is. In different ways, they both refuse "to affirm the private horizon of personal entitlement as the cause of their suffering," and instead hold America directly accountable for the tyranny of sexual exploitation and the system of slavery, which blurs the line between personal and national tyranny. The nation and its laws suffuse and shape the private experience of people of different statuses, right down to the way they feel, think, and are embodied. And in fact, it is a privilege of "liberal tyrants" like Sawyer to believe that "his relative personal integrity and good intentions place him above moral culpability that he has no need to act morally within the law." In taking politicians off the pedestal of abstract rights and returning them, in Lauren Berlant's words, to the "sensational constraints of citizenship," Harriet and John "subversively transfer the horizon of national identity" to the powerless, giving them room to create "a fantasy of cutting across the space that doesn't exist, where abstract and corporeal citizenship come into their contradictory contact not on the exploited and minoritized body but on *the body of the nation*."[36] Just as Harriet turns the master's tools of misrecognition and deception inside out with her anecdote about an illiterate enslaved woman who believed that the Queen of America had forced the president to free all the slaves, John casts himself as the standard-bearer of Justice, carrying a vision of a future beyond the Sodom and Gomorrah called Washington. "That poor, ignorant woman thought that America was governed by a Queen, to whom the President was subordinate. I wish the President was subordinate to Queen Justice," Harriet calls. "Woe to that country where the sun of liberty has to rise out of a sea of blood," John responds.

Writing from as far away from America as possible, John Jacobs creates a new style for the African American slave narrative. We might call it the "art of refusal." Refusal is not a single act but

an arc and a repertoire, and typically involves stopping produc-
tive or reproductive labor to "leave, suspend use in festival, hide
out, rehearse some new moves, corporealize different habits, inten-
sify use, try out a new world, imagine it, make it real, join up with
others, fight with each other, care for each other, come back and
claim your right to the city, too."[37] *Despots* reveals the extremes to
which Black individuals would go to achieve freedom, and it does
so not through the 1840s art of self-transformation of a slave into
"an 'American hero' and into an agent of his own destiny" (à la
Douglass's *Narrative*), nor through the 1850s art of escape as self-
transformation, in which a "peripatetic" narrator's "migrant trav-
els were put forth precisely to expose the ironies of U.S. domestic
enslavement" (à la William and Ellen Craft's *Running a Thousand
Miles for Freedom*).[38]

We can now return John Jacobs to the heart of an America
that has forgotten him. Looking outside the nation by taking off
the blinders of ideology, as he did, means writing back against the
myth of the United States of America as a nation that progressively
eradicates the legacy of its original sin through the development
of its democratic institutions. If *Despots* is any indication, great
power lies in these narratives. Given that an estimated 5 percent
of all Black Americans left the US after 1850 for Britain, Canada,
Jamaica, Australia, and elsewhere, what other narratives did these
expatriates leave behind?[39] The history of the *global* slave narrative
has yet to be told.

A NOTE ON THE TEXT

The text of *The United States Governed by Six Hundred Thousand Despots: A True Story of Slavery*, by John Swanson Jacobs, is reproduced here in book form almost exactly as it appeared in the *Empire* newspaper on April 25 and 26, 1855. Some typos have been corrected and some paragraph breaks inserted (see the list of emendations).

I present *No Longer Yours: The Lives of John Swanson Jacobs* as a companion piece to support readings of *Despots* and expand understandings of Jacobs's life beyond the events and time line covered in his autobiography.

Bookending these two books are my introduction and my essay "John Jacobs at First Sight: Notes on a Frontispiece," which describes the challenge of identifying the first-known image of Jacobs. The two appendixes contain all known writings by Jacobs, aside from "A True Tale of Slavery," and the most important contemporaneous writings about him. All notes are mine. I only refer to John and Harriet Jacobs by their first names when absolutely necessary.

JDSS

SINCE I CAN-NOT FORGET THAT I WAS A SLAVE, I WILL NOT FORGET THOSE THAT ARE SLAVES.

THE

UNITED STATES

GOVERNED

BY

SIX HUNDRED

THOUSAND

DESPOTS

A True Story of Slavery, Showing:—

1. *That Brutality is inseparable from Slavery.*
2. *That the Constitution of the United States of America is the Bulwark of American Slavery.*
3. *That the only hope of abolition of Slavery is in separation from the Union.**

by a Fugitive Slave.

---

* With this trio of claims, Jacobs aligns himself with the abolitionist positions of Frederick Douglass and William Lloyd Garrison, and distinguishes himself

from the position set out by James Gillespie Birney in *The American Churches, the Bulwarks of American Slavery* (1840), a work that John R. McKivigan described as "an uncompromising exposé of proslavery church practices." Birney, along with Arthur and Lewis Tappan, founded the Liberty Party in 1840 following a schism in the American Anti-Slavery Society between the moderate Liberty position and the more radical Garrisonians, who called for total withdrawal from membership in proslavery churches and refusal to vote and hold public office. Despite their growing differences, both Douglass and Garrison continued for most of the 1840s to view the Constitution, and specifically the Fugitive Slave Law, as the chief "bulwark of slavery" in America. John R. McKivigan, *The War against Proslavery Religion: Abolitionism and the Northern Churches, 1830–1865* (Ithaca, NY: Cornell University Press, 1984), 146.

[About a month ago, a respectably dressed man came into the Editor's room in *The Empire* Office, and, after a modestly expressed apology, begged to be informed where he could obtain the loan of Hildreth's *History of the United States*, and a correct copy of the American Constitution, stating that he had endeavoured to purchase them at the booksellers, but had not succeeded in his enquiries.* The novelty of the application at once awakened some curiosity; and the person before us had sufficient in his manner and appearance to deepen that feeling into one of abiding interest. He was a "man of colour," whose complexion would be hardly noticeable among the average specimens of the English face, about thirty-five or forty years of age, with bright intelligent eyes, a gentle firm voice, and a style of speech decidedly American. In answer to some interrogatories which the occasion suggested, he said briefly, that he was engaged in writing out his experiences of American slavery, and wanted the books in question for reference, and was prepared to deposit a sum of money in excess of their value with any one who would lend them to him. Hildreth's *History*, and the last edition of

* In 1855, the *Empire* was located at 490 George Street in Sydney, Australia. Founded by Henry Parkes, the paper ran from December 28, 1850, to February 14, 1875. During Parkes's stewardship (1850–59), it frequently published strong denunciations of American slavery and supported the Anglo-American abolitionist movement. "Notice of Removal," *Empire*, May 9, 1854.

the United States' Constitution authorised by Congress, happened to be among our own office books, and they were supplied to our new acquaintance, he, on his own proposition, depositing in the hands of our office porter a bank note for £10 as security for their due return.* A fortnight afterwards, the Fugitive Slave—for such he had acknowledged himself to be—again presented himself at our office to return the books; and at the same time he produced, and left in our hands the following written narrative. In publishing this "unvarnished tale," and, in many respects, really eloquent account of slavery, we have scarcely altered a word used by the writer, or done more than correct the orthography and divide it into readable sentences.† The writer is in Sydney; we understand he has been among the successful gold-diggers, and is now about

* Richard Hildreth (1807–1865) was a philosopher and translator of Jeremy Bentham; a historian and author of *The History of the United States of America*, 6 vols. (New York: Harper & Brothers, 1840–53); a lawyer and founder of the *Boston Atlas*; and an abolitionist and author of antislavery works such as *The Slave: Or Memoirs of Archy Moore* (Boston: John H. Eastburn, 1836) and *Despotism in America; or, An Inquiry into the Nature and Results of the Slave-holding System in the United States* (Boston: Whipple and Damrell, 1840). John Swanson Jacobs and his sister, Harriet Ann Jacobs, sold Hildreth's works at the Anti-Slavery Reading Room in Rochester in 1849. On Hildreth, see Jean Fagan Yellin, *The Intricate Knot: Black Figures in American Literature, 1776–1863* (New York: New York University Press, 1972). Except when noted, all subsequent references to Hildreth are to the *History*.

The edition of the *Constitution* is *The Constitution of the United States of America, with an Alphabetical Analysis; The Declaration of Independence; The Articles of Confederation; The Prominent Political Acts of George Washington; Electoral Votes for all the Presidents and Vice-Presidents; the High Authorities and Civil Offices of Government, from March 4, 1789 to March 3, 1847; Chronological Narrative of the Several States; and Other Interesting Matter; with a Descriptive Account of the State Papers, Public Documents, and Other Sources of Political and Statistical Information at the Seat of Government* (Philadelphia: T. K. and P. G. Collins, 1854). Arranged by William Hickey, a member of the Senate clerical staff, the manual was in its seventh edition at the time; Jacobs refers to Hickey's revised edition at the beginning of chapter 9.

† Shakespeare, *Othello*, 1:3:106. Othello: "I will a round unvarnished tale deliver."

changing his occupation by going to sea. We shall be much mistaken, if his narrative is not read with a lively interest.—ED. E.*]

I WAS BORN IN EDENTON, NORTH CAROLINA, one of the oldest States in the Union, and had five different owners in 18 years. My first owner was Miss Penelope Hanablue, the invalid daughter of an innkeeper. After her death I became the property of her mother. My only sister was given to a niece of hers and daughter of Dr. James A. Norcom.†

My father and mother were slaves. I have a very slight recollection of my mother who died when I was quite young, though my father made impressions on my mind in childhood that can never be forgotten. I should do my dear old grandmother injustice did I not mention her too; for there was too great a difference between her meekness and my father's fury, though slavery had caused it.‡

---

* Perhaps Alfred Ellis (1825–1901), subeditor of the *Empire* under Parkes. "Obituary," *Goulburn Herald*, April 19, 1901.

† Jacobs lists four, not five, owners in "A True Tale of Slavery," hereafter cited as TT: (1) Margaret Horniblow (1797–1825, here called Penelope Hanablue), the invalid daughter of tavernkeeper John Horniblow (CA. 1748–99) and (2) Elizabeth Horniblow (CA. 1755–1827); (3) Dr. James A. Norcom (1778–1850); and (4) Congressman and father of Harriet Jacobs's two children Samuel Tredwell Sawyer (1800–1865). The fifth owner listed in *Despots* is the slave trader Law, who bought Jacobs from Norcom with the intention to sell him to Sawyer. In her will of April 8, 1825, Margaret Horniblow bequeathed to her mother, Elizabeth, "one negro Girl named Harriett one negro boy named John," as well as their uncle Mark Ramsey. On July 3, 1825, in a deathbed codicil, Elizabeth gave Harriet to her niece Mary Matilda Norcom (1794–1863), second wife of James Norcom. Norcom became John's third owner on January 1, 1828. Samuel Tredwell Sawyer bought Jacobs around 1836 from Norcom, through a slave trader. Will of Margaret Horniblow, 1825, Chowan County Wills and Estate Papers, 1663–1978, North Carolina State Archives, hereafter cited as NCSA; A List of the Property belonging to the Estate of Elizabeth Horniblow sold on the 1st January 1828, Estate of Elizabeth Horniblow, Chowan County Wills and Estate Papers, 1663–1978, NCSA; *Harriet Jacobs Family Papers*, hereafter cited as *HJFP*, 1:17–21. (See abbreviations list for full citations of abbreviated sources.)

‡ John and Harriet's parents were Elijah Knox and Delilah Horniblow. Elijah (CA. 1798–CA. 1826), was owned by Dr. Andrew Knox, and after 1816, by his widow,

To be a man and not to be—a father without authority—a husband and no protector—is far pleasanter to dream of than to experience.

Such is the condition of every slave throughout the United States; he owns nothing—he can claim nothing. His wife is not his—his children are not his; they can be taken from him, and sold at any minute, as far as the fleshmonger may see fit to carry them. Slaves are recognised as property by the law and can own nothing except at the consent of their masters. A slave's wife or daughter may be insulted before his eyes with impunity; he himself may be called on to torture them, and dare not refuse. To raise his hand in their defence, is death by the law. He must bear all things and resist nothing. If he leaves his master's premises at any time without a written permit, he is liable to be flogged; yet they say we are happy and contented.* I will admit that slaves are sometimes cheerful; they sing and dance, as it is natural for any one to do when placed in their position. I myself had changed owners four times before

---

Sarah Penelope Knox, and by 1824, by their daughter, Lavinia Matilda Knox. Delilah (1798–CA. 1819) was the daughter of Molly Horniblow (CA. 1770–1853), the slave of Elizabeth Pritchard Horniblow, who gave Delilah to her daughter Margaret. Will of Dr. Andrew Knox, May 20, 1816, Pasquotank County Wills, 1720–1941, NCSA; Inventory and Account of Sales of the Personal Estate of Dr. Andrew Knox, 1816, Pasquotank County Wills and Estate Papers, 1663–1978, NCSA; Estate of Elizabeth Horniblow; Answer of James Norcom to Bills of Complaint of Frederick Hoskins and His Wife Eliza, Apr. 7, 1834, *HJFP*, 1:29–34.

* Slaves were neither allowed to own real property nor to receive legacies. In 1741, the North Carolina General Assembly passed a series of acts prohibiting slaves from owning livestock and weapons. The acts severely circumscribed slaves' mobility, requiring a written "certificate of leave" to "go off the Plantation," prohibiting the use of boats, and setting up procedures for capturing, imprisoning, and returning fugitive slaves. The state's Supreme Court "refused to hear arguments of self-defense or accidental homicide in an 1857 appeal from a slave husband who was condemned to die for the attempted rescue of his wife, which resulted in the death of the overseer, who was beating her." See Thomas Cunningham's Heirs v. Thomas Cunningham's Executors, I N.C. 519 (1801), *The Public Acts of the General Assembly of North-Carolina* vol. 1, ed. James Iredell and François-Xavier Martin (New Bern, NC: Martin & Ogden, 1804), 45–66; Robert McNamara v. John Kerns et al., 24 N.C. 66 (1841); Thomas Waddill v. Charlotte D. Martin, 38 N.C. 562 (1845); State v. David, a Slave, 49 N.C. 353 (1857); *HJFP*, 1:317–18.

I could see the policy of this. My father taught me to hate slavery; but forgot to teach me how to conceal my hatred.

The deepest impression ever made on my mind was by my father when I was about 7 years old. Mrs. Hanablue and himself one day called me at the same time.

I answered her call first, then my father's. What his feelings could have been I know not, but his words were these—"John, whenever I call you again, come to me, I care not who else may call."

"Sir, my mistress had called me."

"If she is your mistress, I am your father."*

He said no more—it was enough—I knew the remainder—"Honour thy father and thy mother as the Lord thy God hath commanded thee, that thy days may be prolonged, and that it may go well with thee in the land which the Lord thy God giveth thee."†

What has Slavery to say to this? Does she allow children to obey their parents? No: nor the God that created them, when it does not serve their ends. The doctrine they preach to slaves is blasphemy—telling them obedience to their earthly masters is obedience to God, and that they must be obedient servants here on earth if they ever hope to enjoy eternal life hereafter.

When a little boy, my father used to take me with him to the Methodist church. I continued to go, when I could, until one Mr. Moumon came there to preach; he preached to the whites in the morning, and to the slaves in the afternoon.‡ His discourse to the slaves was invariably about robbing henhouses and keeping everything about your master's house in good order. This is what they

---

* In her *Incidents in the Life of a Slave Girl*, Harriet Jacobs reproduces this scene from a third-person point of view. "You are *my* child," replied our father, "and when I call you, you should come immediately, if you have to pass through fire and water." Harriet A. Jacobs, *Incidents in the Life of a Slave Girl, Written by Herself; with "A True Tale of Slavery" by John S. Jacobs*, ed. Jean Fagan Yellin (Cambridge, MA: Belknap Press of Harvard University Press, 2009), 11.

† Deuteronomy 5:16. The version of the Bible quoted is the Authorized Version (also known as the King James Bible) throughout.

‡ Samuel Tucker Moorman (1803–87) became pastor of the Edenton Methodist Church in 1835.

call religious instruction given to slaves. Not a Sunday school nor a Bible class throughout the south where a slave dare put his head in to learn anything for himself. It is unlawful for any one to teach him the alphabet, to give, sell, or lend him a Bible; yet they profess to be Christians they have churches, Bible and Tract Societies. They steal infants from their mothers to buy Bibles to send to heathens, and flog women to unpaid toil, to support their churches. This is what they do for the glory of God and the good of souls.

In 1850, I was in one of the railway coaches going from Boston Mass to Rochester N.Y. There were several ministers in the coach that had been to Boston to attend the missionary meeting, where the slave question had been discussed.* Two of their number were either cut off or cut themselves loose, to save them the trouble, for having said that slavery was anti-Christian. This was bringing things too near home. They were dealing in human flesh and as a matter of course must make it appear all right in the eyes of the world. Well the Bible is taken for it. They first prove that slavery existed in the days of Christ and the Apostles; secondly, their course was non-interference, and that it was their firm belief, that a man could be a slaveholder and yet a worthy member in a Christian Church. Knowing that these gentlemen professed to be of the latter opinion, I begged leave to ask a question, after having quoted

---

* The meeting that Jacobs refers to is the 1848 annual session of the American Board of Commissioners for Foreign Missions, held at Tremont Temple in Boston. The recording secretary read a letter from the Choctaw Mission (a particularly contentious issue for abolitionists that year) that said that "they had wished to preserve a strict neutrality in reference to all exciting subjects. They found slavery there, when the mission was first established—it was a civil institution, and, as such, they had no concern with it. They were not citizens, and were liable at any time to be expelled from the country. Our Savior and his Apostles (they say,) did not interfere with the dreadful evil of slavery, and they were satisfied to follow such example." "Anniversaries," *Boston Semi-Weekly Atlas*, September 20, 1848.

Jacobs had already developed a version of this story by spring 1849. See "The Anniversaries: American Anti-Slavery Society; Third Day," *New York Herald*, May 11, 1849, in appendix 1, 252–54.

these words, "Inasmuch as ye have done it unto one of the least of these my brethren, ye have done it unto me."*

"Now, sir, will you tell me which of the two are the greatest sinners in the sight of God, those who bow down and worship the image of God carved out in wood or stone, or those who sell Christ in the shambles in a human being?"†

Said he, "It depends altogether upon the light they have had on the subject."

"Well, if the south has not had sufficient light on this subject, why send your missionaries from home while the people at home are in greater darkness than those to whom you send them?"

I could get no further answer from him. The fact is, there is more knaving than ignorance among them. A man that will sell his own offspring, which thousands of them have done, has shown himself unnatural enough to do anything. They admit that a negro has a soul, but it must be a very painful acknowledgment to a nation whose prejudices are so strong. Go into the free States, or rather the so-called free States, for there is not a spot in that country, from one end to the other, whence I could not be dragged into slavery. I begin at the schoolhouse, I suppose myself a father living in one of these so-called free States. We have town schools in the different wards, I am always ready to pay my tax to help support these schools, but when I send my children they are told, "We don't keep school here for niggers."

There is my poll-tax I have paid. Am I not allowed to vote? "No, we don't allow niggers at the ballot box here."

Having grown sick of such treatment, I take my wife and children and go in search of a State where they will treat us according to our behaviour and not our colour. I have paid my passage on the

---

* Matthew 25:40.
† 1 Corinthians 10:24–26: "Let no man seek his own, but every man another's *wealth*. Whatsoever is sold in the shambles, *that* eat, asking no question for conscience sake. For the earth *is* the Lord's, and the fulness thereof." According to the *Oxford English Dictionary*, a "shambles" can mean a meat-market, flesh-market, or slaughterhouse.

steamer. As soon as I step foot into the saloon, with my wife and children, I am told that "niggers are not allowed here."

"But, sir, I have a cabin-ticket."

"I don't care for that, I tell you niggers are not allowed here." The boat lands. I go to an Hotel.

"Sir, can I be accommodated here?"

"Whom are you with?"

"No one but my family."

"No, we don't accommodate niggers here."

I go to another, "Can I get supper and lodgings here to night?"

"Yes, yes,—walk in."

The bell rings, I take my wife and children, and start for the tea room.

"Where are you going?"

"To supper, sir."

"We don't sit niggers down with white folks here."

We will suppose the next day Sunday. The church-bells are ringing, and the cold reception we have met with hath made my heart sick and my life a burthen. What say you if we go to church? It is agreed on. We enter. In going down the aisle I am politely touched on the shoulder—"There is a seat in that corner for niggers."

"Sir, my wife is a member of this sect, of good and regular standing in her own church. This being Communion-day, she wishes to be with you."

"Oh, yes, brother; well, she must come this afternoon; we are going to take it this forenoon—this afternoon we will give it to the niggers."

I will suppose one of my children dead. It has been christened in this church. I apply to the church for the privilege of burying my child in their ground.

"Oh no, that will never do; we cannot allow niggers to be buried with white folks."

Poor foolish man! Here your reign of tyranny is over. Can you prevent us from entering the kingdom of heaven or the gates of hell with white folks? You follow us to the grave with your prejudices, but you can go no further.

When asked why we are treated thus, the answer is, "They are an ignorant, degraded race." Why are we ignorant and degraded? Are not the avenues to knowledge closed against us, and we made to black your boots, scrape your chin, cook your food, and do the rest of your dirty work, or starve? Do we not see it everywhere staring us in the face, as plain as though it were written—"No admittance here for niggers." True, your demoralising and brutalising process for three hundred and thirty-three years is enough to have unfitted us for society, but are you still afraid to give us and our sons an equal chance with you and yours?* Yes, you see as clear as that king whose knees smote together with fear, from the writing on the wall, that ignorance is the only hope of slavery, that to enlighten the slaves would be to liberate them.†

* Jacobs is concerned here with the beginning not of slavery in the United States, in 1619, but of the transatlantic slave trade. In August 1518, Emperor Charles V of Spain granted a charter to Laurent de Gorrevod allowing four thousand slaves to be purchased directly from Portuguese slave traders in the Cape Verde Islands and transported to the New World. In abolishing a provision requiring slaves to be born under Christian dominion, he effectively created the transatlantic slave trade; the first known transatlantic slave ships arrived in Hispaniola, Puerto Rico, and Cuba in the mid-1520s.

† At Belshazzar's feast, the fingers of a human hand are seen writing on a wall *MENE, MENE, TEKEL, UPHARSIN*. In the book of Daniel, the words are defined as: "MENE; God hath numbered thy kingdom, and finished it," "TEKEL; Thou art weighed in the balances, and art found wanting," and "PERES: Thy kingdom is divided, and given to the Medes and Persians." Adam Clarke, *The Holy Bible: Containing the Old and New Testaments*, vol. 4 (New York: T. Mason and G. Lane, 1837), 588.

ONE

THE DEATH *of*
MRS. HANABLUE,
and THE SALE *of*
HER SLAVES
at PUBLIC AUCTION

Here they are, old and young, male and female, married and single, to be sold to the highest bidder.* My father, who belonged to a Mrs. Knox, is now dead; and I have no one to look to for parental

---

* See *Incidents*, 12–14. Elizabeth Horniblow died on August 24, 1827. On January 1, 1828, her executors, Dr. James Norcom and William R. Norcom, auctioned off her property. In *Incidents*, we read that Elizabeth had promised that, upon her death, Harriet and John's grandmother, Molly Horniblow, would be freed. James Norcom, however, "offered to sell Molly privately, ostensibly to save her embarrassment, but she rejected his offer because she knew that 'her mistress intended she should be free, [and] she was determined the public should know' of her sale and condemn Norcom for acting against the dead woman's wishes. Apparently using the money she had saved from years of midnight baking, Molly arranged for Hannah Pritchard (?–1836), Elizabeth Horniblow's sister, to buy her and her older son Mark." Pritchard bought Mark for $406 and Molly for $52.25 (*HJFP*, 1:19–20). Pritchard owned no property, and John suggests that it was to Congressman Alfred Moore Gatlin (1790–1841), Pritchard's attorney, that Molly entrusted her savings. Gatlin served in Congress for one term (1823–25). Molly's daughter Betty was the property of Mary Horniblow Norcom. John does not mention Molly's other daughter, Becky, the property of Elizabeth Horniblow Hoskins, who had left Edenton. See Will of Elizabeth Horniblow, 1827, Chowan County Wills, 1760–1942, NCSA; Estate of Elizabeth Horniblow; Chowan County Deed Book G-2, 395 [1817], NCSA; Answer of James Norcom.

affection and advice save my grandmother, whose gray hairs and many years' service in the public-house did not excuse her from the auctioneer's hammer.* But she was not without a friend. She placed some thirty years' savings of money in his hands to purchase her and her son. She had two other children, a son and a daughter, but they were owned by other parties.

They began to sell off the old slaves first, as rubbish; one very old man sold for one dollar; the old cook sold for 17 dollars; from that to 1,600 dollars, which was the price of a young man who was a carpenter.

Dr. Norcom, whose daughter owned my sister, bought me for a shop boy. It would be in vain for me to attempt to give a description of my feelings while standing under the auctioneer's hammer; I can safely say, such will not be the case again. The sale is over, and each slave moves slowly along to his new home—some in one direction, and some in another.†

The man, to whom my grandmother trusted to do her business for her, acted very honourably. As soon as it could be done, after the sale, he procured her free papers and the bill of sale of her son, to show that he was her property by right of purchase. It may seem rather strange that my grandmother should hold her son a slave;

---

* In his will of 1816, Andrew Knox bequeathed Elijah, or "Lyde," to his wife, Sarah Penelope Knox; by 1824, Elijah "had become the property of his young mistress, Lavinia Matilda Knox" (1806–1828). After Lavinia married James Coffield on June 22, 1824, Elijah was moved to Greenhall Plantation 6.5 miles north of Edenton and was prevented from seeing his children. Elijah died sometime between 1826 and 1827. Molly Horniblow worked at Horniblow's Tavern. *HJFP*, 1:lxxiv. In TT, Jacobs writes that this displacement "added another link to his galling chain—sent another arrow to his bleeding heart. My father, who had an intensely acute feeling of the wrongs of slavery, sank into a state of mental dejection, which, combined with bodily illness, occasioned his death when I was eleven years of age."

† "Records indicate that a slave named Bridget brought the lowest price; she was bought by Dr. James Norcom for $17.50. Charles was sold to Joseph H. Skinner for $630, the highest price of the day. Norcom bought John S. for $298.50. Tom, Esther, and Mourning brought $279, $80, and $130, respectively." *HJFP*, 1:318, Estate of Elizabeth Horniblow.

but the law requires it. She must give security that she will never be any expense to the town or state before she can come in possession of her freedom. Her property in him is sufficient to satisfy the law; he can be sold at any minute to pay her debts, though it is not likely this will ever be the case; they have a snug home of their own, but their troubles are not yet at an end.

My uncle Joseph, who was owned by Mr. J. Collins, ran away about this time and got as far as New York, where he was seen and known by Mr. Skinner of Edenton, who had him taken and sent back to his master. He was lodged in gaol and put in heavy irons, where he remained for most of the winter and was then sold to go to New Orleans.*

My uncle Mark, whom my grandmother had bought, was steward on board of a packet or vessel of some kind at that time, and some months after my uncle Joseph had been sold, my uncle Mark met him in New York. He had made his second escape. The vessel was about to sail and they had but little time to spend with each other, though my uncle Joseph told him he had not come there to stop. His intention was to get beyond the reach of the Stars and Stripes of America. Unwilling to trust his liberty any longer in the hands of a professed Christian, he promised to seek safety among the Turks. Since then we have not heard from him, but feel satisfied

---

* See *Incidents*, 21–32 ("The Slave who Dared to Feel like a Man") for Joseph/ Benjamin's escape. At the second division of John Horniblow's property in 1813, the slaves were grouped into four shares of equal value, except for Joseph, who was not valued because he was to be divided later between Horniblow's daughters Margaret and Elizabeth. In 1817, James Norcom petitioned on behalf of his wife, Mary Horniblow Norcom, and her younger sisters that Joseph be sold, and on January 1, 1818, Joseph, "aged twelve years or thereabouts," was sold to Josiah Collins II (1763–1839), a wealthy London-born planter, merchant, and banker, for $675. In 1817, Collins willed his 4,000-acre plantation, Somerset Place, to his son, Josiah Collins III (1808–63); this place, called in *Despots* "the lake of hell," was home to several hundred enslaved people and is probably where Joseph was sent to live. In New York, Joseph was apprehended by Collins's attorney, Joseph Blount Skinner (1781–1851); Petition of James Norcom, 1817, Estate of John Horniblow, 1799, Chowan Wills and Estate Papers, 1663–1978, NCSA; Bill of Sale no. 463, Chowan Deeds, 1696–1878, Book G2, p. 375; *HJFP*, 1:6–8, 12–17.

that he is beyond the reach of slavery, which is the greatest satisfaction that can be given to us, his friends. Since that time both my uncle and myself have travelled a great deal, and never failed to inquire after him whenever we saw any one that we knew—that being the only hope we have of hearing from him.

My grandmother's mind had scarcely got composed about my uncle, before I began to be a source of trouble to her. The older I grew the greater was my hatred to slavery, and I could not conceal it. I had called Mrs. Hanablue mistress, because I heard everybody about the house call her mistress; but when I went to the doctor who bought me, I could not call him master nor his wife mistress. They were members of Mrs. Hanablue's family. I have always called him doctor, and his wife Miss Mary; this they may not have noticed. The next to master were the children. Some slaveholders will make their slaves "Master" and "Miss" their children from the cradle; but such was not the case with the doctor; his boys were not "mastered" until they were 10 or 12 years old. But when they got it from others, and expected it from me, I was not ready to do it. I could not make myself believe that they had any right to demand any such humiliation from me. They saw it and often thumped me over the head for it. I used all possible means to avoid calling them by name; whenever I had to address them I would go right up to them—"Your father" or "your mother," as the case might be, "wants you." It was not long before they began to take notice of that, and would question me—"Want who?" said they. "You." "Who am I?" Here they got me in a corner. But I took a turnabout—sometimes I would "master" them, and at other times I would take a rap.

The old doctor was a tyrant, and his wife was no better. His children were chips off the same block, some a little larger than others.*

Here my grandmother used to teach me a doctrine that I could not appreciate then though it was not without effect. How it was that we could love slaveholders and bear the yoke with patience

* Norcom had at least nine children with his two wives, and, according to Harriet, eleven illegitimate children with his slaves. *Incidents*, 43.

I could not tell; but I must say, that I never saw anything in her, that I could construe into hatred towards anyone. I have seen her treat these very children that were growing up to kick me about, with as much kindness as though they were hers—in fact, they would always look for something good, whenever they went where she was. I could daily see her, practising that which she so much wanted to teach me—love and forgiveness; to love those who loved not me, and forgive those that ill-treated me—a principle though right and just in itself, yet it is all that poor nature can do, and she is often found too weak for that.

TWO

THE

HAPPY FAMILY,

or PRACTICAL

CHRISTIANITY

There are many acts of men that are called acts of Christianity; but the practical Christian need not tell the world what he is.* He is known and felt by all around of a kindred spirit. The words from his lips affect the soul of man, as drops of water the drooping plant. Such I have seen in the Slave States, but they are like lilies among thorns. Having nothing around to reflect back their beauty, they seem to be unfit for this world, or the world unfit for them. Such was the case with the Rev. Mr. Carnes, and his family. They had lived in Alexandria previous to their coming to Edenton. Mrs. Carnes had no children of her own. They had a woman with several children, whose husband was free, but she and the children belonged to Mr. Carnes; but as well as I could learn no longer than

---

* In "Standard of Practical Christianity" (1839), Adin Ballou and other founders of the Hopedale Community set forth a species of Christianity defined by one grand object, "the restoration of man, especially the most fallen and friendless." In eschewing worldly objects and interests, practical Christians put "the love of *Right*" and the "cause of universal righteousness" above all other considerations. See *Autobiography of Adin Ballou, 1830–1890, Containing an Elaborate Record and Narrative of His Life from Infancy to Old Age*, ed. William S. Heywood (Lowell, MA: Vox Populi Press, 1896), 309, 310. For John S. Jacobs's lecture at Hopedale in 1848, see Abby H. Price, "Anti-Slavery Convention at Milford," in appendix 2, 233–35.

they saw fit to stop. Though they belonged to different churches, there seemed to be that love and union which adorns the Christian, and commends him to the world.*

The question about what Paul or Apollos preached did not disturb them; their chief study was their duty to God, and to man.† Mrs. Carnes employed herself in teaching the children how to read and write. Her affection for the children, and theirs for her, in return, made her task a pleasant one. She was more like a mother than a mistress, so much so that their mother and father gave themselves no care about them farther than to keep them clean and neat, knowing that Mrs. Carnes would do more for them than they could possibly do. Mr. Carnes had not been there long before the degraded state in which he found the slaves everywhere around him attracted his attention; and seeing that some of the other sects had given the use of the church to the slaves at stated times for evil, he resolved to get the use of his church, if possible, for their good. It was agreed on by the members, that he could have the use of it every Sunday evening to preach to the slaves. At first, they cared but little to go and hear Mr. Carnes, thinking that no good could be gained by going to the brick church. It was known by this name to all the slaves, and the members were considered a congregation of tyrants; but Mr. Carnes had not preached many sermons before his congregation rapidly increased, and he was satisfied that they appreciated his labours of love. He also took great pleasure in explaining such passages of Scripture as they could not understand to all who would call at his house. The slaves occupied the pews; and their masters, if any of them came, occupied the gallery. His sermons in the evenings were extemporary, which was still more

* See *Incidents*, 92–93. In 1836, Rev. William Douglass Cairns (1803–50), the new rector of St. Paul's Church, came to Edenton with his wife, Mary Catharine Cairns, a native of Alexandria, Virginia. Connecticut-born and a Yale alumnus, William Cairns would spend one year in Edenton. See Franklin Bowditch Dexter, *Biographical Notices of Graduates of Yale College* (New Haven, CT: n.p., 1913), 103–4.

† Apollos was a first-century Alexandrian Jewish Christian who played an important role in founding the early churches at Ephesus and Corinth. Since Martin Luther, scholars have proposed that he, rather than Paul or Barnabas, was the author of the Epistle to the Hebrews. On Paul, see the following footnote.

pleasing to the slaves. They look upon written sermons as being stale and dry, but there was nothing dry about these, they were animating and instructive. In the course of Mr. Carnes's labour among the slaves, he preached a series of sermons on the Lord's Prayer, which gave great satisfaction to his hearers. The slaveholders would come at times to hear whether he was preaching after the manner of their fathers—"Servants, obey your masters and mistresses;" or the seditious doctrine for which Paul was tried before Felix; or like the doctrine he preached to Philemon, his exhortations to brotherly love and Christian kindness. I mention this case of Onesimus, because it has been so frequently used to prove that Paul the Apostle was a slave-catcher; but let their opinion of Paul be what it may, they heard nothing here at Mr. Carnes's church that could be construed into anything but brotherly love and Christian fellowship.* Indeed they thought there was too much of it, and began to complain, saying that Mr. Carnes took more interest in preaching to the niggers than he did to them. Several of them were quite displeased, but they had heard of nothing coming from his lips respecting their condition as slaves.† He had laboured to enlighten

---

* After the Methodist Episcopal Church split over the question of slavery in 1844, "a range of antiabolitionists—northerners and southerners, from proslavery ideologues to antislavery gradualists—found biblical support for their very different political agendas. After the passage of the 1850 Fugitive Slave Law, these various antiabolitionists intensified their appeals to the Epistle of Paul to Philemon, in which the author sends back the slave Onesimus to his master. Both slavery's supporters and antislavery unionists appealed to this text as the appropriate response to what they claimed were abolitionist attempts to undermine the nation's legal foundations." Radical abolitionists fired back, arguing that the "principles of the gospel are opposed to" slavery, that Onesimus was not a slave, but a freeman (given that doulos/δοῦλος could refer to either), and that Christian conscience appealed to a higher law. Steven Mailloux, "Political Theology in Douglass and Melville," in *Frederick Douglass and Herman Melville: Essays in Relation,* ed. Robert Levine and Samuel Otter (Chapel Hill: University of North Carolina Press, 2008), 162. For the pro-slavery argument, see, for example, Moses Stuart's *Conscience and the Constitution, with Remarks on the Recent Speech of the Hon. Daniel Webster on the Subject of Slavery* (Boston: Crocker & Brewster, 1850); for the antislavery argument, see, for example, Joseph P. Thompson's *The Fugitive Slave Law; Tried by the Old and New Testaments* (New York: Mark H. Newman, 1850).

† Cairns's dispute with the vestrymen, one of whom was James Norcom, came to a head after he wrote and witnessed the will of a wealthy parishioner, Mary Mare

and elevate them, saying nothing to create excitement among the slaves or their masters. To stop him from preaching to them without some better cause than they had as yet been able to find, while other Churches were allowing this privilege to their slaves, would look rather anti-Christian, and appearance is about all with them; but that good woman, Mrs. Carnes, had not been with us long before she left the field to receive of her father the reward for the few days she had laboured in his vineyard. This world seemed not her home, she was here to teach those little ones how to love and how to live, and above all how to die; then left them to mourn her loss not alone, but in common with all who knew her.*

In yon churchyard her body lies,
Confined beneath the sod;
Her spirit dwells beyond the skies,
With its father—God.

How refreshing it is to the soul to call the past life of such spirits to mind. Though dead, they yet live in our memory, and often seem to rebuke us for our slothfulness and want of humanity. Whether they ever said anything to Mr. Carnes about his preaching or not I cannot say, but soon after the death of his wife he left Edenton for Alexandria, but with the satisfaction that he had done some good, and had not left a slave behind who knew him who did not believe him to be his friend.†

I will give another case of a Christian character, which I think

---

Bissell (1785–1836), that emancipated her eight slaves and provided the funds to send them to Africa with the American Colonization Society. See pp. 20–22 of this volume; see also *Harriet Jacobs: A Life*, hereafter cited as *HJAL*, 52–53, 282 (see abbreviations list for full source citation).

* Mary Catharine Cairns died on September 11, 1836, "from a bilious fever, after an illness of seven days, in the 35th year of her age." "Obituary," *Southern Churchman*, September 23, 1836.

† Shortly after his wife's death, and after his dispute with the vestrymen, William Cairns offered his resignation on March 14, 1837, and removed to Trinity Church in Columbus, Georgia. "Clerical Changes," *Southern Churchman*, May 26, 1837.

was partly caused by his influence. It was a widow lady; Mrs. Basill was her name; she owned some eight or ten slaves, left to her by her husband at his death.* He was a seafaring Captain, and being the most of his time from home, Mrs. Basill's life was rather a retired one. She was seldom seen from home, and after the death of her husband still less so. She was somewhat of a delicate con-stitution, and advanced in years. Not long after the death of Cap-tain Basill she was taken to her bed, where she remained gradually sinking under her disease. At last finding her time of departure near at hand, and that it was necessary for her to see how things stood between her and Him before whom she would shortly have to stand, she had all her slaves called in to her room. After telling them all that she was about to leave them, but leaning on Him who was able to save, she was not without hope of a brighter world, she said—"I have given you that which I never had a right to with-hold from you—your freedom. It is yours by nature."† After having divided the most of the property among them, she called a very old woman to her—"Here is my rocking chair; you are old, and past labour; let your children and grandchildren wait on you, as you have waited on them, while you enjoy the little comfort that this world can afford; but let it not be the means of robbing you of the happiness that awaits us in the world to come." A few days more of suffering passed, and Mrs. Basill felt the last fond link of nature

* Captain Nathaniel Bissell (1778–1834) left Mary Bissell eight slaves in his will after his death in 1834. See Helen Burr Smith and Elizabeth V. Moore, "John Mare: A Composite Portrait," *North Carolina Historical Review* 44, no. 1 (1967): 18–52.
† In Mary Bissell's will of October 31, 1836, she writes that "My negro servants Molly and Maria and Maria's two children Mary and John and three other chil-dren Nancy, Priscilla and Lucy be made over to the American Colonization Soci-ety, to be sent to either of their colonies in Africa, and the expense to be paid out of the money arising from the sale of two vacant lots in Edenton." Two lots on East Gale Street were to be sold to defray their expenses. Additionally, "One hundred dollars was set aside for the care of her old nurse Hagar, who was to be allowed to decide for herself where she wished to live, since she did not wish to go to Africa." See *North Carolina Historical and Genealogical Register* 1, no. 4 (1900): 532; on Hagar, see Smith and Moore, "John Mare," 50.

break and her captive soul set free. They all gathered around her dying bed with weeping eyes and throbbing hearts, to take their last farewell of one for whom a new spring of love had been opened in every bosom. This last act of her life had satisfied them that she was their friend, the greatest friend they had on earth, one with whom they were now loth to part, not knowing where to look for protection in time of need. Mrs. Basill, after this business had been attended to of freeing her slaves, took her leave of them all, asking each one to meet her in the promised land, where there would be no more sickness nor death, no more sorrowing and mourning, no more weeping around the beds of dying friends; but one continued hosannah to our King, who has given us the victory over death. With this last request she bade them all farewell, and left the world, I trust, for a better.

Mr. John Cox was one of the guardians for the slaves, I do not know any other, though I suppose there were others. Whether these poor slaves, which were all women and children, ever got all that their mistress left them or not, it is hard to say; but this much I know—they were talking of making slaves of them again before I left there. It is not the least unlikely that they are all slaves again long before this. The law is against them, it does not favour abolition. They are at the mercy of the people, and the people are without mercy.*

---

* John Cox (1788–1856). Although the North Carolina Supreme Court finally ruled that Mrs. Bissell's bequest was legal nine years after her death, there is no record that her slaves ever left the state. Furthermore, it had not been decided whether a will could validly emancipate a slave via expatriation. In validating the will, the presiding judge also included a caveat: that it must be determined if the slaves have the capacity to consent to or refuse their freedom, because, as the judge put it, Bissell's "gift" was "to a corporation, with an express limitation on its capacities." See James Iredell, *Reports of Cases in Equity Argued and Determined in the Supreme Court of North Carolina*, vol. 4 (Raleigh: Weston R. Gales, 1847), 15–19, for a summary of John Cox, Executor of Mary Bissell vs. William J. H. B. Williams & Al., 39 N.C. 15 (1845); see HJAL, 282.

THREE

BRUTALITY

and MURDER

AMONG SLAVES

I am not writing of what I have heard, but of what I have seen, and of what I defy the world to prove false. There lived about two miles up a river, emptying into the Albemarle Sound, a planter, whose name was Carbaras. His plantation was called Pembroke. At his death his slaves were sold. I mention this, because slaves seldom ever have more than one name; their surname is most generally that of their first master's. The person I am now about to allude to was known by the name of George Carbaras. After the death of his old master, he was owned by Mr. Popelston; after that by young John Horton, who sold him to a negro trader, whose name was Ham. I think this Mr. Ham was from Georgia.

George was chained in the gang with other slaves, and dragged from his wife and his friends. After a few days' travel on the road, by some means or other he made his escape and returned back to that spot where he knew he could find one heart to feel for him, in whom he could confide; but he had not been there long before the bloodthirsty negro-hunters got on his trail, one beautiful Sunday morning, about midsummer, while the church-bells were ringing.*

---

* Born in Bayonne, France, Stephen Cabarrus arrived in North Carolina in 1776, acquired by marriage the estate of Pembroke, one mile west of Edenton, and twice served as speaker of the North Carolina House of Representatives. Upon his

Willy Ray, Elisha Besell, Rob Keaton and Tom Man were pulling up the Albemarle to murder a brother; this, no doubt, they did
with fiendish relish.* The next question with them was, whether the
mere gratification of killing a man and cutting his head from his
body was the only pay they were to receive or not.

"If he is outlawed, we only need show his head, and the reward
is ours; but if he is not outlawed, what then? Why, they may try to
make us pay for him; but we will not be fools enough to say that
we shot him, unless we are to be paid for shooting him." His body
is put into a canoe; his head thrown in, which lies on his breast.
These four Southern gentlemen now return to the town, leaving
the canoe to inquire how the advertisement reads. On finding that
the reward was to be given to any one who would apprehend and
confine him in any gaol in the State, they saw that they could not
publicly boast of their fiendish work; but the Sunday following they
brought him down for exhibition.†

---

death in 1808, he bequeathed "the negroes named Joe, George, Affy, and Rachael
the four children of Marian the washing woman" to his nephews Thomas and
Augustus Cabarrus. Augustus died in 1817, and Pembroke plantation was put
up for sale in November 1819 and then two more times in front of Horniblow's
Tavern, on March 14, 1820. At the second sale, the sellers also "disposed of 3 or
4 negroes" (*Edenton Gazette and General Advertiser*, March 7, 1820). In 1822 the
plantation went up for sale again. On June 20, 1829, hurt by the bank closings,
John Popelston sold thirty-five-year-old George Cabarrus to Jonathan B. Haugh-
ton. Haughton probably sold George to the trader in 1832 or 1833. Will of Stephen Cabarrus, Chowan Wills, Book 1, 1760–1811, NCSA; Chowan County Deed
Book 1–2, p. 247, NCSA; *HJFP*, 1:324.
* Two of these men can be identified as William Rea and Thomas Mann. Elisha
Bessell and Rob Keaton have not been identified.
† *Incidents*, 400: "On Sunday, September 16, 1833, Thomas V. Hathaway, Chowan
County Coroner, testified that an inquest was held at Haughton and Booth's
wharf over 'the body of a negro Man (name unknown) . . . found in a canoe up
the creek, in a coave, near Pembroke, lying dead . . . The Body burried under the
direction of the coroner . . .' Chowan County Miscellaneous Records–Inquests
(various dates, 1803–1834), NCSA. Harriet Jacobs had reported this atrocity in
her pseudonymous letter to the New York *Tribune* of July 25, 1853: 'It was a slave
that been a runaway from his master twelvemonths. After that time a white
man is justified in shooting a slave, he is considered an outlaw. This slave man
was brought to the wharf, placed in a small boat, by two white men, early in the

Now, the question is, what had this man done that he should be so inhumanly butchered and beheaded? The crime that he had committed, and the only crime, was to leave the unnatural trader in slaves and the souls of men, to return to his natural and affectionate wife. Nothing is done to the murderers. They only made a blunder. Slaves are outlawed and shot with impunity, and the tyrant that shoots them is paid for it; but in this case George was not outlawed, so their trouble was all for nothing, and the glory only known to themselves.

Tom Hoskins was a slave belonging to James Norcom, the son of Dr. Norcom. This slave was found just out of the town in the scrub, said to have been shot by William Ray. He was shot in the back, and must have been killed instantly. There was no pay for this—only a feast of blood. Tom's crime was running away from one whom I know to be an unmerciful tyrant.* Another was shot, but not killed. Sirus Coffield—There were three brothers of the Coffields, William, James, and Josiah; I know not which of the three this slave belonged to.† They had been out that day with their bloodhounds hunting slaves. They shot Sirus a little before dark. By some means or other he made his escape from them, and reached Dr. Sawyer's shop soon after dark. He was taken in, and as many

---

morning, with his head severed from his body, and remained there in an August sun until noon, before an inquest was heard.' Writing to Amy Post concerning this letter, she commented, 'I was at home when the poor outlawed was brung in town with his head severed from his body.'" Harriet Jacobs to Amy Post, October 9, 1853, Isaac and Amy Post Family Papers, hereafter cited as IAPFP (see abbreviations list for full source citation).

* Harriet Jacobs ran away from James Norcom Jr.'s Auburn plantation in 1835 (*Incidents*, 124–25). A year later, Tom Hoskins ran away as well. Three days later he was shot and killed near Edenton. An enslaved woman named Abigail, owned by Martha Blount, told the coroner that on Thursday, June 16, near the Chinquapin Chapel on the outskirts of Edenton, "she saw Mr Wm Rea Shoot a gun off . . . [and] she heard the groans of what she thought to be some human being." Chowan County Miscellaneous Records—Inquests (1836), NCSA; *Incidents*, 400.

† The three Coffield brothers were named William, James, and Josiah. Dr. Matthias E. Sawyer's shop was located in East King Street to the west of Dr. Norcom's shop where John Jacobs had served as a shop boy. Deed from Samuel T. Sawyer to Sarah M. Webb, 1837, Chowan Deeds, 1696–1978, Book M-2, p. 453, NCSA.

of the shots taken out of him as they could get at, and his wounds dressed. This being done, Dr. Sawyer sent a despatch to Mr. Coffield to let him know that the slave that they had shot had come in to him, and got his wounds dressed. As soon as they received this intelligence, they mounted their horses, and rode off in fiendish glee for town. They came up to the shop, hooting and yelling as if all Bedlam was coming. When they had reached the door, the first cry from them was, "Bring him out—finish him—I shot dat nigger—whenever I put my gun at a nigger, he's boun' to fall." This man, who was taking so much glory to himself, was not one of the Coffields. I would give his name, but it is so nearly connected with the name of one of Mr. Coffield's slaves, that I do not know which is his. The doctor came out and said to them, "Gentlemen, the negro has given himself up to me, and I will be responsible for his safe delivery to you as soon as he is able to be moved from here; but at present he is not." Seeing that the doctor would not let them have him they returned home.

The Coffields were very rich, they owned a great many slaves, and shooting with them was common.* They did not feel the loss of a slave or two; it was a common thing for them to offer 50 or 100 dollars' reward for a slave, dead or alive, so that there be satisfactory proof of his having been killed. I came very near being torn to pieces one day by Coffield's bloodhounds. I was sent to my master's plantation with a message to the overseer; the plantation was about one and a half miles from town; I knew what part of it he had the slaves at work on, and took a short cut through the bush; when I had got in sight Coffield hallooed to me to keep off, and get over the fence, otherwise I should have them on me. He was then trying to strike the track of a slave. They have been hunted so much that they have learnt to baffle the hounds when they can get means;

* In 1830, Josiah Coffield (1760–1837) owned 116 slaves; in 1840, James Coffield (1790–1843) owned 300 slaves; 1830 US Census, Chowan County, North Carolina, microfilm, Series M19, Roll 119, p. 342, Family History Library Film 0018085; 1840 US Census, Green Hall District, Chowan County, North Carolina, microfilm, Roll 357, p. 214, Family History Library Film 0018093.

to cut and rub an onion on the bottom of the foot is one way, to sprinkle cayenne pepper in their track is another.

I could mention other slaves that have been shot to my knowledge, but why should I? If one has been shot, and the laws justify the shooting of that one, every slave in the States is liable to be shot.

Your air with misery howls,
The negro groans, the bloodhound growls;
Like demons wild you take their flesh,
And human rights beneath you crush.

FOUR

THE DIFFERENT

WAYS *of*

PUNISHING

SLAVES

Just at the back of the courthouse and in front of the gaol is a whipping post, with stocks and pillory attached. The pillory is not intended for slaves, it is a place where they put men or women when they want to pelt them with rotten eggs; the platform of the pillory is about 8 feet from the ground, 6 or 8 feet square, with a post in the centre—having in the centre of it a board firmly placed 3 feet from the platform, with 3 half circles on each side—two for the wrist, and one for the neck—and a corresponding slide board to let down and fasten them in; the person who is in the pillory stands in a stooping position. The stocks are made on the same principle, the lower part being the groundwork; at each end is a large post with iron straps to fasten the hand in; they are about as high as one can well get their hands in the required manner; this is done to tighten the skin on the back, that the cowhide they flog with may cut the deeper into the flesh. Here I have seen men and women stripped and struck, from 15 to 100 and more. Some of them whose backs were cut to pieces were washed down with strong brine or brandy, this is done to increase pain.*

But the most cruel torture is backing; the hands are crossed

---

* Called "pickling." See Moses Grandy, *Narrative of the Life of Moses Grandy; Late a Slave in the United States of America* (London: C. Gilpin, 1843), 41.

and tied, then taken over the knees and pinned by running a stick between the arms and legs, which tightens the skin and renders the slave as helpless as a child. The backing paddle is made of oak, about 1¼ inch thick, and 5 by 8 inches in the blade, with about 12 inches of a handle. The blade is full of small holes, which makes the punishment severer than it would otherwise be. I have seen the flesh like a steak. Slaves flogged in this way are unable to sit down for months. This was Mr. Collins's favourite way of punishing slaves. Mr. Collins was a member of the ——— Church, and to a stranger would seem to be a very kind-hearted, good man. Every slave that met him would pull off his hat and make a polite bow, which Mr. Collins would return. If he was a day or two from home, when he returned, his slaves that were about the house, would take his hand and inquire after his health. Is it love, that his own and other people's slaves have for him? No, but fear. Mr. Collins always has at hand a little cane, to teach politeness to such as have not learnt it. I have known him to flog others' slaves for not taking their hats off to him, when he has been on the opposite side of the street; and on one occasion he met a slave with a quarter of mutton in each hand, and flogged him because he did not shift the two into one hand, until he could raise his hat. Where the slaves cannot see the necessity of being deceitful, such treatment soon makes them see it.

I was an eye-witness to more than one hundred blows each, being given to two lads belonging to Mr. Collins, and they were then sent to the Lake Farm, a place that will well bear the name I once heard a poor slave mother call it, who was taking leave of her son—"He is going," said she, "to the lake of hell."*

I will give you but one more case of flogging detail, that will be Agnes, the slave of Augustus Moore.† She was hired to John Beas-

* Josiah Collins II was a member of the Episcopal church, and his Somerset Plantation was built on the banks of Lake Scuppernong on the southern shore of Albemarle Sound. See William S. Tarlton, *Somerset Place and Its Restoration* (n.p., 1954).

† Yellin writes: "Agnes (1800–?), a slave belonging to Augustus Moore, was whipped by the man who hired her sometime between 1830 and 1835 . . . Judge Moore's great-granddaughter Elizabeth Vann Moore recalled that in the 1930s she and

ley; she was some six months advanced in pregnancy at the time. Being in an unfit state for field labour, she could not do as much as other slaves. For this cause, Beasley tied her up and commenced whipping her. With my own hands have I dressed her back, and I declare, before God, that she had not a piece of skin left on it as wide as my finger. She was a hired slave. If Beasley had killed her at a single blow, her master could have punished Beasley if he could have got white witnesses to that effect, which is not likely; but she may have died in an hour after being cut down, and there was no

---

her father spoke with an old man who identified himself as Agnes's grandson. He was living in a house his father had built before the Civil War on one of Augustus Moore's former farms near Albemarle Sound, and he said he remembered his grandmother as a skilled seamstress and a 'high-tempered' woman. He recalled that when although only a lad, he had saved the farm from the Yankees. The federal gunboats came up the sound after the fall of Roanoke Island, he explained, and a landing party told him to take them to Moore's plantation house, but he instead led them through swamps until they abandoned their mission. Asked why he had protected the family, he answered that earlier, after his grandmother was severely whipped by a man to whom she had been hired, Augustus Moore had given her a place to live and had set her free—thus ensuring the freedom of the child she was carrying, of her subsequent children, and all of their children, including himself.

Elizabeth Vann Moore never expected that story to be confirmed . . . But she judges John S. Jacobs's version of Agnes's whipping inaccurate and worse, false, because partial. She writes: 'Every person in Chowan County knew that Aggy was emancipated at once, and knew why. And John Jacobs suppressed that fact. Presenting himself as a witness to the truth, he deliberately did not tell the whole truth. The omission of half the story in order to make the other half a more damning indictment falsifies the whole thing. The fact that John Jacobs omitted what was for Aggy the most important part of her story invalidates his testimony, as far as I can see.'

A careful search through Chowan County Superior Court records—which are very incomplete for this period—has yielded no record of Agnes's emancipation. Nor does an examination of the censuses of 1850 and 1860 identify a free black family living in the area of the Moore farm that fits the description given by Miss Moore's narrator—a grandmother, a father, a mother, and their children. It is certainly possible that, without formally emancipating Agnes, Moore could have given her a place to live and manumitted her from further labor, and that her entire family could have lived as a de facto free family while still legally enslaved." *HJFP* 1:325n50.

law to harm him. It would have been death caused by moderate correction, which North Carolina does not punish a slaveholder for.*

I know that the picture I have drawn of slavery is a black one, and looks most unnatural; but here you have the State, the town, and the names of all the parties. Prove it to be false if you can. Take one who has never felt the sting of slavery, he would naturally suppose that it was to the slaveholder's advantage to treat his slaves with kindness; but the more indulgent the master, the more intelligent the slave; the more intelligent the slave, the nearer he approximates to a man; the nearer he approximates to a man, the more determinate he is to be a free man; and to argue that the slaves are happy, or can be happy while in slavery, is to argue that they have been brutalised to that degree that they cannot be considered men. What better proof do you want in favour of universal freedom that can be given? You can find thousands of ignorant men who will lay down their lives for their liberty; can you find one intelligent man that would prefer slavery? These thousands are not men—they are only children to what they should be. I am yet a child; I can see the things that I want, but have not attained to the stature of a man; they are beyond my reach, though I would be ashamed of myself to offer these acts of wanton cruelty as a reason why slavery should be abolished. If they can be considered an evil, they are a necessary evil, and you can only remove the evil by removing the cause. All the chains and fetters in North Carolina would not hold me if I was able to carry them off. God created me a freeman and with His assistance I will die one. If any man has a right to my limbs, he also has a right to use all necessary means to make them available

---

* Technically, the death of a slave subsequent to a severe whipping could be considered "a murder if a person died within a year and a day of being wounded. Had Agnes died . . . Moore could have brought a criminal prosecution against John Beasley. But the law was on the side of John Beasley . . . In 1829, the state Supreme Court, overturning a verdict of a Chowan County jury that had found a temporary master guilty of battery committed on a hired female slave, ruled that temporary masters had the same authority over their slaves as did owners." State v. John Mann 13 N.C. 263 (1829); *HJFP*, 1:326n50.

to him. I deny the former; and declare it as an act of Christian duty, in regard to the latter, that the slaveholder who gets my labour shall pay as much as it is worth for it, and his life, if possible, with it.

The last thing that remained to be done to complete this hell on earth was done in 1850 in passing the Fugitive Slave Law. There is not a State, a city, nor a town left as a refuge for the hunted slave; there is not a United States officer but what has sworn to act the part of the bloodhound in hunting me down, if I dare visit the land of Stars and Stripes, the home of the brave, and land of the free. You can extort submission to the gratification of your lust from our wives—you can take our daughters, and sell them for the basest use that can be made of woman. Yet you declare it to be a self-evident truth that all men are created by their Creator free and equal, and endowed with certain inalienable rights—life, liberty, and the pursuit of happiness. Where are the coloured man's rights to-day in America? They once had rights allowed them. Yes, in the days that tried men's souls, they had a right to bleed and die for the country; but their deeds are forgotten, their swords and bayonets have been beaten into chains and fetters to bind the limbs of their children. To your shame and disgrace, the first man that was seen to fall in the city of Boston, in the revolutionary struggle for liberty, was a coloured man; and I have seen one of his brethren, who had fled from his whips and chains, within sight of that monument erected to liberty, dragged from it into slavery, not by the slaveowners of the south, for they knew not of his being there—but by northern men.*

---

* On March 5, 1770, Crispus Attucks became the first person to die in the Boston Massacre. In *The Colored Patriots of the American Revolution* (Boston: Robert F. Wallcut, 1855), William Cooper Nell writes: "In April, 1851, Thomas Sims, a fugitive slave from Georgia, was returned to bondage from the city of Boston, and on Friday, June 2d, 1854, Anthony Burns, a fugitive from Virginia, was dragged back to slavery,—both marching over the very ground that ATTUCKS trod" (18). In 1851, the State of Massachusetts rejected Nell's petition to erect a monument to Attucks.

FIVE

MY SISTER
HAS RUN AWAY,
MY AUNT,
TWO CHILDREN,
and MYSELF
SENT TO GAOL

Here I am! looking through the grates of your prison. What have I done? What has my aunt done? What could those little children do? We are not accused of anything.*

The old doctor, no doubt, thought that this would be the means of bringing my sister back; but you will by-and-by see, that she did not leave with the intention of returning. She had not yet been called to make her back bare for the lash; but she had gone to live on the doctor's plantation, where she daily expected it. Her mental sufferings were more than she could longer bear. With her it was, in the language of one of our fathers, "liberty or death."†

---

* Cf. *Incidents*, 130–38.
† The quote is from Patrick Henry's speech to the 1775 Virginia Convention. See *Incidents*, 191: "My restlessness increased. I had lived too long in bodily pain and anguish of spirit. Always I was in the dread that by some accident, or some contrivance, slavery would succeed in snatching my children from me. This thought drove me nearly frantic, and I determined to steer for the North Star at all hazards."

The doctor offers 100 dollars reward for her, and threatens to punish to the extreme penalty of the law, any person or persons found harbouring, or assisting her in any way to make her escape.* He then wrote a letter to a gentleman living in New York, who had formerly lived in North Carolina, by the name of Tredwill. I am not prepared to say that Mr. Tredwill took an interest in this letter. I rather believe he did not.† But the news was soon circulated among the slave catchers of the north, and they were sticking their unwanted faces in every coloured man's door, on account of my sister. The doctor pretended to sell me and the two children to a negro trader. In two or three weeks he received a letter from New York, stating that my sister was taken, and safe lodged in gaol. This calls the old man from home. He has got to prove property and pay expenses. Now that the old doctor is gone, I am having a jolly good time. Mr. Lamb, the jailer, was an old acquaintance of mine. Though he was a white man, and I a slave, we had spent many hours together in Mr. Johnson's family. We had taken tea there. To make my story short, and go back to the doctor, Mr. Johnson had a very fine daughter, and we were very fond of each other. Mr. Lamb had been a visitor of Mr. Johnson's for many years. Now that he had me under the lock and key, knowing that it was not for any crime that I was there, he could not be otherwise than kind. He allowed me every indulgence. My friends could call and see me whenever they pleased, such as could come, and stop as long as they liked; he would never turn the key on them. Sometimes he would give me the key on the inside. While the doctor had me here for safe

* Cf. *Incidents*, 125. Dr. Norcom advertised for Harriet's capture in the daily *American Beacon* (Norfolk, Virginia) from June 30 to July 13, 1835, offering a reward of $100. In a broadside, he offered a reward of $150 if she was captured in North Carolina and $300 if taken outside the state.

† Cf. *Incidents*, 134–35. Yellin writes, in *HJFP*, 1:319: "In 1834 James Iredell Tredwell (1799–1846)—first cousin to Samuel Tredwell Sawyer, the father of Harriet Jacobs's children—was living at 81 Chambers Street in New York; by 1836, he had moved to 371 Broadway. Dr. Norcom's absence from Edenton in July 1835 is documented."

keeping, I could have made my escape every day or night; but in the first place, if I had wanted to go, I would not have taken the advantage of Mr. Lamb's kindness; in the second place, I saw no chance of bettering myself.* I knew he would not get my sister, because she had not left town. My uncle-in-law, who was a seafaring man, had intended to take her to New York, but the doctor's threats frightened him so, that he did not dare make the attempt.

While the old man was gone I had a negro trader call with others to see me. His name was Gaskins; he said he would buy me if the old doctor would sell me; I told him I thought he would—that he told me he intended to do so when he put me in.†

After some two weeks the doctor returns home without my sister. The woman that had been taken up and put in gaol was a free woman, but what could she do with the wretch who put her there. America is a free country and a white man can do what he pleases with a coloured man or woman in most of the States. They may have a few friends now who would not allow this if they knew it; but they are hated by the nation at large who do it.

My aunt is taken out of gaol and sent home to the doctor's house, the children and myself are left in. The old man comes to have a little talk with me about my sister.

"Well, John, I have not got Harriet yet, but I will have her yet. Don't you know where she is?"

---

* "George Lamb, an immigrant from London, England, became a U.S. citizen in 1825 and, following William Grimes's death in 1831, succeeded Grimes as jailor. Evidently he had taken tea with John S. at the home of Gustavus Adolphus Johnson (1790–1842), the son of an unknown slave woman and Congressman Charles Johnson of Bandon Plantation. Gustavus A. Johnson occupied an unusual position in Edenton: manumitted in early childhood by private act, under the guardianship of Samuel Tredwell, he was educated by private tutors and taught cabinetmaking by James Borritz, a master craftsman. In 1814 he purchased and married Elizabeth. Johnson lived with his wife and their six children (emancipated by him or born free) at the northeast corner of Broad and Albemarle, where he established his home and cabinetmaker's shop." *HJFP*, 1:319.

† Note: Because TT censors surnames, Yellin identified the wrong trader, Joseph Granier.

"How can I know, sir? I have been in gaol ever since my sister left you. Mr. Gaskins was here while you were away, sir, and said that he wanted to buy me."

"Buy you! I don't want to sell you."

"You told me when you put me here that you did."

"Yes, but not if you will go back to the shop and behave yourself. Mr. Gaskins has not got money enough to buy you."

"I do not know how to behave differently from what I have done."

"Your behaviour will do; but I am afraid you are going to run away from me."

"I have not said anything about running away from you, sir."

"I know that; but your sister is gone, and you will be going next."

With this we parted. About this time my uncle-in-law returns. The doctor forbid his going to see my aunt. Her husband was owned by another man. They had lived together for twenty years, and I had never heard them quarrel; and now they are to be separated, not for anything they had done, but for the acts of another. But such are the laws and customs of the country; and as hard as it is, yet we must bear it; there is no help for us. My uncle-in-law's name was Stephen. His master, Mr. Bozman, was owner of the vessel he sailed in, and though he had several chances to make his escape from slavery, yet he had returned on every voyage.* What was next to his liberty to him was that in slavery his wife was with him. When that union between him and her was broken, the charm of slavery was lost, and he returned no more. His wife to him was dead—ay, worse than dead; he could see her living spirit, but dare not approach it. "That which God hath joined together, let no man put asunder," saith the Scriptures.†

At the doctor's last visit to the gaol, he laid before me the wretchedness of the free people of colour in New York, stating

---

* Probably Captain Joseph Bozman (1762–1838) of Edenton, a wealthy merchant who owned several ships.
† Mark 10:9.

that they had not the comforts of his slaves and how much better off we were than they. To this I said nothing. My mind was fully made up on this subject—first, that I must, in order to effect my escape, hide as much as possible my hatred to slavery, and affect a love for my master, whoever he might be; the doctor and myself knew each other too well for me to hope to better my condition with him; I must change hands in order to do that. Secondly, let the condition of the coloured people of New York be what it may, I had rather die a free man than live a slave. The doctor evidently does not want to sell me, neither does he want to run any risk of losing me; neither was it from any particular fondness that he had for me; it was that he could not replace me for the same money that a trader would give for me. Before he left the gaol he told me that he did not want to keep me in gaol any longer, and would let me out at any time when I would get my uncle Marcus to stand my security that I would not run away from him. When leaving, he told me to send for my uncle and see if he would not do it for me. To all this I was dumb. I was in no particular hurry to get out of gaol. I wanted a little serious reflection, and here was the only place where I could get an opportunity of the kind.

A few days passed, and he heard nothing from me. He saw my uncle and told him that I wanted to see him at the gaol. He accordingly came and asked me if I wanted him to stand my security. I promptly told him no; that I wanted my liberty, and I would make good the first opportunity to get it; that he might do as he pleased, but God being my helper I would die a free man. This satisfied my uncle at once that he had as well take the money out of his pocket, and pay for me, as to stand my security, and if I could get a chance to make my escape without bringing any expense on him so much the better. Here we parted. The old doctor waits for an answer, but gets none, which satisfied him that I no longer had a desire to make his shop my home.

There were two or three slaveholders in the town that would give him more for me than he could get from a trader, but he would not sell me to any one in the town. Mr. Sawyer, who afterwards bought me, came to the gaol, and asked me if I would live with him, if he bought me. I told him that I would, but the question was not asked how long.

I had been here just two months when Mr. Sawyer got a negro trader, whose name was Law, to buy the two children for my grandmother and one for himself. The doctor at first tried to bind the trader not to sell me to any one in the State, but this he would not agree to, saying, he sold his slaves where ever he could get the most for them—he finally agreed to take me out of town in irons, but to sell me the first chance he could get. The old man did not think that he had bargained for me before I was sold. This important part of the business being settled we were sold, the two children for 500 dollars, I believe, and I for 900 dollars. Now for the remnant of our father's old bayonets in the shape of handcuffs; the blacksmith's tools, handcuffs and chain are all in readiness at the gaol. The chain is 30 or 40 feet long, with handcuffs every two or three feet. The slaves are handcuffed right and left on each side of the chain. In the gang there was one who was free by birth. He was born not more than fifty miles from Edenton. He had been put in gaol here for some trifling offence; not being able to pay the fine he was sold for six months or a year to William Roberts, a planter, who was so cruel to him that he ran away from him. He was caught, and after being flogged, was put in irons and set to work. He attempted to cut the irons off, and was caught in the act, sent to gaol, and finally sold to a trader. I saw the irons that he had been made to work in, they were fetters for the ankles, weighing from 15 to 20 pounds in weight.*

Now we are all snugly chained up, the children in the cart, and the women walking behind; your friend weeping and taking a

---

* Although there were many people named William Roberts in North Carolina, a likely candidate is William Bennett Roberts (1802–35), who according to the 1830 census owned 25 slaves and lived in Edenton. In 1830, Roberts placed a runaway slave advertisement for "an excellent Sawyer" named Henry. 1830 US Census, Chowan County, North Carolina, microfilm, Series M19, Roll 119, p. 332, Family History Library Film 0018085; "$15 Reward," *Edenton Gazette and North Carolina General Advertiser*, January 2, 1830.

farewell shake of the hand with you; wives of their husbands, and parents of their children. I went with the gang as far as Mr. J. B. Skinner's, the man that had my uncle taken in New York. Here the cart was stopped and the blacksmith's tools taken out, and Mr. Law began to hammer away at my irons. When they were off he told me to take the children and go home to Mr. Sawyer; the children went to my grandmother, and I to Mr. Sawyer, not the dealer in sausage meat, but S. T. Sawyer of North Carolina. I make this explanation, because they were both members of Congress.*

* John's chains were removed at the home of Joseph Blount Skinner, who at retirement had moved to a farm one mile from Edenton. Richard Benbury Creecy, "Joseph B. Skinner," *Grandfather's Tales of North Carolina History* (Raleigh: Edwards and Broughton, 1901), 132–35. Sawyer's uncle, Lemuel Sawyer (1777–1852), was an eight-term member of Congress; the moniker "Sausage" was given to a congressman from Ohio, William Sawyer, by an anonymous writer named "Persimmon" in the *New York Tribune*, who described "Sawyer's daily routine of flouting House rules while feeding his appetites." "The Saga of 'Sausage' Sawyer," *Whereas: Stories from the People's House* (blog), History, Art & Archives: United States House of Representatives, August 12, 2015, https://history.house .gov/Blog/2015/August/8-11-Sausage-Sawyer/?utm_source=rss.

SIX

MY FIFTH
and LAST
MASTER

By this time I had seen enough of slavery to make my life bitter, but I had resolved to hide it if possible. When I met Mr. Sawyer I saluted him as my master. It came rather hard to me at first to "master" a man, and act the deceitful part of a slave, to pretend love and friendship where I had none. As unpleasant as it was thus to act, yet under the circumstances in which I was placed, I feel that I have done no wrong in so doing; I did everything that I could to please my present master, who treated me with as much kindness as I could expect from any one to whom I was a slave. He had a brother, Dr. M. E. Sawyer, who was subject to fits. My master was a lawyer, my business was to wait on the lawyer and take care of his brother when sick. Sometimes when recovering from his fits he would be perfectly mad for four or five days. On such occasions I visited the sick slaves on the plantation.* This part of my

---

* The plantation on Hertford Road was about a mile from downtown Edenton, where Dr. Sawyer lived. In *Incidents*, Harriet discusses learning that Samuel Sawyer had bought her brother and the children; she also describes Norcom's threats against John and the arrest of Mark Ramsey (139–42). Deposition of James I. Tredwell in response to interrogatories submitted to him on January 5, 1831, in the suit, M. E. Sawyer v. James C. Johnston, Chowan County Road Records, 1830–1839, NCSA.

work caused the overseer a great deal of unpleasantness; he would sometimes want to give them oil or something of the kind, saying they were not sick; at other times he would say they were well enough to go to work, and if they were too sick to work, they were too sick to eat. Knowing that he would not strike me for having my own way in what I was sent there for—to see if they were sick and give them what they needed—I took great pleasure in differing with him on all occasions whenever I thought my patient dangerously ill. If Dr. Sawyer was not in his right mind I would call in Dr. Warren.* My judgment in regard to such diseases as are most common on a plantation was considered very good for one of my age; so much so, that a young planter who was studying medicine at the time offered my master one thousand five-hundred dollars for me. The way I came to know this was this: he asked me one day if I wanted to be sold. This woke up a little of the old feeling, and I had almost forgot myself for a minute.

"No sir," I said, "I am not anxious to be sold, but I know I have got to serve some one." Here he made me a promise which I shall never forget, though it was not consoling to me. He said, "you shall not serve any one after me, I have been offered a handsome price for you; but I don't want to sell you." True, I was glad to hear him say that I would serve no one after him; this required a little consideration; he was but a few years older than me, and to wait for him to die looked to me too much like giving a man who was in want of his daily bread a cheque on the bank to be paid when he is dead. To have prayed for his death would have been unkind; to have killed him would have been worse; so finally I concluded to let him live as long as the Lord was willing he should, and I would get rid of him, as soon as possible. My pride would not allow me to let a man feed and clothe me for nothing, I would work the ends of my fingers off first.

* Dr. William C. Warren (1803–50). In her will of 1840, Molly Horniblow bequeathed her entire estate to Warren and Josiah Collins III.

I have said nothing about Mr. Sawyer's plantation slaves; I have only spoken of his treatment to me.* I am willing to acknowledge kindness even in a slaveholder wherever I have seen it; but had he treated all of his slaves as he treated me, the probability is that they would have been of as little value to him as I was. Some might try to make out a case of ingratitude of this, but I do not feel myself under the slightest obligation to any one who holds me against my will, though he starved himself to feast me. Doubtless he meant to do me a good turn; but he put it off too far.

I must drop Mr. Sawyer for a few minutes, the Doctor is not satisfied yet. He has had my uncle arrested, and lodged in gaol; I too am an eyesore to him; the first time that I met him after he sold me, he stopped me. I had crossed the street twice to avoid him, but in vain. He told me to stop. I replied that I was on an errand and could not stop. He insisted on my stopping. I did so, but some distance off. He began very calmly to ask me several questions about my sister, to which I gave no satisfactory answer; finally, he got in such a rage I thought it best to leave. The last words I heard from him were—"I will butcher you, you. . . . ."

In the evening I went to see my uncle at the gaol. I was obliged to pass by the Doctor's shop doors, or go round a square out of my way. He saw me when I passed. I was on the look-out all the while at the gaol for him, and on my return he had taken his stand in the tavern, between his shop and the gaol. When I got abreast of him, he made a bolt for me, and I made one from him. We had quite a foot race for two or three hundred yards. The old doctor, finding his legs, though longer, not quite as supple as mine, gave up the chase. This may be all imagination, but I had made a study of the old doctor's ways so long that I really thought I could sometimes

---

* Samuel Tredwell Sawyer lists 27 adult and 23 child slaves in his 1835 inventory of his property. Some of his human property served the family in town, others worked on Sawyer's 250-acre plantation producing crops of clover, oats, corn, and cotton. "An Inventory of the Property of Matthias E. Sawyer, which came to the hands of Saml. T. Sawyer his Executor," Estate of Matthias E. Sawyer, 1835, Chowan Inventories, vol. A1, 1811–1868, NCSA.

tell what he was thinking about. Whether I could or not, I baffled him four times when he had thought to catch me. It was near two years before the doctor could let me pass him without giving me a look that meant anything but friendship. He sees my grandmother has some friend, and takes my uncle out of gaol for trial. The only charge that he could bring against him was that he was going about looking like a gentleman, having as much money as he had. The Court said, that unless the doctor could prove that he came dishonestly by this money, they could not find him guilty of any crime; and yet my grandmother had to pay the expense of the Court.

Here the doctor seemed to give up all further intentions of trying to revenge himself on us for what my sister had done. Three long years are passed and gone, and my sister not yet free. She is still within five miles of the spot where she was born, seeing her master almost every day through the cracks of her place of concealment.

Dark and gloomy is the captive's cell,
No light of day e'er enters there;
The feelings of a broken heart no one can tell;
It sickens, it weakens, it sinks in despair.

SEVEN

DR. SAWYER'S DEATH—

HIS BROTHER'S

ELECTION *to* CONGRESS—

and MARRIAGE—

and MY ESCAPE *from* HIM

My master, after being elected, sent his brother to the plantation, to remain there until he returned from Washington.* He had been there but a few days before he had a fit. In the morning, while dressing, he had gone to the fire to warm his hands; while there, and alone, the fit came on him; he fell in the fire, and remained there until the fit was over. He had got out of the fire before he was seen by any one; the first to see him was one of the women, who gave the alarm. The overseer sent a slave in haste for his brother and the doctor. I then took the horse, and after getting such things as were necessary, I was on the spot as soon as possible. One of his arms was

---

* Sawyer was elected to the 25th Congress as a Whig on August 10, 1837, defeating Dr. Godwin C. Moore by a vote of 2,111 to 1,706 statewide (see *Incidents*, 159). He served one term. In 1839, as a result of the "loco-foco notions avowed by their Representative," the Whig party ran a candidate, Kenneth Rayner, in opposition to Sawyer, who ran on the Republican ticket of Martin Van Buren. Rayner won, receiving a majority of the 661 votes cast. "North-Carolina Election. For Members of Congress," *North Carolina Standard*, August 30, 1837; "Nomination!!" *Weekly Standard*, February 6, 1839; "Republican Candidate for President, Martin Van Buren," *Tarboro (NC) Press*, August 17, 1839.

completely baked. When I went up to his bed, he looked up and said, "It is too late; I am beyond all cure," though he allowed me to go on as I had begun, applying a little oil to some burns on his neck, while other arrangements were being made previous to the arrival of the doctor, who soon came and dressed his wounds. The doctor told my master that his brother could not live—that his case was an incurable one; and that death must soon follow. His brother and myself stopped with him until he died. He lived twelve or fifteen hours.* At the remark that he made when I first went to his bed, before the doctor or his brother had arrived, I could not help from weeping. This was a sad accident; but no blame could be attached to any one. His brother had been like a father to him.

This misfortune being over, I am ordered to get ready for Washington City; this being done, we start off on our journey. We were not many days getting to this place, that I so much wanted to see. At the head of Pennsylvania Avenue, a little on the hill, is seen the capital of the United States—the place where they make laws for a nation of freemen. Down the Avenue a little, and on the left-hand side, is the slave-pen where they fat Americans for the market.† The upper crust of the place consists principally of woman-whippers,

---

* Dr. Matthias Enoch Sawyer died "suddenly, on Tuesday evening the 5th inst. [December 5, 1837] at the plantation of his brother, near the town of Edenton . . . in the 33d year of his age." *Weekly Standard*, December 25, 1837.

† Multiple slave pens were located on Pennsylvania SE within view of the Capitol. In 1854, Abraham Lincoln described the view from his home: "The North clamored for the abolition of a peculiar species of slave trade in the District of Columbia, in connection with which, in view from the windows of the capitol, a sort of negro-livery stable, where droves of negroes were collected, temporarily kept, and finally taken to Southern markets, precisely like droves of horses, had been openly maintained for fifty years." Abraham Lincoln, "October 16, 1854.—Speech at Peoria, Illinois in Reply to Senator Douglas," in *Abraham Lincoln: Complete Works*, vol. 1., ed. John Nicolay and John Hay (New York: Century, 1894), 185. On April 2, 1841, Solomon Northup was staying at Gadsby's Hotel when he was drugged and taken to Williams's slave pen on the corner of Seventh Street and Independence Avenue SW. See *Twelve Years a Slave: Narrative of Solomon Northup, a Citizen of New-York, Kidnapped in Washington City in 1841 and Rescued in 1853, from a Cotton Plantation near the Red River, in Louisiana* (Auburn, NY: Derby and Miller, 1853) and "The Kidnapping Case," *National Era*, February 3, 1853.

blacklegs, blackguards, and dough faces. If a lady comes and rings the doorbell, and you, on answering it, tell her that the mistress is not in, the reply most invariably is, "Go and tell her who it is, and she will be in." Just as well say, "Go and tell her she has lied, not knowing who has called to see her." The same is the case of the gentlemen. Here is a bill before the House that they have spent weeks in discussing its merits and demerits; it is now to be voted on at such an hour. The sergeant-at-arms is sent out in search of the absent members; some of them are having a little game of cards— could not think of waiting until after 4 o'clock; the pay is just the same for playing cards as though they were making laws, only you must lie a little when the sergeant-at-arms calls, and say that you are not in. I could not bear this system of lying. I avoided answering these calls whenever I could.

Here I had a chance of seeing some of the great men of the country. Mr. Van Buren, the bloodhound importer, and Henry Clay, the great polka [poker] player. He was a man of extraordinary talent; well understood public opinion; never helped to make it, but went with it; Dan Webster, one of the master-workmen on the Fugitive Slave Bill, was there; Graves, the butcher, was there; and the Honorable John Q. Adams was there, attending to his business.[*]

[*] Martin Van Buren (1782–1862), eighth president of the United States. In 1840, Van Buren endorsed the use of Cuban bloodhounds to hunt fugitive Native Americans in the Second Seminole War. Abolitionists believed that the policy was intended to hunt runaway slaves. Henry Clay (1777–1852), was a senator from Kentucky, three-time Speaker of the House, and secretary of state (1825–29). William Jordan Graves (1805–48) was a three-term congressman from Kentucky who killed his fellow congressman, Jonathan Cilley, in a duel in 1838 after Cilley criticized him on the House floor. Daniel Webster (1782–1852) was a senator from Massachusetts and two-time secretary of state. John Quincy Adams (1767–1848) was the sixth president of the United States.

Webster and Clay were both known as avid poker players, and Clay was even credited with having invented poker: "Close by us was a party playing *poker*," one author writes in 1844. "This was then exclusively a high-gambling Western game, founded on *brag*, invented, as it is said, by Henry Clay when a youth." Joe Cowell, *Thirty Years Passed Among the Players in England and America* (New York: Harper & Brothers, 1844), 94. For "Polker" as a dig at Clay's relationship to James K. Polk

After my master had been there a short time he went to board with Mrs. Payton, who had two young nieces here. He got over head and ears in love, and soon they were engaged to be married. As good luck would have it, this young lady had a sister living in Chicago, and no place would suit her like that to get married in.* I admired her taste much. I wanted to go there too. My master could not do otherwise than give his consent to go there with her. The next question to be settled was about taking me with him into a free State. Near the time for him to leave, he told me that he intended to marry. I was pleased at this, and anxious to know who the fortunate lady might be. He did not hesitate to tell me what he intended to do, stating at the same time that he would take me with him if I would not leave him. "Sir," said I, "I never thought before that you suspected me of wanting to leave you."

"I do not suspect you, John. Some of the members of the House have tried to make me believe that you would run away if I took you with me; but my belief of you is that you would follow me to ―――― and back."

"Well, sir, I would follow you back, sure, but if I could get out of the job of going there with you, I rather think I should."

"Well! get my things all ready; we are to leave on the first day of next week, I will try you anyhow."

Everything was ready, and the hoped-for time came. He took his intended, and off we started for the West. When we were taking the boat at Baltimore for Philadelphia, he came up to me and said, "Call me Mr. Sawyer, and if any body asks you who you are,

---

(and not a misspelling), see "Who Was the Inventor of Poker?" *North Carolina Standard*, October 16, 1844.
* During the first and second sessions of Congress (September 4–October 16, 1837, and December 4, 1837–July 9, 1838), Sawyer lived at H. V. Hill's fashionable Congressional Boarding House. Sawyer likely met Lavinia Peyton (CA. 1818–?) at her aunt Ann Eliza Peyton's Congress Boarding House. Sawyer and Peyton were married on August 11, 1838, by Rev. Dr. Johnson in Chicago, where Lavinia's sister, Cornelia Peyton Russell, lived. *Congressional Directory of the Third Session of the Twenty-Fifth Congress of the United States of America* (Washington, DC: Thomas Allen, 1839), 36; *HJFP*, 1:321.

and where you are going, do you tell them that you are a free man, and hired by me." This I agreed to do with all my heart.

We stopped two or three days at the Niagara Falls; from thence we went to Buffalo, and took the boat for Chicago; Mr. Sawyer had been here but a few days before he was taken sick. In five weeks from the time of his arrival here he was married, and ready to leave for home. On our return we went into Canada. Here I wanted to leave him, but there was my sister and a friend of mine at home in slavery; I had succeeded in getting papers that might have been of great value to my friend. I had tried, but could not get anything to answer my purpose. I tried to get a seaman's protection from the English Custom House, but could not without swearing to a lie, which I did not feel disposed to do.*

We left here for New York, where we stopped three or four days. I went to see some of my old friends from home, who I knew were living there. I told them that I wanted their advice. They knew me, they knew my master, and they knew my friends also. "Now tell me my duty," said I. The answer was a very natural one—"look out for yourself first."

I weighed the matter in my mind, and found the balance in favour of stopping. If I returned I could do my sister no good, and could see no further chance for my own escape. I then set myself to work to get my clothes out of the Astor House hotel, where we were stopping; I brought them out in small parcels, as if to be washed. This job being done, the next thing was to get my trunks to put them in. I went to Mr. Johnson's shop, which was in sight of the Astor House hotel, and told him that I wanted to get my trunk repaired.† The next morning I took my trunk in my hand with me; when I went down, whom should I see at the foot of the steps but

---

* Jacobs's friend's identity is unknown, though it is possible that he is the same friend that Jacobs wrote Sydney Howard Gay about in 1845. See John S. Jacobs to Sydney Howard Gay, September 7, 1845, in appendix 1.

† Built by John Jacob Astor, the 309-room Astor House opened in 1836 at the corner of Broadway and Vesey (later the site of the World Trade Center). Jacobs most likely visited George Johnson's shop at 211 Pearl Street, which, among

Mr. Sawyer. I walked up to him, and I showed him a rip in the top of the trunk, opening it at the same time that he might see that I was not running off. He told me that I could change it, or get a new one if I liked. I thanked him, and told him we were very near home now, and with a little repair the old one would do. At this we parted. I got a friend to call and get my trunk, and pack up my things for me, that I might be able to get them at any minute. Mr. Sawyer told me to get everything of his in, and be ready to leave for home the next day. I went to all the places where I had carried anything of his, and where they were not done, I got their cards and left word for them to be ready by the next morning. What I had got were packed in his trunk; what I had not been able to get, there were the cards for them in his room. They dine at the Astor at 3 o'clock—they leave the room at 4 o'clock, at half-past 4 I am to be on the board of the boat for Providence.* Being unable to write myself at that time, and unwilling to leave him in suspense, I got a friend to write as follows:—

"Sir—I have left you not to return; when I have got settled I will give you further satisfaction. No longer yours, John S. Jacob [*sic*]."

This note was to be put into the post-office in time for him to get it the next morning; I waited on him and his wife at dinner. As the town clock struck four I left the room. I then went through to New Bedford, where I stopped for a few months.

There were some things connected with my leaving which caused me a very unpleasant feeling. In the first place, he trusted me with anything and everything; his money and, I might say, his

---

other things, sold "seal and horse hide Trunks" and "Leather Traveling Trunks." "Saddles, Bridles, Harness, and Collars," *New York Daily Express*, August 24, 1839.

* The steamers *Rhode Island*, *Providence*, and *Narragansett* departed from Pier 1 at Battery Place at 5:00 p.m., for Stonington, Connecticut, where passengers took railcars for Newport, Providence, and Boston; the *Massachusetts* sailed at 5:00 p.m. direct for Providence twice weekly. Tickets cost three or five dollars. "New Arrangement: Regular Mail Line for Boston," *Commercial Advertiser* (New York), April 18, 1839; the *Lexington* sailed from Pier 4 at 5:00 p.m. for Newport and Boston. "Fare Reduced to Three Dollars: No Monopoly," *Morning Herald* (New York), June 25, 1839.

life. In the second place, he was willing that I should enjoy life a little, if there can be any for a slave. I have come off without bidding him farewell, without telling him where I am going, or why I go. I have got his pistols with me, that I have carried north and south. A robber, some would say, but stay a little; let us see how far I am a robber. The law of the land says that I am Mr. Sawyer's property. When I left New York I did not know but this piece of property of my master's might be disturbed by someone. I had taken the pistols for its protection. But if I had had the money to have bought others I never would have brought his away. I do not wish to be understood to blame slaves, under ordinary circumstances, for taking anything that they want and can get from their masters. I would take it, and thank God for the chance. But where a man is denied nothing, and entrusted with everything—denied nothing, did I say? He is denied the only thing that could justify him in betraying such trust, that is his liberty, the fountain of all our joy, without which we are the most miserable of all created beings.*

Thank God! I am now out of their reach, the old doctor is dead; I can forgive him for what he did do, and would have done if he could. The lawyer I have quite a friendly feeling for, and would be pleased to meet him as a countryman and a brother, but not as a master. Though my mental sufferings had become such that it made life a burthen to me, yet I bear but one scar from the hand of my oppressors, and that not unrevenged.†

* Cf. Hildreth, *Despotism in America*, 54–56.
† In the context of *Despots'* original publication, in the pages of the *Empire* newspaper, this is where the first installment ended.

EIGHT

MY VOYAGE *to*

THE SOUTH SEAS,

and THE OBJECT *of*

THE VOYAGE—

MY SISTER'S ESCAPE,

and OUR MEETING

The first thing that I strove to do was to raise myself up above the level of the beast, where slavery had left me, and fit myself for the society of man. I first tried this in New Bedford by working in the day and going to school at nights. Sometimes my business would be such that I could not attend evening schools; so I thought the better plan would be to get such books as I would want, and go a voyage to sea. I accordingly shipped on board the *Frances Henrietta*, of New Bedford.*

This was a whaling voyage, but I will not trouble you with any fishing stories. I will make it short. After being absent three years and a half we returned home with a full ship, 1700 barrels of sperm oil and 1400 whale oil.†

* Jacobs initially found work managing the horses and stables at William Rotch Rodman's estate. Henry Howland Crapo, "Memorandum of Tax Delinquents," 1837–1841, New Bedford Free Public Library.
† The *Frances Henrietta* "sailed August 4, 1839 for the Pacific Ocean" and returned to New Bedford on February 16, 1843, carrying 1,700 barrels of sperm whale oil

I had made the best possible use of my leisure hours on board, and kept the object that drove me from my friends and my home before me when on shore. I had promised myself if what money I had coming to me would be an inducement to any one to bring my sister off from the south, I would have her; but there was better news than that, in the bosom of an old friend, waiting to be delivered. The ship dropped her anchor, and the shore boats came off with friends of different persons on board, among whom was R. Piper.* He had scarcely spoken to me before he began to tell me about my sister; her going to New Bedford in search of me, and her going back to New York, where, he told me, I should find her. This news to me was quite unexpected. I said, if my sister was free from her oppressor, I was a happy man. I hurried on shore, drew some money of the owners, and made my way to New York. I found my sister living with a respectable family as nurse at the Astor House.† At first she did not look natural to me, but how should she look natural after having been shut out from the light of heaven for six years and eleven months; the most of this time spent in a place not more than three feet six inches in height! I did not wish to know what her sufferings were, while living in her place of concealment. The change that it had made in her, was enough to make one's soul cry out against this curse of curses, that has so long trampled humanity in the dust. She had in her possession two letters from the south, one written by the old doctor to Mr. Tredwill, who was then living in New York. After my sister had made her escape from the south, Mrs. Tredwill gave her this letter, that she might see what the doctor's feelings were. I am sorry that I have not got the letter, that it might be copied in this little narrative; when William

---

and 1,420 barrels of whale oil. See "Abstract of the Voyage of the *Frances Henrietta*," New Bedford Whaling Museum, hereafter cited as NBWM.

* In 1841, Robert H. Piper (1814–75), son of William and Amelia Piper, was working aboard the ship *Jefferson*. For Harriet's account of her trip to New Bedford in search of her brother, see *Incidents*, 214.

† In June 1842, shortly after her escape, Harriet Jacobs found work as a baby nurse after interviewing with Mary Stace Willis, wife of the author Nathaniel Parker Willis.

Lloyd Garrison was about to leave the States for Europe on an anti-slavery mission, the coloured people of Boston met and passed some resolutions bearing testimony to their confidence in him as the uncompromising friend of the slave.* I gave him this letter at the same time, and told him that he could use it for the good of the cause. It was read several times, and published once or twice. In the letter the doctor offers 100 dollars reward for my sister, and after giving a description of her, he says—"I want to get her, to make an example of, for the good of the institution." The other letter was written by Caspar W. Norcom, a son of the old doctor.† He tells my sister that if the family ever had entertained anything differing from a friendly feeling, that it no longer existed; they would be glad to see her once more happy at her old home with her friends around her.

Harriet, doubtless before this you have heard of the death of your Aunt Betty. Around her dying bed we all poured forth our tears in one common stream. She was a member of Mr. Johnson's Church. Oh, too high the price of knowledge! In her life she taught us how to live, and in her death she taught us how to die. This was the aunt of mine they so cruelly separated from her husband. My sister, while in the south, was secreted by a lady who is still living there, which prevents me from giving many of the facts of her confinement.‡

Miss Mary Matilda Norcom, to whom my sister had been given,

---

* "On a hot July evening in 1846," Yellin writes, "black Boston staged a public farewell for the crusading Garrison, who was sailing to England to join the campaign demanding that the Free Church of Scotland return money collected for them in churches in the American slave south. John S. Jacobs' role in this meeting demonstrates his prominence. In crowded Belknap Street church, it was he who offered the official series of resolutions 'in the name of three millions of American slaves.'" Jean Fagan Yellin, "John S. Jacobs' 'A True Tale of Slavery' and Harriet Jacobs' *The Deeper Wrong*: A Brother's Story," in *Monuments of the Black Atlantic: Slavery and Memory*, ed. Joanne Braxton and Maria Diedrich (Münster, Ger.: Lit Verlag, 2004), 53; "Crowded Meeting of the Colored Population of Boston," *Liberator*, July 24, 1846.

† Caspar Wistar Norcom (1818–72), son of Dr. James Norcom.

‡ The uncle referred to in this passage is Stephen Bozman, who was also one of the people who helped Harriet Jacobs hide. When Harriet Jacobs first went into hiding in 1835, she was secreted by a slaveowner, Martha Hoskins Rombough

got married to a northern man, whose name was Mesmore. He knew that my sister had been living in New York, and also knew the name of a young man there who knew my sister. He wrote a letter to this Mr. Burke offering to pay him for any information that he could give him that would enable him to get her. It was but a short time after this that I saw Mr. Burke in New York. He showed me the letter. I asked him if he would allow me to answer it. He said I might. I was then living in Boston. It was before Daniel Webster had assisted in making it a penal offence for a Christian to give a crust of bread, or shelter from the bitter blast, to the perishing traveller. I told him where and when he could find her, but he did not make me a call.*

This unparalleled demonstration of American liberty and brotherly love was just being felt among the people of colour when I was

---

Blount, and Blount's cook, Nancy; by 1837, after her hiding place was threatened, she entered into hiding in her grandmother's garret.

* See *Incidents* (219–21 and 239–40) for the Messmore letters. In one of only two extant letters written in his hand, John S. wrote to abolitionist Sydney Howard Gay that Harriet had "received a very affectionate letter lass week from her young mistress—Mrs Mesmore," in which Messmore "reminds my sister of her former love and in that affectionat manner so peculiar to this no soul Nation." He likewise mentioned that letters to Harriet were written by other members of the Norcom family, and that Dr. Norcom had written the New York City police offering a reward of $100 for her. See John S. Jacobs to Sydney Howard Gay, June 4, 1846, in appendix 1 of this volume.

According to Yellin (*Incidents*, 389n6), "[Daniel] Messmore married Norcom's beloved daughter Mary Matilda in 1846 without obtaining Norcom's consent, following a series of violent episodes that split the Norcom family and the Edenton community: On January 7, 1845, Messmore assaulted Norcom's son Caspar Wistar with a stick and cowhide. Two days later, when Messmore was released from jail, young Norcom shot and wounded him and Messmore shot back. On March 1, a group of thirteen young men, including Dr. Norcom's son James, mobbed Messmore. In consequence, Messmore was indicted for perjury and Caspar Norcom was imprisoned. Daniel and Mary Matilda Norcom Messmore left Edenton, and in 1848 moved from Cincinnati, apparently to Norfolk; they eventually settled in New York. Norcom never forgave his disobedient daughter." See *Incidents*, 239–40. President Millard Fillmore signed the Fugitive Slave Act into law on September 18, 1850. Soon after, John Jacobs left for the territory of California, where the law was not in effect.

about to leave the land of the free and home of the brave, for fear of being kidnapped. Mrs. W. sent for me to her room, and gave me her word that if I would be satisfied in leaving my sister with her she should not be carried off by any slaveholder.* Feeling somewhat indignant at the idea of their coming, she said, "No, I will stop them myself at the door with a pistol first."

"Mrs. W.," said I, "I do not doubt your resolution; but how do you think you would act when it became necessary to fire?"

"I think I have nerve enough to do it," she replied.

But thanks to God it never came to this. The fleshmongers came, but they were not allowed to see her until she had been bought and paid for. Six years and eleven months she had been shut in in a cage; eight years after her escape from that she is hunted by the newly-manufactured bloodhounds of the north, and her friends made to pay 300 dollars to save her from being made the example spoken of in the doctor's letter.

The whole country was scoured from one end to the other. The southern planter would find his slave, and say to the northern man, "Go you and seize him;" and he dare not refuse.

---

* Nathaniel Parker Willis married Cornelia Grinnell Willis (1825–1904) in September 1846. This is the second Mrs. Bruce of *Incidents*. In March 1852, after the Messmores came to New York to capture Harriet and her children, Cornelia Willis "contacted the Colonization Society and authorized an agent to offer Messmore $300 to relinquish all claims on Jacobs and her children." Messmore agreed. *HJAL*, 115–16.

NINE

THE LAWS *of*

THE UNITED STATES

RESPECTING

SLAVERY

In the original Constitution the word "slave" cannot be found; but it was well known by the nation that it was there, and that it was not in the power of Congress to wipe it out. In 1848, the Congress of the United States ordered a revised edition of the Constitution.* First, I will give you a copy of the Declaration of Independence.

"We, the people of the United States, in order to form a more perfect union, establish justice, insure domestic tranquillity, provide for the common defence, promote the general welfare, and secure the blessings of liberty to ourselves and our posterity, do ordain and establish this Constitution for the United States of America."

I believe Henry Clay is as good an authority as I can find for

---

* In 1847–48, the Senate and House ordered a clerk named William Hickey to prepare a revised edition of the Constitution "and other public documents" and distribute more than fifteen thousand copies of the edition "for use" by members. Hickey placed his corrected "Constitution at the front of a 225-page manual of the national government that he had produced, which in the course of several editions he expanded to 521 pages." Henry Bain, "Errors in the Constitution— Typographical and Congressional," *Prologue Magazine* 44, no. 2 (2012), https://www.archives.gov/publications/prologue/2012/fall/const-errors.html. See also *Constitution of the United States of America, with an Alphabetical Analysis*, v–vi; full citation appears in the first footnote to *Despots* on p. 4.

the introduction of slavery into the United States, which was at that time one of the British colonies. At least, he has said as much against slavery and done as little for liberty as any man. If his statements are correct, slavery must have been introduced into the States in 1522, two hundred and sixty-five years before the adoption of the Constitution of the United States.

In 1791, four years after the adoption of the Constitution, the census of the States, as given in Hildreth's *History of the United States*, sets the Slaves down at...................... 697,697

In 1802, 11 years after, they had increased to......... 896,749

An increase of.............................. 199,052

The present number is supposed to be........... 3,000,000

A still greater increase of..................... 2,103,251*

In the infancy of their independence they passed a law in the United States Congress allowing the slave trade to be carried on between the United States and Africa for twenty years. This of itself was not sufficient for the slave-breeding part of this body of statesmen; they looked on abolition as a growing evil; they wanted a guarantee that slavery should not be touched in limb or branch until the twenty years had passed. In order to do this, they passed the following Act:—"Section 9.— The migration or importation of such persons as any of the States now existing shall think proper to admit shall not be prohibited by the Congress prior to the year One thousand eight hundred and eight; but a tax or duty may be imposed on such importation not exceeding ten dollars for each person."†

How they do try to hide their infamy from the world! The mere passing of a law, of itself, does not seem so odious, though it be ever so unjust, if left open to the power that made it to amend it; but such is not the case in the law copied above. This ninth section, taken in connection with others of the same character, can have but

---

* The first two totals of the enslaved population are drawn from Hildreth, *History of the United States*, 1:301, 5:436, while the last appears to be Jacobs's own calculation.

† Article 1, Section 9, Clause 1, commonly known as the Slave Trade Clause. *Constitution of the United States of America, with an Alphabetical Analysis*, 10–11; see also Hildreth, *History of the United States*, 4:193–94.

one common-sense construction given to it, and that is—"We, the representatives of the people of the United States, here assembled this 17th day of September, A.D. 1787, do acknowledge the rights and guarantee protection to all such as may hereafter engage in the slave-trade between the United States and the coast of Africa. We further agree that no law passed by the Congress of the U.S. prior to 1808, can stop or check this trade in slaves and the souls of men."* Yet the fleshmongers are not satisfied. They look to their numbers, and the number of their victims, and find themselves in the minority. They remember the blood that had just been spilt by their fathers about some tea, a little paper, and such-like things, which the more they were contrasted with the wrongs of the slave, the more insignificant they grew. They call on Congress not to protect the property, but to protect them against the evil that must and will, as sure as God rules the earth, grow out of it. It was given:— "Section 4, the United States shall guarantee to every State in this Union a republican form of government, and shall protect each of them against invasion, and on application of the Legislature or of the Executive (when the Legislature cannot be convened) against domestic violence."†

---

* For "slaves and the souls of men," see Revelation 18:13. The phrase was a favorite of abolitionists.

† Article 4, Section 4, commonly known as the Guarantee Clause. Though "perfectly innocent in themselves," Wendell Phillips wrote, the clauses of Article 4, "being made with the fact directly in view that slavery exists among us, do deliberately pledge the whole national force against the unhappy slave if he imitate our fathers and resist oppression—thus making us partners in the guilt of sustaining slavery." Wendell Phillips, *The Constitution a Pro-Slavery Compact; Or Selections from the Madison Papers* (New York: American Anti-Slavery Society, 1845), vi–vii. "The abolitionist William Lloyd Garrison," Paul Finkelman writes, "thought the U.S. Constitution was the result of a terrible bargain between freedom and slavery. Calling the Constitution a 'covenant with death' and 'an agreement with Hell,' he refused to participate in American electoral politics because to do so meant supporting 'the pro-slavery, war sanctioning Constitution of the United States.' Instead, under the slogan 'No Union with Slaveholders,' the Garrisonians repeatedly argued for a dissolution of the Union." Paul Finkelman, "Garrison's Constitution: The Covenant with Death and How It Was Made," *Prologue Magazine* 32, no. 4 (2000), https://www.archives.gov/publications/prologue

Here is another piece of northern recreancy. Though many of them had opposed the slave trade, and some of them were trying to get rid of it in their own State, yet they would let every Bill that was brought before the House for the support of slavery become the law of the land. There is another Bill connected with others, as if to hide it, which is very necessary to complete this peculiar institution—it is a part of the 2nd section—"No person held to service or labour in one State, under the laws there, if escaping into another, shall, in consequence of any law or regulation therein, be discharged from such service or labour, but shall be delivered up on claim of the party to whom such service or labour may be due."*

This law has direct reference to fugitive slaves, and no other class of persons; that law was not amended until 1850, when Daniel Webster and H. Clay, after a long struggle in Congress, finally succeeded in passing the amendment, which was the Fugitive Slave Law.

Now, my countrymen, for such you are, show me if you can, since the days of Adam, anything in which the laws of God and of nature, and the cries of humanity, were ever so little regarded as they were in that Bill; there was weeping and mourning from one end of the land to the other. All who could not be dragged into slavery— whether white or black, rich or poor, male or female—were threatened to be fined or imprisoned if they dared to give shelter, bread, water, or any aid whatsoever to the hunted slave. Every man in the United States employ was obliged to give his assistance when called on by the slave-hunters, and those who were not employed were made to honour and respect the law as the supreme law of the country. What says Isaiah x. 1, 2? "Woe unto them that decree unrighteous decrees; and that write grievousness which they have prescribed, to turn aside the needy from judgment, and to take away the right from the poor of my people, so that widows may be their

---

/2000/winter/garrisons-constitution-1. See also *Constitution of the United States of America, with an Alphabetical Analysis*, 20.

* Article 4, Section 2, Clause 3 (the Fugitive Slave Clause). *Constitution of the United States of America, with an Alphabetical Analysis*, 20; Hildreth, *History of the United States*, 3:522.

prey, and that they may rob the fatherless." And, Isaiah lviii. 2–6, 7, "Yet they seek me daily, and delight to know my ways, as a nation that did righteousness, and forsook not the ordinances of their God; they ask of me the ordinances of Justice, they take delight in approaching to God. Is not this the fast that I have chosen, to loose the bands of wickedness, to undo the heavy burdens, and to let the oppressed go free, and that ye break every yoke? Is it not to deal thy bread to the hungry, and that thou bring the poor that are cast out to thy house; when thou seest the naked, that thou cover him, and that thou hide not thyself from thine own flesh?"

There are the laws of the United States, forbidding the nation to do a single act of humanity toward the most helpless and most needy known to man; here are God's laws, every one of which are written on our own hearts. And a man may as well attempt to deny his existence, as to deny his conviction of the rights of man, and the duty we owe to each other. But another word, from the Acts of the Apostles, iv. 19, "Whether it be right in the sight of God, to hearken unto man more than unto God, judge ye." This institution thinks there is nothing too holy to be made subservient to it. There is nothing in the catalogue of crime but what can be found in this unnatural hell on earth. The slave's life is a lingering death. The last glimmer of hope that cheered their sinking soul is gone. Their backs lacerated and bleeding; their limbs galled with chains and fetters; fleeing from slavery, when hunger and thirst compels them to stop; they see before them a large city; they see churches, hear the bells ringing, and see the people going in. They hear them call on God, and ask him to visit the sick and afflicted, the poor and the needy, and the distressed everywhere. The people all go home to enjoy the blessings of this life, so bountifully bestowed by their heavenly father, upon whom they have so lately called. The slaves drag along after them, and enter as Lazarus entered the rich man's premises. "Who are you, and what is your business here?"*

---

* The parable of Lazarus and the rich man appears in Luke 16:19–31. The quotation is from John Bunyan, *The Pilgrim's Progress* (London: Ingram, Cooke, and Co., 1853), 272.

"We have fled from the prison-house of bondage, and ask protection from the bands of our pursuers."*

"Then you are runaway slaves?"

"We are, and ask your sympathy in the name of Him who tells us to remember those that are in bonds as being bound with them."

"Well, we do remember you all; we pray for you sometimes. What more can we do?"

"Sir, do we not owe certain duties to each other as men and brethren?"

"Yes, but I owe duties to your masters as well as you."

The one is an act of justice and mercy required by a just and merciful God; the other is not an injunction, but an unnatural prevention of the free exercise of your own conscience, in the elevation of bleeding humanity, whose sighs and groans have rent the air of heaven and sickened the soul of man. Hear Matthew xxvi. 42, 43, 44, "For I was an hungered, and ye gave me no meat. I was thirsty, and ye gave me no drink. I was a stranger, and ye took me not in; naked, and ye clothed me not; sick, and in prison, and ye visited me not."† Oh you willing and obedient slaves, how long will you be traitors to liberty and rebels against God? For shame, arise, and shake off your chains. It is you that stand between the southern slave and his liberty. It is you that have held him there for 68 years. Dare you make any pretensions to liberty or honesty while you are holding these men and women till the planters of the south can rob and plunder them? Dare you make any pretensions to the Christian religion while members of that body are sold to support the church? Who is the God that you worship? Is he a God of slavery, or a God of liberty? "No man can serve two masters; for either he

---

* The "prison-house of bondage" was a favorite image for abolitionists, but particularly for Frederick Douglass. John Jacobs was probably in attendance for Douglass's "The Right to Criticize American Institutions," a speech before the American Anti-Slavery Society (May 11, 1847) and may have helped print "An Address to the Colored People of the United States" in September 1848 at the *North Star* office. See *Report of the Proceedings of the Colored National Convention held at Cleveland, Ohio, on Wednesday, September 6, 1848* (Rochester, NY: John Dick, at the *North Star* Office, 1848), 17–20.

† Matthew 25:42–43.

will hate the one and love the other, or else he will hold to the one and despise the other. Ye cannot serve God and Mammon."* "He that says he loves God whom he has not seen, and hates his brother whom he has seen, is a liar, and the truth is not in him."† Where is the love that you have shown for the oppressed of your country? Is it for your adherence to that Constitution, which, I declared before, contains and tolerates the blackest code of laws now in existence? Your prayers and your petitions are alike; the one mockery to God, the other an insult.

I do not mean to cast any reflection on the Quakers, for they have done more than any other sect for the African race; and there are but few, if any, among them who have any reverence for that devil in sheepskin called the Constitution of the United States— the great chain that binds the north and south together, a union to rob and plunder the sons of Africa, a union cemented with human blood, and blackened with the guilt of 68 years. Ye northern slaves and petty tyrants, how long will you be driven by your southern masters? How long will your homes be the hunting-ground of slaveholders? Do you ever expect to have one foot of ground under the American flag sacred to liberty? Such you have not now; and you dare not claim it. Do you ever expect to see the day when every man can sit under his own vine and fig-tree among you, and no one to molest or make him afraid?‡ Do you ever expect to see the day when the stranger and sojourner with you will not be dragged from your doors? Do you believe that God holds you guiltless of the blood of the three million slaves? The people of the north can- not plead ignorance to the sin of slavery; and, let their opinion

---

* Matthew 6:24.
† A variant of 1 John 4:20: "If a man say, I love God, and hateth his brother, he is a liar: for he that loveth not his brother whom he hath seen, how can he love God whom he hath not seen?"
‡ The phrase "vine and fig tree" is used three times in the Old Testament: Micah 4:4, 1 Kings 4:25, and Zechariah 3:10. George Washington used the phrase over fifty times in his writings and considered Mount Vernon his own personal vine and fig tree, or place of refuge.

have been what it may before the passing of the Fugitive Slave Bill, they can no longer say, "This sin does not lie at my door;" they can no longer say, "I am not my brother's keeper."* The blood of your coloured countrymen cries out against you—the laws of God condemn you. The civilised and Christian world is arrayed against slavery. Let them build their ramparts as high as they please, they must and will be pulled down, and the oppressed let go free.

* Genesis 4:7, 9.

TEN

THE AGREEMENT *between* THE NORTH *and* SOUTH *at* THE ADOPTION *of* THE CONSTITUTION

At the time when the Constitution of the United States was adopted, Massachusetts was the only free State in the Union, though several other States were looking for the day when they would be freed from this curse. Georgia, North Carolina, and South Carolina were the three principal States that were in favour of perpetual slavery. The debates in Congress show beyond all doubt that those States would not unite with the other States until Congress passed certain laws to secure to them the right of property in their slaves in any of the States, and other laws of a similar character. It is very evident that those men who framed the Constitution of the United States, felt that they were doing deeds disgraceful and unjust. They hid it as much as possible from the eyes of the world by giving the word "slave" a pleasanter name. It is "person" or "persons" throughout the Constitution.

ELEVEN

THE DECLARATION
of AMERICAN
INDEPENDENCE,
with INTERLINEATIONS
of UNITED STATES
and STATE LAWS

When, in the course of human events, it becomes necessary for one people to dissolve the political bonds which have connected them with another, and to assume among the powers of the earth the separate and equal station to which the laws of nature and of nature's God entitle them, a decent respect to the opinions of mankind requires that they should declare the causes which impel them to the separation.

"We hold these truths to be self-evident:—That all men are created equal; that they are endowed by their Creator with certain unalienable rights; that among these are life, liberty, and the pursuit of happiness. That no slave held to service or labour in one State, under the laws thereof, escaping into another shall, in consequence of any law or regulation therein, be discharged from such service or labour; but shall be delivered up on claim of the party to whom such service or labour may be due. To secure these rights, governments are instituted among men, deriving their just powers from the consent of the governed, excluding Indians and free negroes.

That whenever any form of government becomes destructive of these ends, it is the right of the people to provide that no amendment which may be made prior to the year one thousand eight hundred and eight, shall in any manner affect the legalisation of the slave trade, between the United States and the Coast of Africa, a part of the price of the Union, paid to the South by Congress, in 1787. To alter or to abolish it, and to institute a new provision: any person maliciously killing or dismembering a slave, shall be made to suffer the same punishment as if the acts had been committed on a free white person, except cases of *insurrection*, or unless such death should happen by *accident* in giving such slave *moderate correction.*"*

With a Constitution and Union like this, what hope of freedom is there left for the slave? When shown your oppressive laws, you point us to the Congress of the United States, as if something could be done there. What has Congress ever done for freedom? In 1808 it stopped the slave trade between the United States and Africa. When it had done that, there was not another Act to be found in the Constitution of the United States that would allow them to take another step towards freedom. They have opened new markets for the extension of slavery and increase of the slave power.

John C. Calhoun, in speaking of the rights of the south, in a speech he made in Congress, said:—"So long as the States confine themselves to the exercise of constitutional rights, they are to be secured from any direct interference," which nobody denies; "but, also, that they are entitled to the direct countenance and support of the general Government in everything which they are constitutionally entitled to do, even though they may see fit to adopt or to persevere in an obsolete, retrograde, barbarous course of policy, alike disastrous to themselves, and disgraceful to the nation."† Mr.

---

* In the final sentence of this paragraph, Jacobs quotes Article 4, Section 12 of the 1798 Constitution of Georgia. William and Ellen Craft also quote this law in *Running a Thousand Miles for Freedom; or, The Escape of William and Ellen Craft from Slavery* (London: William Tweedie, 1860), 14.

† John Calhoun was in fact quoting an 1804 speech by Republican Speaker of the House Nathaniel Macon (1757–1837): "Here was the germ of the argument afterward zealously urged by Mr. Calhoun, and still in many mouths, but pushed much

Smith, of South Carolina, in the Congress of the United States, said, "To let the slaves loose would be a curse to them. A plan had been thought of in Virginia of shipping them off as soon as they were freed, and this was called humanity. Jefferson's scheme for gradual emancipation, as set forth, in his notes upon Virginia, was derided as impracticable. Emancipation would probably result in an exterminating war. If, on the other hand, a mixture of blood should take place, we should all be mulattoes. The very advocates of manumission held the blacks in contempt, and refused to associate with them. No scheme could be devised to stop the increase of the blacks, except a law to prevent the intercourse of the sexes, or Herod's scheme of putting the children to *death*. The toleration of slavery was said to bring down reproach upon America: but that reproach belongs only to those who tolerate it, and he was ready to bear his share."*

Mr. Smith seemed to be greatly alarmed at the idea of amalgamation—while the blood of American statesmen, from the President downwards, has been sold in the slave markets of the south. Look at the many colours between the European and African races, and you have the proof of this assertion at once.

Andrew Jackson, of Tennessee, speaking on the same question, said—"It is the fashion of the day to favour the liberty of slaves; he believed them better off as they are, and better off than they had been in Africa. Experience had shown that liberated slaves would not work for a living."†

---

further than Macon ventured to go. For we are now gravely told not only that the states, so long as they confine themselves to the exercise of constitutional rights, are to be secure from any direct interference, which nobody denies, but also that they are entitled to the direct countenance and support of the general government in every thing which they are constitutionally entitled to do, even though they may see fit to adopt or to persevere in an obsolete, retrograde, barbarous course of policy, alike disastrous to themselves and disgraceful to the nation." Quoted in Hildreth, *History of the United States*, 5:502.

* Quoted in Hildreth, *History of the United States*, 1:186. The South Carolina congressman William Smith delivered this speech in 1790.

† Quoted in Hildreth, *History of the United States*, 4:94. The speech was not by Andrew Jackson but by James Jackson, a Democratic-Republican Georgia congressman, speaking before the House of Representatives on May 13, 1789.

These reasons why slavery should not be abolished no longer stand good. Several of the States, soon after the adoption of the Constitution of the United States passed laws for the abolition of slavery in their respective States.* The coloured people have not got their rights yet in any of them, as a white citizen. Yet the world must acknowledge, that they can and do take care of themselves, in all the disadvantages they have to labour under. Yet they do not take more than an equal share of gaol or poor-house room from their white brethren. The chances of getting work are, at least, two to one against them. Sailors, mechanics, or day labourers, it is all the same. With all these obstacles in their way, if they can support themselves and families, what might they not do that others have done, if they lived in a free Christian country? I am aware that there are thousands in the States daily offering up their prayers to the God of the oppressed, and using all other means in their power to help the slave whenever he comes within the reach of their mercy; but under the present Constitution of the United States Congress has no power over slavery in the States where it now exists, and to so amend the Constitution as to make it abolish slavery is next to impossible. The following is an article of the amendment, copied from the Constitution:—

"Article 5. The Congress, whenever two-thirds of both Houses deem it necessary, shall propose amendments to this Constitution; or on the application of the Legislatures of two-thirds of the several States, shall call a convention for proposing amendments, which in either case shall be valid to all intents and purposes as part of this Constitution when ratified by the Legislatures of three-fourths of the several States, or by convention, in three-fourths thereof, as the one or the other mode of ratification may be proposed by the Congress, provided that no amendment which may be made prior to the year one thousand eight hundred and eight, shall in any manner

---

* The earliest states to abolish or order the gradual abolition of slavery were Vermont (1777; partial), Pennsylvania (1780; gradual), Massachusetts (1783), New Hampshire (1783, gradual); Connecticut (1784, gradual), Rhode Island (1784, gradual), and New York (1799, gradual).

affect the first and fourth clauses in the ninth section of the first article, and that no State without its consent shall be deprived of its equal suffrage in the Senate."

The first and fourth clauses in the ninth section of the first article referred to in the Constitution of the United States, shows that the Americans were not ignorant of the enormity of the crime that they were committing. For the first twenty years of their independence, had an angel come from heaven, and pleaded the cause of the slave, they had sworn to hear him not. For that length of time, they had agreed with the kidnappers to protect them in robbing Africa of her sons and daughters. But, after the expiration of these twenty years, which ended in eighteen hundred and eight, that traffic which was the corner-stone of the edifice of American republicanism, was considered a crime worthy of death. I am not learned enough to make that nice distinction between two thieves that some men can. If a man steals my horse, he is a horse-thief; but if he steals me from my mother, why he is a respectable slaveholder, a member of Congress, or President of the United States; while in fact he is as far beneath the horse-thief as I am above a horse. I cannot agree with that statesman who said "what the law makes property, is property."* What is law, but the will of the people—a mirror to reflect a nation's character? Robbery is robbery, it matters

* The full quote, from a speech delivered before the House by the Virginia planter and congressman John Randolph in 1828, is as follows:

> Sir, it was settled two hundred years since. It has been settled from the day on which the first cargo of Africans was landed on these shores, under the colonial Government. What new distinction is this, about persons not being property—as if there were any incompatibility between the two? Sir, there is none: there never has been any. Property is the creation of the law. What the law makes property, that is property; and what it declares to be not property, that is not property. There is no other distinction.

Henry Clay later appropriated the slogan, adding that "'two hundred years of negro slavery have sanctioned and sanctified' the principle of property in man." "Case of Marigny D'Auterive," *Register of Debates in Congress* 4, January 7, 1828, 920; William Goodell, *Slavery and Anti-Slavery: A History of the Great Struggle in Both Hemispheres, with a view of the Slavery Question in the United States* (New York: William Harned, 1852), 566. See also Frederick Douglass, "Northern Whigs and Democrats," July 7, 1848, in *The Life and Writings of Frederick Douglass*, ed. Philip Foner (New York: International Publishers, 2021), 1:311.

not whether it was done by one man or a million, whether they were organised or disorganised: the principle is the same. No law, unless there be one that can change my nature, can make property of me. Freedom is as natural for man as the air he breathes, and he who robs him of his freedom, is also guilty of murder; for he has robbed him of his natural existence. On this subject the Church and the State are alike. One will tell a lie, and the other will swear to it. The State says, "that which the law makes property, is property." The Church says, "that organic sin is no sin at all;" both parties having reference to slavery.* With a few exceptions, their politics and religion are alike oppressive, and rotten and false. None but political tyrants would ever establish slavery, and none but religious hypocrites would ever support it. What says Matthew, 15th chapter, 8th and 9th verses:—"This people draweth nigh unto me with their mouth, and honoureth me with their lips, but their heart is far from me, but in vain they worship me, teaching for doctrines the commandments of men."

At the time when the Constitution of the United States was adopted there were but thirteen States in the Union, with more humanity and less hypocrisy than what there is at the present day, with more than twice the number of States and six times the number of people. It was then slavery struggled for its existence, and had not the friends of liberty compromised principle for power it would before this have been numbered among the things that were; but as an inducement to get the Southern States in the Union they were then forming between the several States, a bill was passed of this nature:—"That no future law that may hereafter be passed by the Congress of the United States shall in any manner affect the slave trade now being carried on between the United States and the Coast of Africa, before the year one thousand eight hundred and eight;" giving the South twenty years to import what slaves they wanted into the country; and the number of slaves has increased to

* Jacobs refers to works such as James Dunlop's *American Slavery: Organic Sins; or, The Iniquity of Licensed Injustice* (Edinburgh: William Oliphant, 1846).

upwards of three millions, over which Congress has no control. The States where slavery exists, are the only ones that can make laws for its regulation; and they being so nearly equal in number with the northern States, and with but one feeling on the subject of slavery, it is impossible for the people of the north to effect any change in the Constitution of the United States that would make it favour freedom. The Union was agreed to for the protection of slavery, without which it could not have existed, and even now, as it has been stated in Congress by slaveholders, a dissolution of the Union would be a dissolution of slavery; but the people of the north dare not contend for their own rights. Six hundred thousand legalised robbers rule the country; the laws of the south are paramount over those of the United States. For proof:—The law of the United States pledges its protection to its citizens going from one State into another. On several occasions men have been taken out of northern ships while lying in southern ports, and sent to gaol for no other crime than having a coloured skin; and whenever the captain of the ship failed to pay the expenses of the prisoner, and take him on board when ready for sea, he was sold into slavery. This baneful kidnapping is carried on up to this day. The people of Massachusetts being unwilling to submit longer to so great and unlawful a wrong, petitioned the Legislature of their State to investigate the matter, and, as soon as possible, to bring it before the Congress of the United States. Two of her most respectable citizens were chosen, and sent to the south with official documents stating the nature of their business, which was to test the legality of a law that had made slaves of men that were born free in other States, and entitled to their protection. What did it all amount to? The south drove them home, and one of them, an elderly gentleman, barely escaped with his life. This is the treatment the south gave the north in the latter part of 1847–8. They received it like slaves.*

---

* In 1848, George W. F. Mellen and 193 others submitted a petition to the Massachusetts state legislature calling for laws to safeguard against various kinds of mistreatment of free Black sailors in southern ports. In 1862, John S. Jacobs found

In eighteen hundred and fifty it came to the slaveholders' turn to ask, or rather to demand. Some of the States had refused them the use of their gaols to put their slaves in. The people would give them food and shelter. They asked Congress to unlock the gaols of the north to them, for the reception of their slaves, and punish every man and woman who would dare give aid to any fugitive. Congress granted them all this; yes, and more. "The people of the north shall catch slaves for you. Wherever our Stars and Stripes fly, there the slave power shall be felt, and freedom shall be driven beyond the bounds of our country, to seek a home among those who have the courage to defend it." The people of the north have not. In the City of Boston, the capital of the State that received the insult from the south, the troops were called out by the Mayor of that city to prevent the escape of a slave.* They have taken up arms to force men into slavery, but dare not lift a finger for liberty.

What is to be hoped of a people like this? They are full of lies and hypocrisy. They sell their brother, child, or sister, and if it were possible, I believe they would sell their God, and worship the gold. Give me liberty with a cannibal, rather than slavery with a professed Christian. No man should hold unlimited power over his fellow-Man. From the repeated abuses of this power, he becomes the most brutal wretch that ever disgraced the human species; and the more he himself has been abused, the more eager he is to abuse others.

---

himself on a Liverpool ship that planned to run the blockade for Charleston and was forced to plead his case before a magistrate in the Bahamas in order to leave the ship. Petition of George W. F. Mellen, Massachusetts Anti-Slavery and Anti-Segregation Petitions: House Unpassed Legislation 1848, Docket 2164, SC1/series 230, Massachusetts Archives, Widener Library, Harvard University, https://nrs.lib.harvard.edu/urn-3:fhcl:11005505; Diaries of Frederick William Chesson, August 15, 1862, hereafter cited as DFWC (see abbreviations list for full source citation).

* After Anthony Burns's arrest in Boston on May 24, 1854, "an attack was made upon the Court House by a body of men, with the evident design of rescuing Burns." During the trial, Burns was guarded by at least 125 men. After the ruling went in the slaveowner's favor, Mayor Jerome V. C. Smith ordered that a regiment of Massachusetts infantry be posted on Boston Common "to guard every street, lane, and other avenue leading to the Court Street, State Street, &c. the route through which the slave procession was to pass." See Samuel May Jr., *The Fugitive Slave Law and Its Victims* (New York: American Anti-Slavery Society, 1861), 34–36.

But slavery is unnatural, and it requires unnatural means to support it. Everything droops that feels its sting. Hope grows dimmer and dimmer until life becomes bitter and burthensome. At last death frees the slave from his chains, but his wrongs are forgotten. He was oppressed, robbed, and murdered. Better would it be for the slaves, if they must submit to slavery, if the immortal part of them were blotted out; but, no—the feeling is natural. Nature's God has breathed it into the soul of man, but slavery is the unnatural off-spring of hell—a curse to the human family; hated and shunned by all. Rather let us blot that out of existence which stands between man and his rights; God and His laws; the world and its progress. The Christian religion that binds heart to heart, and hand to hand, and makes each and every man a brother, is at war with it; and shall we, whose very souls it has wrung out, be longer at peace? If possible, let us make those whom we have left behind feel that the ground they till is cursed with slavery, the air they breathe poisoned with its venom breath, and that which made life dear to them lost and gone.

In conclusion, let me say that the experience of the past, the present feeling, and, above all this, the promise of God, assure me that the oppressor's rod shall be broken. But how it is to be done has been the question among our friends for years. After the prayers of twenty-five years the slaves' chains are tighter than they were before, their escape more dangerous, and their cups of misery filled nearer its brim. Since I cannot forget that I was a slave, I will not forget those that are slaves. What I would have done for my liberty I am willing to do for theirs, whenever I can see them ready to fill a free-man's grave, rather than wear a tyrant's chain. The day must come; it will come. Human nature will be human nature; crush it as you may, it changes not; but woe to that country where the sun of lib-erty has to rise up out of a sea of blood. When I have thought of all that would pain the eye, sicken the heart, and make us turn our backs to the scene and weep, I then think of the oppressed strug-gling with their oppressors, and have a scene more horrible still. But I must drop this subject; I do not like to think of the past, nor look to the future, of wrongs like these. God save us from the blood of the innocent; I ask nothing more.

LET ME BREATHE THE FREE AIR OF ANOTHER LAND, AND DIE A MAN & NOT A CHATTEL.

NO LONGER
YOURS

THE LIVES OF
JOHN SWANSON JACOBS

JONATHAN D. S. SCHROEDER

PROLOGUE

Even as it vibrates with the prophetic intonation of the orator and the clamorous protest of the sailor, *The United States Governed by Six Hundred Thousand Despots: A True Story of Slavery* does not tell us about John Swanson Jacobs's time on the podium and at sea. Like nearly all slave narratives, it is silent about its author's life after slavery, about his loves and joys, extended family and friends, and ancestors. Furthermore, in devising an impersonal autobiographical style that refuses the sentimental objectification of the Black body, Jacobs casts even more of his life out of bounds in order to magnetize readers' attention on the slaveowner, the proslavery state, and the power of his own words. And of course, he could not say what lay ahead of him in 1855: a life of near constant mobility that saw him sail across the world on more than thirty-five voyages in seventeen years as a cook or steward, the highest rank that a Black sailor could hope to attain. Defiantly uncategorizable, lives like his are rarely remembered, because they exceed the boundaries of nation, occupation, and status that shape most archives and histories.

This biography reads across borders to bring the lives of John Jacobs back into play. Drawing upon a line of Black feminist historicism running from Toni Morrison through Saidiya Hartman and based on archival research on three continents and four oceans, it reconstructs the parts of Jacobs's life that were unavailable to him in

1855 as resources for life writing. These lives are extraordinary: born a sixth-generation slave, Jacobs emancipated and educated himself. As a free man, he worked as an American and British abolitionist, a Californian and Australian gold miner, and a Black citizen-sailor of the world. He published not one but two autobiographies. If these parts of his life were not written into his narratives, they nevertheless invisibly underwrite them. By foregrounding acts of Black world-building and repair and by supplementing rather than supervising John Jacobs's own words, this volume aims to create a model for undoing the Black message / white envelope structure of the slave narrative. The lives that John Jacobs led cannot be erased if we read wisely and imagine expansively.

 O N E

B O N D S E R V A N T S

of L I B E R T Y

Sailing to Freedom

In 1802, Tom Copper organized the largest slave rebellion in North Carolina history. Not for the first time and not the last, fear gripped the slaveowners of the twenty-eight tidewater counties of Virginia and North Carolina, a fear made all the more explosive by the shock waves generated by the Haitian Revolution and, closer at hand, Gabriel's Rebellion. Subversive letters supposedly penned by Copper and his conspirators were laid before the governors, who read of "the number of men involved, the types of weapons in their possession—muskets, scythe blades, swords, clubs—and their objectives, which was said to involve killing the whites, destroying Richmond, and taking the state."[1] Another letter, found in Elizabeth City and possibly written by Copper himself, sang out the language of American independence, concluding "with a determination that the [rebellion's] result must be Liberty or Death." In Edenton, Enoch Sawyer claimed he heard the conspirators discussing a plan to march to Camden, gather all who would join, massacre all the whites, kill all the Black women, and marry all the white women on their way to Elizabeth City, where they would wait for arms and ammunition from Richmond. On the lips of enslaver and enslaved alike was the prophecy of Copper and his officers, Samuel Overton, Minar, and Caesar: "A warm winter, a dry spring, and a bloody summer." As rumors circulated and expectations increased, slaveowners armed themselves, mounted nightly patrols, arrested and executed alleged conspirators, and every which way doubled down on the perennial strategy of Atlantic slavery: terror.[2]

Before he organized his eponymous rebellion from an Albemarle swamp, Tom Copper was a slave on Andrew Knox's Pasquotank plantation—the same plantation where Athena Knox raised her young son, Elijah.[3] Whether or not Harriet and John's grandmother and father had a role in Copper's plan, they avoided suspicion, unlike six others from the Knox plantation.[4] Tom Copper's Rebellion formed a crucial event in Elijah's childhood and informed the rest of his life. "My father taught me to hate slavery," John Jacobs recalled, "but forgot to teach me how to conceal my hatred."

John and Harriet Jacobs were born into an age of rebellion, and into a family that had resisted slavery for over a century. From the Haitian Revolution till the siblings' escape to the North in 1838–39, slave rebellions rocked Virginia and the Carolinas decade after decade. Names like Toussaint Louverture, Gabriel Prosser, Denmark Vesey, and Nat Turner became swirling centers of controversy and icons of Black resistance that endure as touchstones for understanding and reimagining slavery and antislavery's complex histories. Names that have not endured likely played an even greater role in teaching John and Harriet the weapons of the weak. Did they realize that their autobiographies represented the first chance that their family had ever had to present their side of the story? To understand who John and Harriet Jacobs were—sixth-generation slaves, with stronger claims to American identity than most of their owners—it is necessary to know their family history.

On the Knox plantation, Tom Copper must have sought out Athena for assistance in planning his rebellion, for she had known freedom. A decade earlier, her parents, Jack Cotton and Maria Knox, pulled off one of the largest and most daring escapes on record when they fled their enslavers in North Carolina and sailed to New Bedford with their five children. Incensed, Ambrose Knox, the wealthy merchant who owned Maria and her children, spent over $1,000 (the equivalent of approximately $31,700 today) on recovering them, beginning with the runaway slave advertisement that he placed in papers in northeast North Carolina and Richmond and Norfolk in Virginia (see figure 1.1). The ad ran for three weeks on the front page.[5]

For nearly six years, Jack, Maria, and their children, including Athena—the Theney of the ad—vied for freedom, unwillingly becoming the center of the first case to test the Fugitive Slave Act of 1793. When Knox's runaway ads failed, he sent a slavecatcher named Benjamin Clayton Lowry north. After Lowry discovered three of the family members in New Bedford in the summer of 1792, Knox initiated an action in Massachusetts courts against the Quaker sea captain, David Wilbur, who had allegedly helped the Cottons escape. The case ultimately drew into its net the governors and senators of five states, including Samuel Adams and North Carolina senator Samuel Johnston. Johnston, the chief architect of the Fugitive Slave Act, coached Knox on procedure and protocol while the bill was moving from the House to the Senate, and Knox successfully delayed the trial until after George Washington signed it into law on February 12, 1793. Support from Johnston and North Carolina Governor Richard Dobbs Spaight gave Knox every advantage, and he wrote his attorney that he had "not a doubt in the channel [the case] is in but the property will be restored with damages, & the thieves punished according to their deserts [*sic*]."[6]

Leading up to the trial, New Bedford and Providence Quaker industrialists such as William Rotch Jr. and Moses Brown funded Wilbur's defense while helping the family crisscross state lines, assume aliases to evade detection, and find work and learn new skills—above all in the cotton-spinning industry that was soon to bind New England and the South closer together. When Lowry confronted Rotch at his house, the slavecatcher "asked . . . if he did

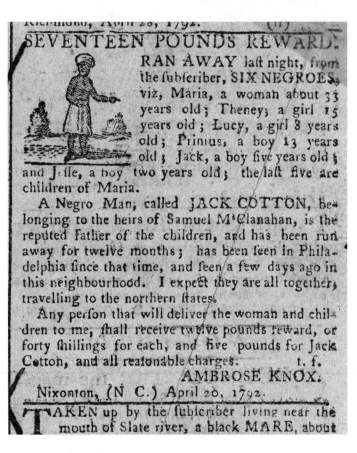

FIGURE 1.1. Ambrose Knox's Runaway Slave Ad, *Virginia Gazette, and General Advertiser*, May 2, 1792. Courtesy of the Library of Congress.

not think it very unjust th[at] a mans property should be stolen in the manner those negroes had been," and Rotch "said no, he did not consider them as any property at all and I shall protect them and all those that come here." Rotch continued:

Genl. Washington would be a man with[out] a fault was it not for his holding slaves, I consider those Blacks would make as good Citizens as any you have in North Carolina if they had a chance. Tho⁵ Hazard said he could come to North Carolina and bring negroes off with him [with] as much propriety as white people if they would

SEVENTEEN POUNDS REWARD.

RAN AWAY last night, from the subscriber, SIX
NEGROES, viz, Maria, a woman about 33 years old;
Theney, a girl 15 years old; Lucy, a girl 8 years old; Primus,
a boy 13 years old; Jack, a boy five years old; and Jesse, a
boy two years old; the last five are children of Maria.

A Negro Man, called JACK COTTON, belonging to
the heirs of Samuel McClanahan, is the reputed father of
the children, and has been run away for twelve months;
has been seen in Philadelphia since that time, and seen a
few days ago in this neighbourhood. I expect they are all
together, travelling to the northern states.

Any person that will deliver the woman and children
to me, shall receive twelve pounds reward, or forty shillings for each, and five pounds for Jack Cotton, and all
reasonable charges.   t.f.

AMBROSE KNOX.
Nixonton, (NC.) April 20, 1792.

come with him, he did not consider that David Wilbur and his crew
stole those negroes, he might bring all the Negroes away if he chose,
as he did not consider them any persons property.[7]

The Rotches and other Quakers successfully put up an antislavery
wall—one of the first in American history—and Knox lost the trial.
As Josiah Quincy would recall after 1850, it was at this moment that
the people of Massachusetts first pledged to disobey the fugitive
slave law and protect any fugitive from reenslavement.[8] Although
the case file of *Knox v. Wilbur* does not preserve the attorneys' arguments, Knox probably lost because the depositions that he provided

BONDSERVANTS OF LIBERTY 83

from two sailors aboard Wilbur's ship did not prove his ownership of Maria and her children. The jury ordered Knox to pay Wilbur's costs in the suit.

After the trial and after he was indicted in an Edenton court, Jack Cotton disappeared on a whaling vessel. He may have changed his name to Jack Freeman, proclaiming his freedom with a free name, as Rotch purchased six spelling books and twelve primers for him that spring—one book for each member of his family.[9] Maria and her children went into hiding in Rhode Island, finding work at one of Moses Brown and William Almy's businesses in Providence and northern Rhode Island. Days after the decision, Knox sent Lowry and another slavecatcher, Andrew Stanton, north to hunt down the family again. Stanton later reported that they discovered Maria, Athena, and two of the children not in Pawtucket at the Almy-Brown textile factory, but in Smithfield in the Blackstone Valley, "at a small shop" adjoining William Buffum's house at 383 Great Road. Stanton testified that "the people of that Neighbourhood assembled about 50 in Number & declared he should not do it without a warrant from the Governor of the State of Rhode Island." Faced with a human wall, the two men were forced to leave.[10]

In Smithfield, Athena and her siblings spent time with William's ten-year old son, Arnold, who in 1832 would found the New England Anti-Slavery Society with William Lloyd Garrison and serve as its first president. She also became attached to "a smart young colored laborer"—probably one of the ninety freepersons and five slaves who lived in the village of 3,600—who threatened to make "pudding" out of the slavecatchers with his knife.[11] The Cotton family presumably had to flee Smithfield and were not discovered again, and so we can only speculate about where they went and what happened to them. But in that spirit of speculation: What if the "smart young" person who was so enamored with Athena was Harriet and John's grandfather? What if his surname was Jacobs? This would solve some mysteries, including who the father of Athena's son Elijah was and who introduced the Jacobs surname to the family.[12] Whatever the relationship between Athena and the young man, if any, it would have been irreparably severed several years later when Athena was captured, reenslaved, and forcibly returned to Nixonton.

Following his loss, Knox immediately appealed the decision to the Supreme Judicial Court and gathered nine new depositions. Two of his oldest neighbors provided testimony that "traces Marias Genealogy back to her grandfather and mother & proves them to be Africans."[13] They had both known Maria's mother, Lucy, for "upwards of fifty years," and had also known her grandmother, Tenea, and grandfather, Primus, who were "both Africa born" and were the "property of John Wyatt."[14] In July 1794, the case went to court. We know nothing about the trial except the verdict: "The Jury find that the appellee is not guilty." Wilbur had won again. Did his attorney, future Massachusetts governor James Sullivan, argue the one thing that the slaveowner never imagined—that Jack and Maria were able and willing to escape on their own? Or did he simply argue that Wilbur had no knowledge of their escape? In losing, Knox lost more than just his money and slaves that year. His wife Mary had died in April at the age of thirty-eight. Two years later, Knox died, too, leaving his family and creditors to fight over his estate. In his will, he left Primus Senior, Maria, and her child Lucy to his son, John Knox; to John and Parthenia Wyatt, he gave Primus Junior. To "Old Lucy," he gave twenty shillings.

In his autobiography, five years after going into exile in response to the second Fugitive Slave Act, John Jacobs declared that "the Constitution of the United States is the Bulwark of American Slavery." Did he know what his ancestors had endured when the first Fugitive Slave Act was passed? Did he know that they were split apart as slaveowners learned how to manipulate an increasingly powerful legal, political, and police apparatus that forced early abolitionists to devise new tactics to thwart their efforts—the kind of scrambling that gave rise to the antislavery movement in the 1830s? It is unclear where Jack and Maria and their children went after 1793. By 1798, Maria, Athena, Primus, and Lucy were back in North Carolina. It is quite possible that they were kidnapped or that

Ambrose Knox's nephew, Andrew, pursued the case through North Carolina courts.[15] Andrew was not Ambrose's heir, but he likely came into possession of the family because Ambrose's son John was underage, and his other son, Robert, was not self-sufficient. By 1802, Athena and her son, Elijah—Harriet and John's father— were slaves on Andrew Knox's plantation, Woodleys Manor. And rebellion was in the air.

The Wisdom of Athena

Born into an Atlantic culture of terror, John Jacobs also received an inheritance: an intergenerational memory of the resistance to slavery. This inheritance can be traced back to the 1720s, when Tenea and Primus were first transported to North Carolina.

For their children and children's children, Tenea and Primus's lives spoke of a time just out of living memory that survived via accents, intonations, the way a meal is prepared, a phrase turned, a ritual performed—all the elements of culture that slaveowners could not eradicate. (Whereas Athena was given her neoclassical name by the Wyatts and Knoxes, she went by Theney, likely as a nod to her grandmother, Tenea. This is one way that Theney and her community took back the power of naming from their owners.) This was the memory of a culture where Black lives mattered as lives and not as objects to be exploited and disposed of.

In the early years of the eighteenth century, Tenea and Primus had been captured, brought to a slave fort on the coast of West Africa such as Cape Coast Castle, stripped of their clothes and, as much as possible, their sense of self-worth, and transported across the Atlantic on a journey of death, disease, and shackled migration called the Middle Passage. For the Royal African Company, Tenea and Primus were numbers on a ledger, two of "the 300,000 captives who departed from the Gold Coast (present-day Ghana) between 1675 and 1725 aboard ships bound for the English American colonies."[16]

Did Athena talk of the Middle Passage? Of fell disease, of conspiratorial whispers between the boat's creaking and the chains' rattling? Of slaves who were taken above deck and forced to dance to music to stimulate their circulation, which European physicians believed would help them fight off scurvy and malnutrition? Did they talk of the slaves who took these opportunities to jump overboard, believing their spirits would fly back to Africa? What ways of knowing the world did they draw upon to make sense of the eighty days and nights on board? Of the land they found afterward? When Tenea and Primus set foot on American shores, they were given only a short time to recover from the illnesses they had contracted at sea.[17] Slavers above all knew that the bodies of the enslaved could heal, but that no one could recover from the violence and degradation that they inflicted to break ties to self, home, kin, and culture, and to prepare men and women for social death in a foreign land. In this state, Tenea and Primus were brought to a place where they would be sold.

They were bought by the scion of one of North Carolina's first settler families, John Wyatt, in the 1720s or early 1730s.[18] Few ships sailed directly to North Carolina, so he probably traveled either to the lower Chesapeake or took the longer route to Charleston, the bigger market. In the 1710s, there were about 800 Africans in North Carolina, 211 of them in Pasquotank Precinct, where John had inherited land after his father died suddenly in 1686.[19] Eight years later, when he turned fifteen, he received a grant for 288 acres on Yeopim Creek, which, like much of the region, was composed of silt sand, as well as mucky peat, a loam-rich sediment that drains poorly, its blackwater flowing directly into Albemarle Sound.[20] By the time of his death, in 1739, Wyatt owned more than 1,000 acres adjoining the plantations of the Harmans and Norcoms—land that had been taken by "agreement" from the Weapemoc ("Yeopim" being the British transcription) and given as headrights to his family, the Calloways, and the Laurences.[21]

Tenea gave birth to a daughter whom she named Lucy—the "one slave named Luci" whom John Wyatt bequeathed to his son, William.[22] By 1743, William owned five slaves, and at his death in 1761, he owned thirteen. When he modified the family's earmark, which was used to brand their livestock, adding an "underbit" to the "crop in ye rite eare and a swallofork on ye left eare" to identify his property, what marks did he leave on his human property?[23] On William's death in 1761, he left eight of his slaves to his daughter Mary, including Lucy and her daughter Maria. One of the slaves given to his son John was a boy named Primus, who was likely Primus's grandson. When the estate was settled, things became even more uncertain for Lucy and her children. John and Mary were minors and so could not inherit their shares of the estate without a legal guardian. Two men, Thomas Leary and Joshua Worley, vied for the position, and the gateway to the Wyatts' wealth. Mary was vulnerable, and her guardian would have an entire childhood to groom her into a wife. With marriage would come the inheritance through the law of coverture, an inheritance that included Lucy and Maria and six other humans. Leary had the upper hand at first, but in 1765, the elder Andrew Knox, who was sheriff of Perquimans County and a member of the North Carolina General Assembly, became both siblings' guardian, a position he held for eight years. Soon after, Lucy and then Athena began to be listed as Andrew Knox's property.[24] Generation after generation, owner after owner, the family would find themselves living out lives as the objects of patriarchy.

Around 1770, Ambrose Knox returned home, likely after amassing a fortune in the West Indies trade that linked the islands and the Carolinas. Little is known about this period of his life, but he was probably in business with his brother, Andrew. When Ambrose landed, he set his eyes on a new fortune: his brother's ward. Approaching forty, Ambrose rapidly bent Mary to his will, probably with the help of his brother and the consent of his new neighbors, the Wyatts, who had their own intermarriage plans. At sixteen, Mary gave birth to her first child, Robert, and would eventually have two more. Soon after, John Wyatt married Andrew Knox's daughter, Ann.[25] Then, unexpectedly, Andrew Knox died, leaving behind a sizeable estate. In his will the merchant requested that his executors, Ambrose Knox and Samuel Johnston, settle all the debts they had amassed. In particular, he asked them to call in all money owed them, use it to pay off the debts, and then, if the books didn't balance, "sell at their discretion either at private sale or public vendue as much of my estate real or personal as shall be sufficient for that purpose." Once again, Lucy, Maria, and now her infant granddaughter, Athena, had to wait out an inheritance that threatened to split them apart.

To his wife, Christian, Andrew Knox gave "her the use & Labour of [his] Negro Girl Thene and her increase during her natural life." At the same time, he wrote that "all the residue of my real Estate & negro Thene & her increase I give divise & bequeath to be equally divided among my three children, Hugh Knox, Andrew Knox, and [daughter] Christian Knox & to the survivor or Survivors of them & their and each for either of their Heirs or Assigns forever."[26] And so in the first record to mention her, the infant Athena enters with her life predetermined, even as that decision would pull at her from multiple directions. Defined as real estate, rather than personal property, or chattel, in keeping with colonial Virginia law, her body was reduced to its capacities for labor and reproduction, assigned a commercial value, and divided between Andrew Knox's widow and, later, the three Knox children. Andrew ensured that Athena and her children's lives would be inextricably interwoven with those of his white, legitimate children.

Athena had to face the letter of the will almost immediately, as Christian Knox died the following year, orphaning Sarah (nineteen), Andrew (seventeen), Hugh (thirteen), and Christian (six). Just a toddler herself, Athena felt the turmoil without making sense of it. And thus, once again, "Thene" was itemized alongside the backgammon table, the heads of sheep, the sugar tub, candlesticks, and the books from a large library that included such texts as *Paradise Lost*, *The West Indian*, and *Defence of the Christian Revelation*. She and Dennis and Will found that their fates were out of their hands. By July 1777, Dennis was sold at vendue for 135 pounds, while Will was hired out. Yet the executors, Samuel Johnston and Ambrose Knox, did not settle the estate, and eleven years later, 1,150 pounds was still owed on it. To complicate matters, Johnston was himself owed more than 4,000 pounds, largely from debts accrued from the coastal mercantile business, Knox & Co., and on their sloop, *Franklin*.[27]

Athena was not sold but during this formative period was passed around with the care one would expect from such owners. Ambrose seems to have followed his late brother's lead and supplanted the two guardians initially appointed for the children, one of whom was Samuel Johnston, then sent Andrew the younger off to Edinburgh, and slowly assumed possession of his guardian's inheritance. The one bright spot was that Athena's mother, Maria, was living with Ambrose and Mary Knox, which gave her a chance once again to be with her daughter.

As Athena grew, she would have noticed how, with the passing of each generation, the skin of the family was getting lighter. She soon learned that skin speaks volumes even when lips remain closed, that it acts as a "monument" to what poet Caroline Randall Williams calls "the rules, the practices, the causes of the Old South," which condoned white masters' rape of Black women who served as their "help" and their "hands," and who were condemned to watch the same thing happen to their children.[28] Furthermore, when rich planters held control of the courts, rape was not considered a serious offense.[29] And yet a woman's light skin betrayed the knowledge that she passed on not only the stain of slavery but also the shame of rape. This is the ordeal that Harriet Jacobs lived through, wrote about, and resisted, as she escaped from the predations of James Norcom, whom she reported had eleven children with his slaves, into the arms of another white slaveowner, Samuel Tredwell Sawyer.[30] The two children she had with Sawyer, which he neither acknowledged nor willingly freed, constituted the price of admission for this most meager of refuges. All of Harriet's and John's biological children were able to pass as white, with both Joseph and Joseph Ramsey Jacobs choosing to do so.

Less intimately but just as important, geopolitics would play a role in the family story. North Carolina Whigs had been organizing resistance to the Crown throughout 1775, and when the

Revolutionary War broke out, Ambrose Knox and his partners took to shipping gunpowder and other supplies to the American army.[31] To throw America into disarray, the British deployed a strategy that Abraham Lincoln and the Union would emulate in the Civil War: emancipate slaves who escaped to their side. This strategy proved to be of signal importance for the Jacobs family. In South Carolina, a young slave named Molly was emancipated in the will of her master, who was also her father. He left her and others with money to go to St. Augustine, Florida, which had been in British hands since 1780, but during the voyage, as Harriet later reported, "they were captured on their passage, carried back, and sold to different purchasers." Molly was sold to an Englishman named John Horniblow, who took her to Edenton, where he had bought a plantation of five hundred acres that he named Horniblow's Point. By 1790, Horniblow owned twenty-seven slaves. In 1797, Horniblow bought Robert Egan's tavern and moved to town.[32] The two sides of the future Jacobs family were converging on Edenton.

Children of the Common Wind

Little is known about Athena and her young son's first years back in North Carolina, but it is quite possible that one of the roles that she and her mother Maria were asked to fill was as healers. Medical knowledge became a hallmark of the Jacobs family, with John and Harriet both working as nurses. Knox's plantation, Woodleys Manor, obliquely hints at the tense system that privileged white male doctors over enslaved healers, and speaks to how "conflicts between masters and slaves over proper treatments and practitioners went to the heart of planter interests in curtailing African American self-determination."[33] When Harvey Harrison began restoring Woodleys Manor in 2015, he found engraved on the doors, studs, and window frames hexfoils, also called witches marks. Drawn to ward off evil spirits by the British- and Scottish-descended slaveowners and laborers, and perhaps even by Knox himself, hexfoils like the daisy wheels that Harrison found (six petals within a compass-drawn circle) testify to the ways that religion, medicine, and slavery took on new shapes in the Americas as subjugator and subjugated struggled to control their own fates. Whether drawn by the builders or an owner of Woodleys Manor, these marks physically testify to the degree to which the institution of slavery was organized around violence and affected not simply the legal and social structure of the nation but also Americans' ordinary ways of being, belonging, and healing.[34]

In such a tense site as Woodleys Manor, Tom Copper drew ideas of revolt from all around him. Try as they might, slaveowners could not prevent news of the Haitian Revolution from making its way to the enslaved, nor the sensational news that their near neighbor, Gabriel Prosser, had led his own rebellion in 1800. Though Tom Copper's rebellion was foiled, it destroyed Andrew Knox's career as a planter, leading Knox to sell many of his slaves—others were hanged, others went missing—but he kept Athena and her child, Elijah. He married a doctor's daughter, inherited the practice, and moved into what became known as the Cupola House in Edenton.

As Elijah grew into a teenager, he trained as a skilled carpenter, probably because Knox subscribed to the widespread racist belief that light-skinned people were naturally more skilled and that these skills were hereditary.[35] So "skilful in his trade" was he, Harriet wrote, "that, when buildings out of the common line were to be erected, he was sent for."[36] Elijah's finish carpentry is still visible in some of the most important historic sites in Edenton: the federal portico at Beverly Hall, the drilled spiral molding of Supreme Court justice James Iredell's double porch, the barrel vault ceiling and square bell tower of St. Paul's, and the cupola that gave Andrew Knox's house its name.[37] In turn, Elijah's skill gave him mobility. Although he was still forced to hand over his wages to his master at the end of the week, he knew he had secured a certain amount of trust from him, which he used to mix with people in town and on shore. Even after Dr. Knox moved away in 1812, Elijah was permitted to remain in Edenton with his wife and children. "By his nature," Harriet recalled, "as well as by the habit of transacting business as a skilful mechanic, [he] had more of the feelings of a freeman than is common among slaves."[38] It was in this small county seat of fewer than one thousand people that Elijah met Delilah, the daughter of Molly Horniblow and future mother of Harriet and John Jacobs. Like her brothers, Joseph and Mark, and her mother, Delilah lived at Horniblow's Tavern, and was owned by John and Elizabeth Horniblow. Elijah probably met Delilah while doing a job for the Horniblows or across the street at the courthouse. Little is known about Harriet and John's mother except that Harriet describes her as "a slave merely in name, but in nature . . . noble and womanly." At some point, they married and Elijah gave Delilah a ring. While the ceremony had no legal force because of slave law, Jean Fagan Yellin writes that "their wedding was not without ceremony."[39]

Some time between 1813 and 1815, Harriet was born. About two years later, John followed.[40] Their time with their parents was short—Delilah died in 1819, the same year as Andrew Knox, and Elijah died in 1826. John and Harriet probably grew up in one of the outbuildings behind Horniblow's Tavern, surrounded by family. Located next to the courthouse, the tavern was where court-ordered business was carried out—shares of a steamboat company purchased, a saltworks auctioned off, or a plantation put up for sale. It also taught John and Harriet about slavery early on, for slaves were sold "before Mrs. Horniblow's door in the town of Edenton," such as "Negro Girl Dolly," who was advertised for sale in the newspaper.[41] As a site of town commerce, it also opened up the siblings' imagination to Edenton's place within the Black Atlantic. In the harbor, "sailors of all nations and colors, both free and slave," like their uncles Mark Ramsey and Stephen Bozman, "sailed not only up the coast to New York, but to the West Indies and even across the Atlantic":

> Revolutionary Haiti was not very far away, and the presence of the Cabarrus Pocosin . . . invited [their] awareness of the maroons of fugitives living freely just beyond the town's boundaries. [The siblings'] Edenton was . . . a multifaceted community of people—black

and white, slave and free—actively participating in the dynamic conglomerate culture of the Atlantic rim.[42]

Yet slavery also made its impact felt at home, particularly as absence, as when their grandmother's mistress celebrated her children's marriages by giving one of Molly's daughters each time to the bride as a wedding gift: "Molly's Betty would go to Mary Matilda, and Becky to Eliza. To Margaret, an invalid who would never marry, Elizabeth had already given Molly's Delilah."[43]

The children felt these absences just as sharply when a family member ran away. With Jack and Maria's escape in hindsight, the siblings grew up with an event looming: the sale of their uncle Joseph. Molly had given birth to five children, but John Horniblow, who died in 1799, only named four heirs in his will, thus creating a problem for the division of assets. After marrying into the family, James Norcom petitioned the court to sell the fifth child, twelve-year-old Joseph, at auction and to split the proceeds among the heirs. Eight years later, Joseph was sold for $675 to Josiah Collins the Younger, one of the largest and most feared slaveowners in the region. John Jacobs recalled the words of a "slave mother, who was taking leave of her son" before he went to Collins's Lake Farm. "He is going," she said, "to the lake of hell."

Not long after, Delilah died. Because of his age, John only had "a very slight recollection of [his] mother," but the death left a deeper impression on his older sister. Without her mother's protection, Harriet writes that she "learned, by the talk around me" that she was a slave, and it was at this time that Molly was forced to become not only grandmother but mother and general protector too.

Delilah's death brought her mistress, Margaret Horniblow, into the picture. In her early twenties and chronically ill, Margaret had been Delilah's foster sister and had been breastfed by Molly as well. "They played together as children, and when they became women, my mother was a most faithful servant to her whiter foster sister," Harriet drily writes. For John, the loss of his mother dramatized how Black parental authority was subordinated to slave-owning mastery and effectively canceled in the eyes of Black children. Margaret promised on Delilah's deathbed to care for little Harriet and John, and "under her protection and surrounded by family, Delilah's children grew finely, their lives enriched by the presence of their father Elijah, who was allowed to stay with them when working in Edenton, as when their mother was alive."[44] Miss Margaret took an interest in Harriet in particular, teaching her the rudiments of spelling and writing and "the precepts of God's word" in 1819—an education that would soon become illegal to provide, as John, who was not so lucky, found out. "It is unlawful for any one to teach [a slave] the alphabet, to give, sell, or lend him a Bible," he recalled, "yet they profess to be Christians they have churches, Bible and Tract Societies."[45]

In the church John found something of a safe haven from radical inequality. While he later learned to distinguish proslavery Christianity, which used doctrine to reinforce hierarchy, from a practical Christianity that lovingly called for its leveling, in Edenton he found no easy distinction. His father began bringing him to the Methodist church at a young age, but he did not see "Widow Horniblow" and her son in another pew, though they also belonged to the congregation. Despite the fact that three-quarters of the congregation was Black, the minister "preached to the whites in the morning, and to the slaves in the afternoon."[46] "Not a Sunday school nor a Bible class throughout the south where a slave dare put his head in to learn anything for himself," John later lamented, because "religious instruction given to slaves" by preachers such as Samuel Tucker Moorman, who became pastor of the Edenton Methodist Church in 1835, "invariably [was] about robbing henhouses and keeping everything about your master's house in good order."[47]

When John writes of the church or his father, he anatomizes the consequences of denying Black people sovereignty as individuals, families, and citizens. In keeping with a Christian worldview that equated justice with love, equality, and neighborliness, John was drawn to rebellion when his nation and its institutions violated these principles and failed him in the process. From the age of five through the Civil War, large-scale rebellions taught him about the immense gray area where the law and violence blurred. In May 1822, in Charleston, a free carpenter named Denmark Vesey organized a massive, coordinated rebellion set to coincide with Bastille Day, a date that he chose with the Haitian Revolution in mind. "There is ample reason for believing, that this project was not, with [Vesey], of recent origin," the editor of the *Raleigh Register* wrote, "for it was said, he had spoken of it for upwards of four years."[48] With each foiled rebellion, slaveowners tightened their grip on the slave caste. This meant passing strict state laws and above all controlling slaves' mobility and access to education. Vesey's plan added a new concern to the mix, as slaveowners increasingly began to see freepersons of color as threats to plantation management and the subjugation of the enslaved. "In no part of the U.S. are *free* blacks of any advantage; and in many sections, they are an intolerable nuisance," one author wrote. "They are interminably inciting the slaves to discontent, insubordination, and not unfrequently, to insurrection."[49] Within this climate, the American Colonization Society, which proposed to send freepersons to Africa, gained serious traction. In sidestepping the prospect of abolition, slaveowners forged a racial contract with groups they were ordinarily opposed to: evangelicals, Quakers, philanthropists, and moderate abolitionists.

Broken Bonds

Not long after Vesey's insurrection was foiled, Elijah was forced to move out of town. Andrew Knox's daughter, Lavinia Matilda Knox, had married a wealthy planter named James Coffield—one of the Coffields named in *Despots*—and moved to Greenhall plantation, about 6.5 miles out of town. With the marriage Elijah lost the mobility that made him feel a little bit less unfree, and John and Harriet lost the opportunity of seeing their father regularly. Even in his new situation, Elijah's "strongest wish was to purchase his children," just as he remained John's chief source of "parental affection and advice."[50] Not long after arriving at Greenhall, he also met a freewoman named Theresa and had a child with her. Elijah

Knox Jr. would later make his way north to New Bedford and start one of the most distinguished and educated Black families of the twentieth century; his descendants are the closest relations of John and Harriet alive today.

Then the vise began to tighten. James Norcom had entered the picture after marrying Mary Horniblow in 1810. Like Ambrose Knox before him, he used marriage as an avenue to wealth. And like Andrew Knox, he was a doctor, a proud alumnus of the top American medical school, the University of Pennsylvania. Norcom even named two of his children after his principal teachers, Caspar Wistar and Benjamin Rush, the latter "the most eminent and distinguished Physician of his day." Norcom proclaimed to the world that he was a slaveowner of the Enlightenment in many other ways, which was no contradiction in an era when slaveowners called for the reform of their own peculiar institution through the introduction of current medical knowledge and management techniques adapted from military training manuals.[51] Before returning to Edenton, he had spent three years sailing around the world on a kind of medical grand tour, "practic[ing] much on shipboard and among the natives of the places he visited."[52] He wrote and published articles, including one on fevers in the Albemarle region and another on the "virtues" of tobacco enemas for slaves. Upon his death, a friend wrote that he was "the best of husbands—the kindest of fathers—inflexible in his friendship to the poor and oppressed," and lavished numerous other platitudes upon him.[53] Not mentioned were the names of his eleven enslaved children.

By 1824, Norcom had set his sights on the slaves of his wife's sister, and particularly on eleven-year-old Harriet. Margaret Horniblow was then preparing her will, and she had bequeathed her five members of the Jacobs family to her mother. On her deathbed, however, something highly suspicious transpired: a codicil was added. "It is my will & desire," it read, "that the foregoing device be so far altered, that my negro girl Harriet be given to my [three-year old] niece Mary Matilda Norcom Daughter of Dr James Norcom."[54] Witnessed only by Dr. Norcom and an obscure figure named

Henry Flury, the codicil was never signed, and it is highly likely that Norcom was responsible for the alteration. From the Jacobses' perspective, all of Margaret's professed fondness and talk of freeing her slaves after her death had amounted to nothing, and now Harriet was going to have to pay the price. Time and again the Jacobses would witness the numerous ways that white women broke their promises or had their wishes overruled by men and the law.

In 1825, Harriet was forced to move to Norcom's house on Eden Alley, to the outbuildings behind the two-story, four-room house with its wraparound porch. The next morning, Harriet heard the crack and cry of a slave being whipped. As she worried about her own future, she also became concerned about her "spirited" brother, who had been loaned to Norcom after his marriage to Mary Horniblow.[55] Raised on his "father's fury" and desire for authority, John found working at Norcom's as a shop boy extremely hard. As he grew older, he was forced into other modes of submission that sought to teach him to "bear all things and resist nothing." In interacting with the Norcoms, John "early detested the name of master and mistress" so much so that they sought to teach him "his first lesson of obedience to a master."[56] In *Despots* he tells of the games he had to devise to prevent the Norcom children from cornering him into calling them master. "I could not make myself believe that they had any right to demand any such humiliation from me," he writes, and when he was finally forced into a corner, he was either able to "master" them, or, at "other times . . . take a rap."

After John and Harriet moved to the Norcoms', their father died and was buried in Providence, the Black cemetery north of town. Now an orphan, John recalled having "no one to look to for parental affection and advice save my grandmother." His new mistress, Elizabeth Horniblow, died less than two years later. As she went into the ground, her slaves were put up for sale: John, Uncle Mark, and everyone else, including Molly, "whose gray hairs and many years' service in the public-house did not excuse her from the auctioneer's hammer."[57] To see her sold in public like livestock was a traumatizing experience for the young children. In both John's and Harriet's autobiographies, the January 1, 1828, division of the family is an epochal event.

Sometime beforehand, James Norcom went up to Molly to convince her to hold the auction in private—to better preserve her dignity, he said—but Molly saw through his deception. Plus, she had a plan that depended on holding the auction publicly. "It was common knowledge that her dead mistress had intended to free her and, aware of the esteem in which she was held in the town, Molly insisted that everyone watch as he sold her off to collect the medical bills he claimed he was owed by Elizabeth Horniblow's estate. Seeing her on the block, the crowd hushed and, as Molly anticipated, refused to bid."[58] Molly had entrusted her savings, hard-earned from years of baking, to a white friend, Hannah Pritchard. Pritchard then bought her (for $52.25) and, with the remainder of Molly's savings, Uncle Mark ($406.00). John, however, was not so lucky, and was bought by Norcom ($298.50). In a characteristic refusal of sentimental depictions of Black suffering, John does not narrate his own experience and instead writes that "it would be in vain for me to attempt to give a description of my feelings while standing under the auctioneer's hammer; I can safely say, such will not be the case again."[59] As had happened time and time again, the Jacobses found themselves staring into a canceled future, in which they nonetheless had to fight to remain enslaved together rather than apart.

In the spring, an attorney, Alfred Gatlin, drafted Pritchard's petition to the superior court to emancipate Molly. Her free papers issued, Molly moved into Gatlin's empty house on King Street, opened a bakery, and bought her son from Pritchard. "It may seem rather strange that my grandmother should hold her son a slave," John writes, "but the law required it," and he added that Gatlin sold her the house and arranged for Mark's sale.[60] She was obliged to give security that she would never be any expense to the town or state before she could come in possession of her freedom. Her property in her son was sufficient to satisfy the law, since in its eyes he could be sold any minute to pay her debts. Harriet would spend seven years under a Norcom roof, seven more hidden in her grandmother's garret.

Not long after the family was sold but before Molly purchased Mark, Joseph had made his first escape attempt. He had been whipped for obeying too slowly, and had fought back, throwing his young master to the ground. He decided to take advantage of his knowledge of the Atlantic waterways and escape. Luck was against him, however, for a hurricane forced his ship ashore, close enough to home that the captain saw a runaway advertisement for him that "so exactly answered its description, that the captain laid hold on him, and bound him in chains."[61] When they arrived in New York, Joseph slipped his chains but was caught again. Joseph Blount Skinner, attorney for Joseph's owner, Josiah Collins III, spotted Joseph, identified him, and had him taken back to his master. In Edenton, Joseph was paraded through the street in chains and lodged in the jail for several months. Harriet and Molly could not visit him during the day, but the jailer let them enter in disguise at midnight, to find Joseph sobbing. John also likely adopted this ruse. Several months later, after being sold to a slave trader bound for New Orleans, Joseph escaped again, and this time he got away, despite being spotted by a Northern-born Edentonian in Baltimore. In New York, his uncle Mark, who worked as a steward aboard a packet ship, tried to convince him to wait until Molly finished raising money to buy him, but Joseph wouldn't wait. For once his "white face did him a kindly service" (it is likely that Joseph's father was white, since in legal documents, Molly, who also had a white father, is classified as a "negro" while he is listed as a "mulatto") and he left the country altogether.[62] "His intention was to get beyond the reach of the Stars and Stripes of America," John writes:

> Unwilling to trust his liberty any longer in the hands of a professed Christian, he promised to seek safety among the Turks. Since then we have not heard from him, but feel satisfied that he is beyond the reach of slavery, which is the greatest satisfaction that can be given

to us, his friends. Since that time both my uncle and myself have travelled a great deal, and never failed to inquire after him whenever we saw any one that we knew—that being the only hope we have of hearing from him.[63]

Losing Joseph hit the family hard: Molly broke down in tears, and John and Harriet lost an uncle who was like an older brother. Whether Joseph intended to go to the Ottoman empire or whether John is simply reproducing an abolitionist-orientalist trope to underscore the extreme despotism of the South, his uncle's disappearance only strengthened John's "resistant spirit."[64] More than anyone in the family, Joseph was responsible for leading John to associate the water and foreign lands with freedom. They had lost a family member but could still rejoice that Joseph was free. Later, they ensured that they would not forget him either: the siblings both named their only sons Joseph.

Insurrection Acts

Amid so much loss and turmoil, Harriet was learning how to live in the Norcom household. Her aunt Betty taught her the ropes and surely warned her of the snares that Norcom set for young girls. Norcom failed over and over to rape her, yet Harriet's victories were tempered by the fact that the next day might bring another round of assaults. Not surprisingly, Harriet used the language of weather to describe her life and to emphasize how slavery entrapped the enslaved in cycles of abuse. The intensity of her desire to protect herself from Norcom eventually led her to become the mistress of a local aristocrat named Samuel Tredwell Sawyer and to become pregnant with her first child. Becoming Sawyer's mistress later proved to be a delicate subject to address to a white readership, who often expected heroic acts in impossible circumstances. Consequently, Harriet Jacobs and Lydia Maria Child went to great lengths to demonstrate that ideal womanhood was unrealizable for enslaved African Americans because of slavery's corrupting influences.[65] They thus prepared readers to understand why Jacobs had to make such a nonideal, weak alliance, one that saw her trade sex for the dubious chivalry of a white slaveholder.

In 1828–29, Edenton was hit especially hard by the recession, since, with the opening of the Dismal Swamp Canal, ships and revenue were diverted to Elizabeth City. Dr. Norcom, a notorious spendthrift, was soon "among those in desperate need of relief." As Norcom's debts mounted, John and Aunt Betty were "repeatedly itemized for sale and reprieved when Norcom paid up." John's silence about this period of his life is deafening, his one-word estimation of Norcom loaded: "tyrant." On August 26, 1830, Harriet learned that she and her new baby were listed to be sold to pay Norcom's debts. Just as the first record of Athena's existence is in a will bequeathing her as property, the court authorization for the sale of Harriet's son "was the closest thing to a birth certificate that Jacobs's son Joseph would ever have."[66] Somehow, though, Norcom came up with the money and John, Harriet, and Joseph were spared the auction block. Whether Sawyer did anything to help his mistress and their child is unknown. The month they were marked for sale, August 1830, he was reelected to represent Edenton in the state legislature and moved to Raleigh, returning between sessions to Edenton and to Harriet.

During the downturn, sailors began carrying revolutionary pamphlets and newspapers from the North, sometimes sewing them in their coat linings. David Walker's plan was working, for his *Appeal to the Colored Citizens of the World* was designed to be read in public, its typography and punctuation functioning like stage directions for the literate to read the pamphlet aloud to others: "Hear your language, proclaimed to the World, July 4th, 1776— ☞ 'We hold these truths to be self evident—that ALL MEN ARE CREATED EQUAL!!—that they *are endowed by their Creator with certain unalienable rights*; that among these are life, *liberty*, and the pursuit of happiness!!'"[67] Not long after a freeperson was discovered with Samuel Cornish's *The Rights of All* in his possession, white Edentonians found that copies of the dreaded *Appeal* had reached

North Carolina. On New Year's Day 1831, the first issue of Garrison's *Liberator* was published, with a motto that John later lived up to: "our country is the world—our countrymen are mankind." Of the "secret agents" who supposedly carried the paper to the South "under the pretext of peddling," one North Carolina paper instructed its readers to "keep a sharp look out for these villains, and if you catch them, by all that is sacred, you ought to *barbacue* them."[68] In response, the state legislature, Sawyer among them, "created a storm of repression" designed to prevent the circulation of seditious publications.[69]

As Joseph Jacobs celebrated his first birthday, an enslaved Methodist exhorter named Nat Turner was carrying out a rebellion less than eighty miles northwest of Edenton, which ultimately took the lives of fifty-seven whites. As in previous insurrections, the reprisal was swift and brutal. Turner and twenty-eight of his followers were executed, patrols were mounted to terrorize the local Black population, and "low whites" led pogroms across the South, including in Edenton.[70]

Harriet and John prepared Molly's house to be searched and ensured that Harriet would be protected by Sawyer and Molly's patrons. Edenton probably followed the example of nearby New Bern, which requested that troops be sent in. When Josiah Coffield led the patrol to Molly's house, the family gritted their teeth for the violent intrusion and the inevitable breaking and stealing of their things. At night an armed mob took to the streets and passed by the house. Less than a week after Turner's Insurrection, rumor circulated of another slave "conspiracy" in Sampson and Duplin Counties, and reprisals were swift. "Extravagant reports" circulated that "Wilmington and Clinton had been captured and destroyed, that the intermediate country was laid waste," and that the bridge across Cape Fear had been blown up.[71] In Edenton on September 1, 1831, authorities examined a slave called Small's Jim under oath, who described a conspiracy "to kill the whites" and named more than a dozen names. Martial law was declared over the town's enslaved and free Black population for a week, and "by the end of the month, nineteen men—the property of ten local slaveholders—were in the old jail," with eight eventually "indicted for conspiring 'to rebel and make insurrection'" despite there not being "the slightest evidence."[72] Slaves were forbidden to visit loved ones on plantations, and the most important Black church, Providence, was pulled down. In a chapter of her *Incidents in the Life of a Slave Girl* called "Fear of Insurrection," Harriet Jacobs describes how "all day long these unfeeling wretches went round, like a troop of demons, terrifying and tormenting the helpless," at night "forming themselves into patrol bands, and went wherever they chose among the colored people, acting out their brutal will." Less than a year later, she gave birth to her second child, whom she christened Louisa Matilda at St. Paul's Church after Louisa Matilda Knox.

Of the fifteen- or sixteen-year old John during this period, however, we know almost nothing. He is silent about the rebellion, about the brutality and terror, about his fellow slaves who were jailed, about the untold number of unsanctioned reprisals, about the men who were charged with conspiracy to "rebel and make insurrection." What we do know is that while working in Norcom's shop and office, he used every means at his disposal to resist. He stepped out as frequently as possible, which caused Norcom to complain that "no persuasion, no menaces, no punishment, can confine [John] to the scene of his duty!" In retaliation, John later declared, Norcom's sons were explicitly "instructed . . . to see that I did not learn to write."[73]

The politicians and masters of Edenton used methods other than terror to control the Black population too. After Turner, the American Colonization Society received a groundswell of support, as moderate Southerners sought to send freepersons of color and slaves alike to the colony of Liberia. Earning the hatred of both the planter class and radical abolitionists, ACS members argued that the South would not become modern until it eliminated unfree labor and introduced capitalist incentives. When she emancipated her eight slaves in her will on the condition that they be sent to Africa with the ACS, Mary Mare Bissell set the controversy ablaze. Witnessed and written by Rev. William Douglass Cairns, the rector of St. Paul's Church, soon after the clergyman and Yale alumnus had moved from Connecticut to Edenton with his wife, Mary Catharine Cairns, the will created an immediate dispute with the vestrymen, among whom was James Norcom. When they suspected that the minister held grave doubts about the spiritual authority for slavery, they accused him of improperly influencing Mrs. Bissell. On March 14, 1837, Cairns tendered his resignation, saying that he would remain at St. Paul's only if the vestrymen unanimously asked him. Instead, they unanimously accepted his resignation.[74]

When Louisa turned three, Harriet tried to refuse to move into James Norcom Jr.'s Auburn Plantation, located six miles out of town. When she was ordered to sleep in the big house, she found that her work forced her to neglect her daughter. Norcom's grip was tightening around her once again. Swallowing her pride, she persuaded Sawyer to buy her and her children. Yet Norcom instantly refused the proposal, in part because of the enmity between the two men. When she started walking at night from Auburn to see her grandmother and John, she came up with another plan. She would outwit the cunning doctor. Her plan to entomb herself in her grandmother's garret above the storeroom is the stuff of legend.

The Garret and the Gaol

When she reached her grandmother's, Harriet quietly kissed her sleeping children goodbye, closed the door, and went into hiding. When morning came and her disappearance was discovered, northbound vessels were stopped, patrols issued, night watches scheduled, and a broadside put up, offering $150 if she were captured in North Carolina, $300 if not. A week of intense search turned up nothing. Somehow, Harriet got word to her grandmother to ask an old family friend and sympathetic slaveowner, Martha Hoskins Rombough Blount, to help. Blount's cook, Nancy, hid her in a small, locked room above the mistress's bedroom. In her chamber, Harriet waited for Sawyer to buy John and her children. She would be kept waiting far longer than she expected.

Norcom threw John, Aunt Betty, and the children in jail in

order to extract information from them. When they were less than forthcoming, he sent a slave trader to pretend that he was selling them to the Deep South. Now an adult, John dictated a note to encourage his sister and had an ally get it to Harriet, probably via Nancy. Though "scarcely legible," Harriet recalled, she was able to read his warning:

> Wherever you are, dear sister, I beg of you not to come here. We are all much better off than you are. If you come, you will ruin us all. They would force you to tell where you had been, or they would kill you. Take the advice of your friends; if not for the sake of me and your children, at least for the sake of those you would ruin.

As they wrote each other, John and Harriet began to realize that they could use letter writing to outwit their enemy. If "cunning" is "the only weapon of the weak and oppressed against the strength of their tyrants," they knew that the surest way to fool the racist doctor was to use the intelligence that he believed they were incapable of.[75] And given that they were both incarcerated and consequently immobilized, letter writing proved the only way that Harriet could trick Norcom into thinking that she was on the move between Boston and New York, as their grandmother, Athena, had been a half century before.

The seafaring men in the Jacobs family helped make this scheme possible, since each letter had to be posted from the North. Of the six people who kept the secret of Harriet's whereabouts, three were sailors: Uncle Mark, their uncle-in-law Stephen Bozman, and a man known only as "Peter." Because all of them regularly sailed on packet ships and commercial vessels to New York, they were able to make it look as if Harriet was writing from there. Remarkably, the Jacobs men's revolutionary act consisted not of smuggling subversive materials like *Walker's Appeal* to the South but carrying an enslaved woman's letters the other way.

Supported by her sailing kin, Harriet pitted her and John's knowledge of the first Fugitive Slave Act against Norcom's medical tactics. As *Despots* reveals, her first letter to Norcom states that she had been captured and jailed. "This calls the old man from home," John writes, "He has got to prove property and pay expenses."[76] And when the dependably cash-poor Norcom paid a visit to his in-law Martha Blount's house, he gave Harriet valuable information. Within earshot, he asked to borrow five hundred dollars, which she quickly inferred was to pay for his travel expenses to New York, notarized depositions, slavecatcher and attorney fees, and the myriad other expenses that Ambrose Knox had long ago incurred. Athena was surely standing behind them as the siblings learned how to fight to be free.

During the two weeks the doctor was away, John reflected on how unjust his incarceration was, even by Southern standards, and took certain liberties as his right. The jailor, Lamb, was his friend, as they had both spent time at the home of Gustavus Adolphus Johnson, a prominent freeperson of color and son of congressman Charles Johnson (their uncle Mark would marry a Johnson, and John was at the time attached to another member of the family). In jail, he worked out a plan to get himself and his sister out of slavery as quickly as possible. Uncle Stephen planned to take Harriet to New York around this time but abandoned the plan when he heard the doctor's threats "to punish to the extreme penalty of the law, any person or persons found harbouring, or assisting her in any way to make her escape." Consequently, Harriet pivoted back to letter writing as a safer course of action.[77] Between the garret and the jail (the "gaol" in *Despots*, which was published in British English), the siblings continued to correspond, conspire, and collaborate.

Harriet's next letter did more than send Norcom on a wild goose chase; it also drained his wallet when he was already cash-strapped. Accordingly, it helped the Jacobses in two ways. First, it pressured Norcom to sell his human property to pay off his growing debts. When a slave trader named Gaskins visited the jail, John was able to tell him with some confidence that he expected Norcom to sell him in the near future. Second, with his funds dwindling and a mounting jail bill, Norcom was forced to write from the North to release Aunt Betty and, two months later, John and the children. Frustrated, Norcom refused to let Stephen see Aunt Betty, even though they had lived together for twenty years; with "the charm of slavery . . . lost, . . . [Stephen] returned no more," jumping ship when he reached New York sometime later.[78] This is how John and Harriet did everything in their power to effect his own sale and that of the children. By orchestrating Norcom's financial misfortune by dangling Harriet as fugitive property, they assumed as much control as was possible for two incarcerated slaves in 1835.

There was one weak link in their plan: Sawyer. For their plan to work, the slaveowner had to buy John and the children. Fortunately, after two months, Sawyer sent a trader named Law to offer $1,700 for them. Norcom hastily agreed and the contract was drawn up. As they were leaving, Joseph showed Aunt Betty "a long row of marks" and told her that John had taught him to count out the days of their imprisonment. Outside, John was shackled to a chain gang, in a "scene that seemed too much like reality" for Molly, who fainted and had to be carried away.[79] The gang was transported by wagon to a hotel, where several men came forward with offers to purchase John, which were surprisingly rejected. Many of the gang were sold there, separated from their loved ones, before the remaining men and women were put back on the wagon and rolled out of town. At an old farmhouse owned by Joseph Blount Skinner, the man who had helped capture Joseph in New York, the wagon stopped, and John was let off along with his nephew and niece. As his shackles were hammered off, John must have appreciated the farce he was living. Far from an act of emancipation, his broken shackles signified that he was now the property of S. T. Sawyer, the white man who had had two children with his sister and who himself owned fifty slaves, who grew clover, oats, corn, and cotton on his 250-acre plantation.[80] This is what being saved meant—exerting one iota of control over one's own fate. "America is a free country," John writes, "and a white man can do what he pleases with a coloured man or woman in most of the States."[81]

Nevertheless, when Uncle Mark procured a wagon and brought

them back to Molly's house, there was rejoicing, for they had collec-tively pulled off a feat that bordered on the miraculous. Confined in Martha Blount's attic, Harriet was not so lucky, and she passed an agonized night with no news. When Norcom found out who had bought Harriet's children, he had Uncle Mark arrested on a charge of aiding her escape. The charges were dropped, but the search was renewed, and Martha Blount's housemaid was found trying to get into Harriet's room. Betty soon brought Harriet a jacket, trousers, and a tarpaulin hat, and, dressed as a sailor, Harriet walked the streets of her hometown undetected. Peter, who remembered Elijah not simply as his mentor but also his "best friend," went with her to Uncle Stephen's boat and then to a vessel offshore. Near dawn, she was rowed three miles across Albemarle Sound to Cabarrus Pocosin, next to Great Dismal Swamp. She and Peter spent the day there, but she grew so sick that it was necessary to bring her back right away. Luckily, Molly had prepared a hiding space that even Harriet didn't know about. It was then and only then that she entered the "loophole of retreat," the phrase she borrowed from William Cowper's *The Task* (1785) to describe the coffin-shaped garret above her grandmother's storage room.

Washington City

By August 1837, Harriet had manipulated Norcom into making three trips to New York City. He returned from the last one in time to vote against his rival, Samuel Sawyer, who was running for Con-gress, and he even crossed party lines to support the Democratic opponent, Dr. G. C. Moore.[82] Sawyer won in a landslide. With the House entering session in a month, Sawyer quickly packed his bags for Washington to join a North Carolina delegation of eight Feder-alists (i.e., Whigs) and five Administration (Democrats), a balance that later became a bare Democratic majority when Sawyer and fellow congressman Charles Shepard crossed party lines to support President Martin Van Buren's plan for an independent treasury.

Sawyer left John behind to care for his epileptic brother, Dr.

Matthias E. Sawyer. Jacobs was quite capable as a caretaker, having picked up medical knowledge under Norcom and during his time working for Dr. Sawyer. He was also surreptitiously caring for his sister. The following winter, Harriet suffered horribly from the cold and inaction incidental to her cramped, confined, drafty room, and at one point she lost consciousness for sixteen hours and became delirious. When John and Mark came to help her during the six-week illness that followed, John came up with the plan of going to a Thomsonian doctor and complaining of exactly her symptoms. After returning with "herbs, roots, and ointment," he brought coals up from the fireplace and applied the ointment.[83]

Around this time, while John was out of the house, Dr. Sawyer suffered a seizure, fell into a fire, and died from his burns. After the funeral, John was ordered to come to Washington. Sawyer had secured lodging at Mrs. H. V. Hill's fashionable boardinghouse in the old Capitol building; "so many politicians (plus 'dashing young men and transient bachelors') frequented the establishment that it was known popularly as the 'Congressional Boarding House.'"[84] While most senators and representatives lodged with members of their own state delegation, Sawyer lodged with the leading politicians of Virginia and South Carolina, including John Calhoun, Robert M. T. Hunter, and James Murray Mason, who would soon wield extraordinary power in antebellum Congress, which they used to strengthen the peculiar institution.[85] As Drew Gilpin Faust writes, "these legislators dined together, passed their leisure time together, and shared political ideas and strategies over dinner or breakfast or before the evening's fire; the 'mess' was the basic social and political unit of congressmen's lives."[86] At Mrs. H. V. Hill's, John was horrified by the private behavior of Washington politicians, as he repeatedly saw them abdicate their civic responsibilities in favor of cards and other trivial pursuits. To add insult to injury, as a gentleman's servant he was made to lie for them. In *Despots*, John reserves some of his most acidic barbs for his descriptions of politicians.

Back in Edenton, Harriet was still keeping Norcom off-balance. In winter 1838, she wrote two letters, dated from New York, which

Peter carried and sent there to make it appear that she was in Boston. Her aim now was to have Sawyer emancipate their children, but on that front, she had cause to worry. At the state convention in 1836, Sawyer had voted yes to "abrogat[e], *in toto*, the right of free colored persons to vote," thereby helping to take the vote away from free Black Americans. Did he also believe, along with other members, that "the God of Nature has put his mark upon the negro as a separate cast, and in that cast he wished to keep him"?[87] Beyond the buffer he gave her from Norcom, Sawyer was very much a Southern white slaveowner, and most of them kept their sexual relationships with "slave girls" private. While there was little hope of putting her relationship with Sawyer on more equal standing, from her garret Harriet also discovered that her chances of getting Sawyer to free her children were growing slimmer by the day. For to take the unusual act of emancipating Joseph and Lulu would be virtually equivalent to acknowledging them as his children. Thus, Sawyer's proposal to send Lulu to New York to live and work for his relatives was about all she could hope for. Was it then that she began to see her loophole of retreat as an embodiment of her impossible condition as a fugitive slave: a human capable of freedom in a nation that made no space for Black freedom?

At some point, Sawyer fell for Lavinia Peyton, whom he probably met at her aunt Eliza Peyton's boardinghouse. When they decided to hold the wedding in Chicago, Lavinia's sister's home, Sawyer thought twice about bringing John to a free state, and even made him promise to call him "mister" and not "master." A decade before the first train line reached it, travel to Chicago was accomplished largely by boat, and so they proceeded by steamboats along the seaboard, up the Hudson River, across the Erie Canal, and through the Great Lakes. At Niagara Falls, where they stopped for a few days, John had time to consider how far he was from home and just why his relatives had always taken to the waters to escape slavery's grasp. He had decided that now was the time. After the wedding on August 11, 1838, the Sawyer party traveled back through the Great Lakes. At a stop in Canada—likely Sault Sainte Marie or

Toronto—John went to the English customhouse to procure seaman's protection papers. That same month, in Delaware, another slave, who was not yet known as Frederick Douglass, was obtaining his own seaman's protection papers. John, however, decided against it, since he did not want to lie about his name on the certificate in order to pose as a free man.[88] They were also New York–bound, and Sawyer was the sort of master he could break away from when the time was right. John had spent four years putting on a good face for Sawyer. It was time to break the mask.

No Longer Yours

In New York City a few days later, while Sawyer was out, John left the Astor House hotel with his suitcase in hand at 4:00 p.m. He walked the three-quarters of a mile to Battery Place to catch a 5:00 p.m. steamship for Providence. Because "he was scrupulous about taking any money from his master on false pretenses . . . he sold his best clothes to pay for his passage," though he did take two of Sawyer's pistols.[89] When Sawyer returned, he found a note in the hotel room:

> Sir—I have left you not to return; when I have got settled I will give you further satisfaction. No longer yours, John S. Jacob [*sic*].

Four years of John's carefully constructed persona crumbled in Sawyer's face. As a declaration of independence, the note explodes the master-slave relationship by informing Sawyer that John has emancipated himself and is now in a position to tell *him* what's going to happen. Through a play on words, John also calls for reparations, as "settled" often meant putting things in a desired order and closing an account. (In fact, "settled" was written at the foot of bills once they were paid). But Jacobs reserves his best irony for the end, for to give someone "further satisfaction" meant to provide proof to remove doubt and uncertainty, to pay off a debt in full, or to gratify a desire. The satisfaction that John will give Sawyer this time is his own, for he tells him, in the language that, as a politician, Sawyer likely used in his own letters, his absence from Sawyer will be the best proof of his freedom and a continual reminder of the debt owed him.

When Sawyer arrived back in Edenton, he sent a boy to Molly's to tell the Jacobses that "the abolitionists had decoyed [John] away." Harriet reports the boy also saying that "he felt confident she would see [John] in a few days," which suggests that Sawyer may have attempted to recapture him. "The slaveholders," Harriet writes, "pronounced him a base, ungrateful wretch, for thus requiting his master's indulgence. What would *they* have done under similar circumstances?" She continues:

> I afterwards heard an account of the affair from [John] himself. He had not been urged away by abolitionists. He needed no information they could give him about slavery to stimulate his desire for freedom. He looked at his hands, and remembered that they were once in irons. What security had he that they would not be so again? [Sawyer] was kind to him; but he might indefinitely postpone the promise he had made to give him his freedom. . . . [John] had too often known such accidents to happen to slaves who had kind masters, and he wisely resolved to make sure of the present opportunity to own himself.[90]

In Boston, John was put up by "a worth Quaker family." He "told them that he had left his sister in that little garret-cell, where she had been shut up for years"; two years later, the same family would harbor Harriet for a year.[91] After a time, he "went through to New Bedford," where he was to start a new life.

TWO

TOWARD *a*

NEW GRAMMAR

of JUSTICE

Where is the love that you have shown for the oppressed of your country?
Is it for your adherence to that Constitution, which, I declared before, contains and tolerates the blackest code of laws now in existence? Your prayers
and your petitions are alike; the one mockery to God, the other an insult.

JOHN S. JACOBS, *Despots*

This is a band of brothers—let it be
In highest truth, Adelphic. Hand in hand
Explore the paths of knowledge. Heart to heart
In firmest concord stand. Think nought too hard
To be attained by diligence untired.
Action to us belongs—success to heaven;
Intentions, not results, are in our power;
And he who *greatly dares*, will *greatly do*.

HENRY W. WILLIAMS, "A Poem Delivered at the
Commencement of the Seventh Annual Course of Lectures
before the Adelphic Union Library Association" (1843)

When John Jacobs arrived in New Bedford, Massachusetts, in
May 1839, he came to a port town that had long offered fugitives
safe haven.[1] The Rotches, Rodmans, and a few leading families
continued to run the whaling industry and continued to welcome
people of color into it, just as they had welcomed his ancestors a
half century before. Between the 1790s, when Harriet and John's
great-grandfather, Jack Cotton, disappeared on William Rotch's

whaling vessel, and the 1820s, New Bedford had supplanted Nantucket as the world's largest whaling port. Between three hundred and seven hundred fugitive slaves made their homes in New Bedford between 1845 and 1863. Like Jacobs, many of them went to sea to evade recapture.[2]

Yet when John arrived, he stayed in town for four months. He stayed because he had come seeking an opportunity that was worth more to him than gold: an education. Slavery had left him illiterate, a consequence of North Carolina laws that prohibited slaves from learning to read and write. William Piper, who had escaped from Alexandria, Virginia, with his wife Amelia a decade before, helped John get work at William Rotch Rodman's Greek Revival mansion managing the horses and stables, and likely recommended he lodge in one of several boardinghouses for Black sailors, like those run by William Vincent, William P. Powell, and James Dyer. With the time that money bought, John began doing something he'd never been permitted to do. He began to practice being free.

"The first thing that I strove to do," Jacobs writes, "was to raise myself up above the level of the beast, where slavery had left me, and fit myself for the society of man." This line, which recalls Frederick Douglass's famous chiasmus, "You have seen how a man was made a slave; you shall see how a slave was made a man," represents Jacobs's promise that his independence is going to be defined positively, as liberation for himself and others.[3] Though he had told Samuel Tredwell Sawyer that he was "no longer yours," John had been unable to write his own note. In proclaiming his desire to enter into "the society of man," he points to literacy as the threshold for entering public and civic life and asserting ownership of the self. The Black community that John met in New Bedford only intensified these beliefs in the powers of self-cultivation. Douglass, who had arrived in town the year before, had recently given up caulking and day laboring and had begun preaching at the African Methodist Episcopal Zion Church in a little schoolhouse on Second Street—the first opportunity he had, he recalled, to "exercise my gifts," and to "prepare me for the wider sphere of usefulness which

I have since occupied."[4] It is quite likely that Jacobs first met Douglass in New Bedford, as a student and parishioner, and that he was a quick study too; at the end of his life, Douglass wrote that he "long ago remarked the intelligence of the colored men coming from North Carolina."[5]

As Jacobs earned the first money that he could call his own, it became clear that he needed a steady job that would give him better pay and more consistent downtime to attain the learning he wanted.[6] And so he began acquiring "such books as I would want" at sea. In New Bedford, that meant heading to the establishments of William C. Taber, the Quaker abolitionist and printer who helped operate the Underground Railroad between New York and New Bedford. At Taber's, Jacobs could buy blank notebooks and letter paper, as well as "juvenile" literature and works on morality, religion, and abolition, such as Theodore Weld's recently published *Slavery as It Is: Testimony of Ten Thousand Witnesses* (1839).[7] Taber's antislavery bookstore surely served as a model for John and Harriet's Anti-Slavery Reading Room in Rochester, New York. But first, the sea beckoned.

The Voyage Out

"I will not trouble you with fishing stories," John writes at the beginning of the second installment of *Despots*, reluctant to deviate from his narrative arc from enslavement to freedom. Yet the sea occupied a central place in the history of his family, no more so than in his own life. That fall, John signed aboard the *Frances Henrietta* as a steward, effectively the highest position that Black men could hope to attain on a ship (see figure 2.1). "African Americans" were considered "ideal servants, and most easily found work on whaleships as cooks and stewards," just as Native Americans were racialized as natural harpooners.[8] Though without opportunity for advancement, the position paid better and gave Jacobs time off at night when the officers retired. His 1/130th lay was a far cry from the 1/15th share that the captain took of the profits but a sight better than the greenhand's 1/300th lay.

FIGURE 2.1. Rounseville Slocum, from the *Account of Whaling Voyages in the Whalers By Chance, William Rotch, Liverpool, Royal William, Cora, Frances Henrietta, Newton, Dragon, Kutesoff, Russell, 1828–1851*. Courtesy of the United States Merchant Marine Academy, Kings Point, NY. The text reads: "Augt 4th 1839 Sailed in the above named Ship from New Bedford on a whaling voyage to the Pacific Ocean William H Reynard master Rounseville S Slocum first mate Zebedee Davvol [*sic*] second d[itt]o Isaac B Manchester third d[itt]o Randal Himes Wm Tuckerman Jose Valli and John Williams Boat Stearers."

Before he could learn to read, however, Jacobs had to learn his job. His responsibilities were similar to that of a gentlemen's servant, as he catered to the needs of the officer class, tending to many of their personal needs. Some of his tasks included cleaning and scrubbing the captain's cabin and staterooms, "painting and varnishing the walls and wooden trim about the entryways, and scrubbing the floors."[9] He also took care of personal supplies, fetching the captain's pipe and cleaning his dirty laundry. More generally, he served the captain and mates their meals and kept the kitchen pantries stocked, organized, and free of infestation. In addition to calculating rations, a crucial duty when ships were at sea for months at a time, he was responsible for sourcing foods at ports of call around the world that would prevent diseases of nutritional deficiency such as scurvy.[10] While not entirely different than his work as a gentlemen's servant for Sawyer, he now enjoyed far more responsibility in running the ship—and he was free.

Jacobs's position may have also been a source of resentment. The forecastle hands "often regarded stewards as members of the officer's camp," since the steward followed the same daily schedule, usually waking up between four and five o'clock in the morning. On the other side, the officers often resented the fact that stewards made as much as they did. Racism was woven into these tensions. When another Black steward, Charles Benson, sailed from Salem on the *Glide* in the 1860s, he wound up spending most of his time in his cabin or in the galley, passing "time in the company of the cook (the only other black man aboard), who shared the steward's isolation."[11] In this manner, Jacobs learned about the many meanings of race among the multiracial, multinational crew of sailors.

As the *Frances Henrietta* crossed the Atlantic on the way to the Azores and then turned south to Cape Verde, John had the opportunity to see whaling in action for the first time. Ten days in, over the course of two days, he saw the killing of nine "blackfish"—smaller whales such as orcas and pilot whales, which were processed for oil and bone. If he thought that as steward he could merely observe the action, he was sorely mistaken, and he soon found himself baptized into the strange rituals of his new occupation. When a smaller whale or porpoise was killed and butchered for its meat (and brains, which were battered and "fried like fritters"), the steward was expected to "tak[e] possession of the best parts of the 'lean,' for the use of the cabin. He chops it up fine, like sausage meat, mixing in sage, pepper &c. it is then fried in balls, and is justly esteemed a rarity."[12] No wonder that Jacobs later opened an oyster restaurant, or that Douglass could write that "Mr. Jacobs is a most excellent cook, as we can testify; and we have no doubt that he will give perfect satisfaction to all who may be disposed to patronize him in his gastronomic art."[13]

As the ship approached Cape Horn, the crew struck and killed their first sperm whale after a seven-hour chase. This was the monstrous ordeal he had signed up for: a multiyear voyage founded on the idea that Lilliputian humans could dart ropes into forty-plus-foot, 100,000-pound intelligent deepwater behemoths. A few days later, first mate Rounseville Slocum's larboard boat struck and killed a larger sperm whale, butchered and processed it, and stowed 115 barrels of oil in the hold.[14]

Rounding Cape Horn in November, gale-force winds split the sails, setting the ship adrift for two days. At the Juan Fernandez Islands, John Williams, a boatsteerer who had allegedly murdered a Wampanoag woman the night before sailing, went on shore and never came back. Desertion was extremely common. John Jacobs's education was proliferating in many directions. Yet rather than dwell on these scenes, he took out his copy books and taught himself to read, burning the midnight oil that was extracted from the very creatures that his mates were hunting.[15]

When they pulled into port at Paita in Peru in January 1840, John went ashore to buy foods known to help prevent scurvy, such as sweet potatoes and pumpkins. At Callao in May, he may have been asked to ride with the officers to Lima. If he did, he learned about cultures both indigenous and European as they clashed and came together in colonial sites that now catered to the American whaling industry. The first mate was fascinated by the *tapadas*

limeñas—the veiled women of Lima—and particularly their walking dress, the *saya y manto*, the overdress and veil that covered the
face entirely except for a tiny opening barely big enough for a single
eye to peep through. Allowing women to circulate freely around the
city without fear of molestation, the *manto* began as an emblem of
modesty but came to function "as a disguise that freed women from
social constraints and allowed them to engage in playful flirting or
to conduct secret liaisons."[16] Whether he went with the officers or
not, John found that he had to navigate not only his relationship
with them but also their ways of navigating foreign cultures.

As the voyage wore on, sperm whales proved elusive, and what
whales they did meet put up a serious fight. After four boats were
"stove" by a pod of whales, and whales broke away from the lines
holding them fast, Slocum wrote, "I should call it hard luck but the
old women say that every thing is for the best."[17] Three months
later, he was out of patience: "All for the best as the old women
say but if they hang their chemise to the fire to air and it catches
fire and burn they wont say so."[18] Eight months in, the newness of
whaling began to wear off. Whaling was monotonous, with most
of the voyage spent cruising back and forth to "raise" whales. The
putative freedom of the sea also had its limits, as sailors were subject
to a harsh system of discipline that used many of the same instruments of punishment—whips, irons, cat-o'-nine-tails—that John
had seen used in the South.

Toward the end of the year, the *Frances Henrietta* began killing as many as six sperm whales in a day. Their luck had turned,
but not for everyone, and as the weather also turned, six men "took
a boat in the Night and left the ship."[19] In the new year of 1841,
John repainted the ship, killed a pig, hooped a barrel to store the
remaining meat, and waited as the ship sailed up and down the
coast between Ecuador and Panama, killing whales with increasing
frequency and filling the hold with hundreds of barrels of oil.[20] In
the Galápagos in October, the sheathing needed to be removed and
the hull burned to kill the shipworms eating it. Multiple times, John

and others had to smoke the entire vessel out and kill the fleeing rats. The men took in six boatloads of wood, killed three hair seals, and caught about two hundred fish before beginning a new four-month cruise along the equator that eventually took them north to Hawaii.[21] When the ship couldn't raise any more whales, John may have reflected on the ethical bind he found himself in, for the lay system meant that he was personally invested in the ship's success: the more whales they killed, the more money he earned and the more likely he would be able to help his sister get out of Edenton.

Upon reaching Hawaii in March 1842, the ship stopped for almost a month. Slocum once more made note of the women: "We saw the pretty girls all around our ship . . . it was great sport for me to see them swim we could go on shore and go into any of their houses and play with the girls as much as we pleased."[22] With his sister still in hiding from her abuser and master, how did John respond to the officers, who were likely participating in the sex–for–Western goods trade that allowed Hawaiian women to acquire wealth, compensated for "the exigencies that a capitalist market foisted on Hawaiian families dispossessed of their land," and created a syphilis epidemic that resulted in a 47 percent drop in the indigenous population by the 1830s?[23] During his antislavery career, Jacobs reserved a special place for criticizing the American colonization of the islands. "He had been in the Sandwich Islands," Jacobs said at an antislavery convention years later, "and damned our churches for sending the Bible there, when it was so much more needed at home in the South."[24] The three missionaries the ship picked up on its way from Oahu to Maui left a lasting impression, one that he used to connect the Pacific and the South, proimperialist and proslavery Christianity, and Hawaiian and African American lives.[25]

After sailing as far north as the Gulf of Alaska, the *Frances Henrietta* arrived home in New Bedford on a "bittercold day" in February 1843. John Jacobs had celebrated three birthdays at sea, and when the ship dropped anchor, he was three days shy of turning twenty-eight. As he got ready to go on shore, William Piper's son, Robert, came on board and told him something astounding: Harriet had escaped a year ago and had recently failed to find him in New Bedford. John had not seen his sister in almost nine years. Before he could leave for New York, however, he had to unload the vessel—1,701 barrels of oil, 1,413 barrels of sperm whale oil, and 16,372 pounds of baleen. When John collected his earnings—$356.83 (roughly $14,665.00 in 2023 currency), another $10.00 for unloading the ship, $12.78 from the shipowner "for his bills of clothing &c" and, seemingly, a right to two casks of sperm oil on board—he now knew that this money was his own and was no longer needed as an "inducement to any one to bring my sister off from the south."[26] He then hurried to New York.

He found his sister working as a nurse for a Southern family at the very Astor House from which he had escaped. Harriet writes of their reunion:

> One bright morning, as I stood at the window, tossing baby in my arms, my attention was attracted by a young man in sailor's dress, who was closely observing every house as he passed. I looked at him earnestly. Could it be my brother [John]? It must be he—and yet, how changed! I placed the baby safely, flew down stairs, opened the front door, beckoned to the sailor, and in less than a minute I was clasped in my brother's arms. How much we had to tell each other! How we laughed, and how we cried, over each other's adventures! . . . He staid in New York a week. His old feelings of affection for me and [Louisa] were as lively as ever. There are no bonds so strong as those which are formed by suffering together.[27]

In her lengthy autobiography, this is the only moment where John or Harriet laughs. Yet the siblings' mutual laughter is not the product of a joke they had been telling or heard but the laughter of people who know that a joke has been played upon them—a cosmic joke. This laughter of disbelief, a noise that registers the two fugitive slaves' reduction to bare life and exposure to incredible suffering, evinces their awareness that even as they had survived the transition from slave to refugee, they had had no *right* to do so.

Just four years removed from slavery, John Jacobs had sailed around Cape Horn and learned to see the world as precious few ever do: as a single, interconnected planet. He had seen the Galápagos finches that gave Charles Darwin the idea of natural selection; witnessed the arrival of missionaries and plantations in Hawaii; compared the paddles, whips, and irons used to discipline his fellow slaves and shipmates; and circled the world for a company of Quakers who were against slavery but all for killing marine life. And he had learned the liberties of life as a sailor. Jacobs's long years in the Pacific likely drove home the fact that the businesses of whaling and slavery were different modes of killing life for profit. As whale blood, bone, and fat were worked into commas, zeros, and barrels, he learned to see the world as a whole by finding time and space for his own course of education. Part of what allowed him to take this wide-angle view was the fact that he had long been able to distinguish between the people who squeezed the life out of things for profit and those who were forced by circumstances to do so. Returning as an autodidact and a member of the motley crew of pirates, slaves, servants, and outcasts who devised and disseminated radical ideas about freedom and equality, John Jacobs was hungry for a formal education—for a kind of education that he had been denied all his life, an education that would help him speak truth to injustice, that would help him make something of himself. The best place for such an education was Boston, Massachusetts, the cradle of abolition and capital of the American university.

Yours in the Cause of Liberty

When John arrived in Boston, the Supreme Court had just struck down the personal liberty laws, which free states had erected to obstruct the 1793 Fugitive Slave Act. Shortly after *Prigg v.*

Pennsylvania, George Latimer had escaped to Boston from Virginia and become the testing ground for the 1793 law. When he was arrested and Massachusetts chief justice Lemuel Shaw enforced the decision, Boston briefly became the most violent city in America. Knowing that he and his sister were considered fugitives just like Latimer, John was forced to tread cautiously in Boston.

He was by himself, but not alone. He had surely heard of William Lloyd Garrison in the past dozen years. The "worthy Quaker's family" with whom he had briefly stayed in 1839 may have offered him assistance. And many of the Black New Bedfordites had strong Boston ties, such as Jeremiah Burke Sanderson, a close friend of William Cooper Nell, who in turn was the glue that held Black Boston together, and a board member of the Adelphic Union Library Association, a Black self-improvement society that John joined shortly after arriving.[28]

In 1840, about two thousand African-descended people (2.4 percent of the population) lived in Boston, principally in two areas: the base of Beacon Hill and the North End. Whereas North Enders were mostly single, transient men who roomed in boardinghouses and worked as sailors, Black families in Beacon Hill were considerably more affluent, settled, and respectable. As Boston became increasingly segregated, Black life centered more and more around Beacon Hill, which became a genuine beacon for antislavery organizing, politics, education, and society.[29] John moved into Grove Street, just down the hill from the State House, and likely boarded with an older Black woman named Lydia Potter.[30]

Just as he was getting his bearings, he found his sister at his door. Harriet had gotten word that James Norcom was coming to New York after her, but she fortunately was able to get a few weeks off from her mistress to visit her brother. With the protections of distance and her brother, she now worried about her children. After she wrote Grandmother to send Joseph to her, she was thrilled and relieved when the now-teenaged Joseph arrived. And John was equally elated, for he had not seen his nephew in upward of seven years, when he had taught Joseph to count in jail. Did

Joseph still look up to him, as John had once looked up to his own uncle Joseph? His nephew brought the welcome news that their uncle Mark had married and that Grandmother had become a communicant of St. Paul's.[31]

Before she returned to New York, Harriet likely attended the New England Anti-Slavery Society annual meeting with John.[32] For three "spirited" days and nights at the Howard Street Tabernacle and Faneuil Hall, the siblings were immersed in Garrisonian abolition and received their first taste of moral suasion. Because the Garrisonians believed that the Constitution so favored the slaveowners that formal participation in politics was doomed to fail, conversation during the convention revolved around the church, and more specifically whether the entire church should be censured "*as a class,*" or just the proslavery portion.[33] When Garrison took the podium, however, he took a different tack, looking out over a crowd of thousands and speaking directly to fugitives like John, if not as much to a Black woman like Harriet. "You are men," he began in his "Address to the Slaves of the United States":

> Created in the same divine image as all other men—as good, as noble, as free, by birth and destiny, as your masters—as much entitled to 'life liberty and the pursuit of happiness' as those who cruelly enslave you—made but a little lower than the angels of heaven, and destined to an immortal state of existence—equal members of the great human family.

For anyone reduced to the status of expendable life within a corrupt system of labor, justice, education, and religion, Garrison's words must have elicited a powerful response. Garrison did more than affirm the fugitives' humanity, however. He also borrowed a page from *Walker's Appeal* by sounding the difference between the inhuman and human:

> Your masters say that you are an inferior race; that you were born to be slaves; that it is by the will and direction of God, that you are held

in captivity. Your religious teachers declare that the Bible (which they call the word of God) sanctions slavery, and requires you to submit to it as of rightful authority. Believe them not![34]

Finishing with a flourish, Garrison unfurled the Declaration of Independence, his voice rising as he hit the phrases of his speech. "When a long train of abuses and usurpations, pursuing invariably the same object, evinces a design to reduce them under absolute despotism, it is *their right*, it is THEIR DUTY, to THROW OFF SUCH GOVERNMENT, and to provide new guards for their security." When he stopped, the crowd of five thousand erupted "in thunder-tones that shook the venerable pile to its foundations." Only when the hall quieted was Latimer "introduced to the immense multitude . . . creat[ing] a deep sensation."[35] Douglass and Charles Lenox Remond, who had both been on a lecture tour with Latimer that spring, took the stage. Douglass's speech is lost, but he probably spoke from personal experience to embody the hypocrisies Garrison critiqued, and, because it was Douglass, going much further. "I am one of the *things* of the South," he had declared a few weeks before, "and drawing himself up to his full height, and spreading his arms wide, he exclaimed, '*Behold the thing!*'"[36] John had been hailed as a human, rather than reduced to an object, and he had seen his peers stand on apparently equal footing alongside leading whites. His education as an abolitionist had begun in earnest.

Black life on Beacon Hill revolved around the Belknap Street Church. John enrolled Joseph in the Smith School, located in the basement, and spent evenings in the same schoolroom when the Adelphic Union Library Association met. During its eleven-year run from 1836 to 1847, the Adelphic served as the most important self-improvement society for Black men in Boston, who came to Belknap Street to borrow books from the library and take classes in elocution and oratory. On Tuesday evenings between November and February, audiences of all genders could pay a small fee to hear lyceum lectures by Alexander Crummell, Garrison, Douglass,

Theodore Parker, and other speakers who collectively delivered more than 165 lectures. Organized on the principle that "knowledge is power," the union "allowed black intellectuals to articulate their own vision of free African American intellectual life and to provide concrete educational and community service for African Americans in Boston." In doing so, the Adelphic stood at the head of a series of Black organizations that were rejecting Scottish commonsense philosophy and embracing transcendentalist thought, which in Black communities would become known as the philosophy of Elevation.[37] When John writes that he sought to raise himself above the level of the beast and make himself a man, he is speaking the language of the Adelphic, which taught its pupils the universal that all human beings are created equal. This education taught him to push back against not only out-and-out proslavery apologists but also moderates who hid under universals while sharing a belief in the natural inferiority of Black and brown peoples.

The presiding genius of the association, William Cooper Nell, was roughly the same age as John, had been raised free in Beacon Hill, and had founded the Juvenile Garrison Independent Society at the tender age of sixteen. He would come to call John his "adopted Brother" and Harriet and her daughter his adopted "Sisterhood."[38] A fierce supporter of equal rights, Nell helped run virtually every major Black society in Boston in the 1840s, and it is thanks to him, in his capacity as an employee of the *Liberator*, that we know so much about them. Other Adelphic committee members held positions of occupational distinction. Alfred Howard, Thomas Cole, and John T. Hilton were hairdressers, while others were librarians and waiters—some of the best jobs attainable by Black men at the time. In his will, Cole demonstrated their commitment to the association, giving all his books to the Adelphic, naming two fellow committee members as executors, and leaving a sizeable bequest to the Belknap Street Church.[39]

In this space, John found an opportunity for self-cultivation. In elocution classes, which he almost certainly attended, one of the first lessons required engaging with the question, "Does Justice and the good of society require the acknowledgement and exercise of the equal rights of the sexes?"[40] With a summer of practice under his belt, he most likely took part in the "Elocutionary Exhibitions" by class members, which followed Dr. Henry Bowditch's lecture that kicked off the 1843–44 season. Before Bowditch began speaking on "the evidences of design as exhibited in man and the lower animals," Nell introduced him as the chair of the Latimer Committee. Afterward, John would have been called upon to speak about Bowditch's lecture and its relation to the Latimer case.[41] And in fact, part of what the organization taught was to use knowledge of the humanities and sciences to advance abolition and defend Black humanity. The previous month, Bowditch had asked all Massachusetts gubernatorial candidates whether they were in favor of "altering or repealing all laws and constitutional provisions . . . which require the citizens of Massachusetts to assist in upholding or extending slavery" and "prohibiting rail-road corporations from making any distinction among their passengers on account of descent or color."[42] Between the lecture and exercises, Henry W. Williams read a poem on knowledge, at the conclusion of which he addressed his fellow members:

This is a band of brothers—let it be
In highest truth, Adelphic. Hand in hand
Explore the paths of knowledge. Heart to heart
In firmest concord stand. Think nought too hard
To be attained by diligence untired.
Action to us belongs—success to heaven;
Intentions, not results, are in our power;
And he who *greatly dares*, will *greatly do*.[43]

With such encouragement, Jacobs more fully subscribed to the idea that the pursuit of knowledge and truth would help him shape his own future.

That season featured lectures on natural philosophy (a lecture on "the Air," illustrated by a series of experiments), Nell on "The Means for Securing Success and Elevation," Douglass on the significance of the One Hundred Conventions movement, Jerome V. C. Smith on "the function of respiration and the philosophy of Voice," Wendell Phillips on "History" and "Trials in All Ages," Williams on "Electricity, Magnetism, Galvanism, and Electro-Magnetism," Henry Clapp on the "philosophy of reform," and Paul Sweetser on "Elocution." In class, students practiced their elocution before the lectures, which culminated in a student exhibition in March: a presentation of "a choice selection of pieces" and "performances . . . varied by appropriate music."[44]

As the season was getting under way, John learned his sister was in danger again. When Harriet had returned with the Willises from their summer stay in Saratoga Springs and resumed her life as a nurse, her daughter Louisa told her of a torn-up letter she'd found. When they pieced it back together, "they saw it was the draft of a note Blount had written to Dr. Norcom in Edenton, telling him how he could seize Jacobs."[45] While Mary Willis contacted antislavery judge Aaron Vanderpoel and abolitionist attorney John Hopper, John Jacobs quickly departed for New York to take Harriet back to Boston.

Breaking Through

In addition to teaching Black men knowledge, oratory, and politics, the Adelphic was a gateway to Boston antislavery activism writ large. Black "self-improvement," Benjamin Quarles has written, "had antislavery antecedents, for its advocates viewed it as a means of refuting the charge of racial inferiority while at the same time gladdening the hearts of the reformers."[46] If the Adelphic preached elevation, the Black activist organizations that it was connected with took direct action through the protection and aid of fugitive slaves.

Prompted by the dangers hounding his sister, John joined the New England Freedom Association. Formed in the wake of Latimer, the Freedom Association sought to raise funds to aid fugitive slaves—"those of our friends who flee to the land of the Pilgrims for their liberty"—and "to hide the outcast, and deliver

him that is spoiled out of the hand of the oppressor."[47] In particular, Nell helped connect fugitives with individuals who volun-
teered shelter or employment and with sewing circles that donated
clothing—aid that John and his sister may have received when
they first came to Boston. Members staged juvenile concerts, lectures by self-emancipated slaves such as Henry Watson, and levees.
On August 1, 1843, the ninth anniversary of British Emancipation,
members marched under a banner that read "Liberty inherent the
birthright of all" along the streets and through Boston Common
to Chardon Street Chapel to listen to speakers and hear the children's choir.[48] Here John learned another core tenet of the Garrisonians: "not to pay one farthing to any slaveholder for the property they may claim in a human being." Rather, members declared,
"our mission is to succor those who claim property in themselves,
and thereby acknowledge an independence of slavery."[49] Throughout his life, John refused to allow anyone to buy his freedom, for to
do so was to condone slavery.

As John took part in these events, he discovered that the Freedom Association was teaching him to find self-worth by helping fugitives become free on their own terms. If John felt a keen
urgency to do this kind of work, he was also discovering that what
he learned was never only theoretical but served at least three practical ends: redressing the harms of slavery; swaying political opinion among northern citizens; and developing a practical, above all
legal, knowledge of citizenship that might come in handy when a
slaveowner like Norcom came to recapture his human property.

Charles T. Torrey's arrest in the summer of 1844 touched a nerve
on all three fronts throughout the North. A major conductor of the
Underground Railroad who helped approximately four hundred
slaves escape, Torrey was already a well-known abolitionist before
his letters from a Baltimore jail made him an instant martyr, a status he came to share with two other white "slave stealers": Jonathan
Walker, a ship captain from Cape Cod charged with slave stealing
in Florida, and Calvin Fairbanks.

Black Bostonians were among the first to pick up Torrey's case.
An "enthusiastic" meeting of "colored citizens" at Belknap Street

raised twenty dollars, and a committee was formed to help "take further measure" in Torrey's and Walker's cases.[50] Torrey replied from jail to say that he "cherished" the gratitude of the citizens of color all the more, since they, not him, were the "proper *representatives* of the slaves" by virtue of race and kin.[51]

While Harriet was sailing for England in the summer of 1845, John was becoming increasingly visible as an organizer and antislavery activist. He wrote to Sydney Howard Gay in New York, who used his office at the *National Anti-Slavery Standard* as a hub of the Underground Railroad, to advocate for a friend from Edenton, whom he believed was being kept as a slave illegally, and he now signed his own letter, "yours in the cause of liberty."[52] In October, John was appointed to the lecture committee of the Adelphic, and he helped invite James McCune Smith and other speakers for the new season. And in December, he was appointed corresponding secretary of the Freedom Association. After she returned to the US, Harriet moved with her daughter to 87 Charter Street in the North End, while Joseph followed in his uncle's footsteps again, shipping out on a whaling voyage. Around this time, John moved from Boston to Chelsea, just across the harbor from Harriet and Louisa. Based on the range of causes that John subscribed to during this period and after—Irish famine relief, pledges to end the Mexican-American War, petitions against the Chinese "coolie" trade that drew unskilled contract laborers from Asia into conditions closely resembling slavery—it would seem that just as he had achieved a remarkable level of literacy on the *Frances Henrietta*, he had learned a new grammar of justice in Boston.

And then he started breaking through. With his sister likely in the audience, he first received a chance to speak for a Freedom Association benefit in January 1846. "Help the Fugitive," the *Liberator* ad announced, calling on supporters to come to Belknap Street to hear Jacobs and speakers such as Robert Morris, the most prominent Black lawyer in Boston. "*Come as the waves come*," the ad concluded, with a nod to Walter Scott.[53] On the Fourth of July, John helped out with the Rural Fair in Dedham and, at a crowded meeting at Belknap Street Church, was chosen to deliver a series of resolutions against the Free Church of Scotland for its support of slavery. "We, the oppressed of these United States of America," he intoned, "do entreat our anti-slavery friends in Scotland to hear us through our beloved Garrison [then in Scotland], and in the name of God and humanity let their watchword ever be, *No Union with Slaveholders.*"[54] When Torrey died in jail of tuberculosis during his six-year sentence, John helped raise money for a monument in his honor. The Torrey Monument Association would deliver a total of $83.37, which more than covered the cost of the lot at Mount Auburn Cemetery. Although other groups also chipped in and Liberty Party member Samuel Sewall took the lion's share of the credit for the statue, an obscure hint of the Freedom Association's contribution remains on the pedestal of the Torrey monument today in the phrase, "The friends of the American slave."[55]

That fall, John worked to help the fugitive directly. As Nell recalled:

> In September, 1846, the city of Boston was the scene of an exciting battle for liberty. A slave had escaped from New Orleans in a merchant vessel, and landed on the soil of Massachusetts, supposed by him, as by many others also, to be sacred to man and his God-given rights. He was hunted like a partridge on the mountain, secured and sent back to hopeless bondage. The friends of freedom put forth their power to save him, but the wicked slaveholder, aided by *Northern men—Boston men*, triumphed. In the struggle to save this flying victim from the "peculiar domestic institution," many men performed wonders; but none among them was more zealous or more executive than John S. Jacobs. For one whole dark night, (after vainly seeking for help in his chosen plan of rescue,) he was watching on the islands in the harbor, hoping to secure freedom to his brother. None the less praiseworthy was his effort or those of others, because not crowned with success.[56]

Given that this is exactly the kind of work performed by the Boston Vigilance Committee and its ship captain Austin Bearse, it is plausible that Jacobs had become a member of the committee as well.

By the following year, John had so demonstrated his abilities and so proved his dedication "to do all that [he] can for the deliverance of the three millions of Americans that are this day clanking in their chains" that the American Anti-Slavery Society invited him to embark on a speaking tour with Jonathan Walker.[57] In 1844, the Massachusetts shipwright and sea captain Walker had relocated to Pensacola, Florida. That November, he was found guilty of aiding and enticing "two slaves to run away, and stealing two others." Rather than deterring him, however, the conviction emboldened him, and next summer he sailed with seven enslaved men from Florida to the Bahamas. After fourteen days at sea, his boat was discovered by a passing American sloop and towed ashore. After he was convicted a second time, the court ordered that his hand be branded with the letters *SS* for "slave stealer."[58]

The image of Walker's hand became one of the most sensational symbols of the abolitionist movement. In John Greenleaf Whittier's poem "The Branded Hand," the "brave seaman" is celebrated as a throwback to the "old heroic spirit of our earlier, better day." In rebranding Walker's brand, Whittier's poem redefines his stigmata as the "highest honor" a person could hope to attain. The "S.S." on the captain's "branded palm shall prophecy, 'SALVATION TO THE SLAVE!'" and serve as a call to arms to break unjust laws, out of a fidelity to a higher law.[59] And so John went out on the road with a white martyr. Billed as a "'noble man of sable brow,' who, though but nine years since a Carolinian slave, has well improved his self-gained freedom," Jacobs soon found that he had to prove himself all the more because of how Walker's presence affected white audiences. It was time to show them who he had become: a person who was already on his way to speaking with the "fluency and depth of interest scarcely excelled by any of his predecessors—even by Douglass himself."[60]

Speaking Life

The *Liberator* announced Walker and Jacobs's lecture tour on December 3, 1847, the day that the first issue of Douglass's *North*

Star appeared. Nell had moved to Rochester in October to work on the newspaper, and the western New York town of twenty-five thousand was rapidly becoming the capital of the Black nineteenth century, *the* place where Black Americans forged dreams of self-reliance and self-sufficiency into ways of life. Over the next four months, Jacobs and Walker walked from Boston to Rochester, giving forty to fifty lectures at villages, towns, fairs, and conventions in between. Fifteen months later, Harriet would move to Rochester. The siblings' eighteen months in Rochester represent the longest uninterrupted span of time that they were able to live together in one place during their entire postslavery lives. And even that didn't guarantee seeing each other regularly, as John was away on tour for months at a time and Harriet was busy running the Anti-Slavery Reading Room above the *North Star* office at 25 Buffalo Street. Yet it was in Rochester that John, Harriet, and Nell became a chosen family, and that they learned the frank, unsentimental truth-to-power language that characterized Douglass' speech and writing and that white editors such as Lydia Maria Child found too unnervingly radical to put into print. From Douglass, Harriet and John learned "logic," "the powers of ridicule," and "language . . . classically chaste . . . like a piece of finished sculpture beautiful in every outline of its symmetrical, and unadorned simplicity." "We wonder not that Douglass is severe," an admiring auditor wrote after hearing him for the first time. "We applaud him for his boldness. We like to see a man stand erect and plead for himself, for his race and for truth, though blood drip from his blade. Our own shoulders may bleed, but we admire a fearless arm."[61]

In lecturing in over 150 towns with Walker, then Douglass, and finally by himself, John told the story of his passage to freedom, a freedom that remained unfulfilled. He walked roads that other lecturing agents, including Charles Lenox Remond, Lewis Hayden, and William Wells Brown, had traveled before him on the Western New York Circuit, the "Burned-Over District" where so many religious revivals and new religious movements had occurred. Just as in Douglass's *Narrative*, the siblings' narratives cast performance, whether by speech or pen, as a means of demonstrating self-reliance and self-sufficiency within a nation that makes Black autonomy impossible. *Incidents* represented the only way that a Black woman could live autonomously in America: in a nowhere space that disables her body. *Despots* constitutes a powerful philippic on the legal impossibility of autonomy for Black men and women in America altogether. This search for autonomy underwrites John's life of migrant labor, in the hinterlands of New York, the mines of California and Australia, and the open oceans.

As they made their way to Rochester, Walker and Jacobs took turns writing letters to Garrison for the *Liberator*. For Walker, they were "carry[ing] on a warfare at our own expense, against slavery and oppression, and consequently against this plundering and murdering government." Armed with words, the abolitionists disseminated the "melancholy facts" of slavery by "presenting the condition, the claims and the wrongs of the victims of oppression; urging a strict and candid investigation of American slavery, with its horrible realities, pecuniarily, politically, socially and morally, on this guilty nation." In response, the duo encountered a few instances of the "mobocratic spirit": a pistol was fired outside their lecture hall and gunpowder was sprinkled on Walker. More often, however, they found the people simply apathetic. Yet a war was coming that would be fought with more than words, and that would swallow them all. "The days of quiet repose, and union as a nation" are over, Walker prophesized, and the "dreadful conflict between freedom and slavery is ere long . . . to be fought in this country; and though I dread the consequences, I am anxious for the event to take place, that it may the sooner be over."[62]

Both Walker and Jacobs were asked to lecture because of what they represented. After hearing them speak in Norway, New York, one Baptist minister wrote that Walker's "simple, truthful story impressed upon the mind the fact, which multitudes are slow to admit, that the North *has* something to do with slavery," and in fact assists "the South to forge the fetters of the poor bondman."[63] Walker brought this structural claim home to audiences because his hand was branded not by a slaveholder but by a federal marshal, with a branding iron paid for by taxpayers. Rather than bury his head in the sand, he had gone to Florida to combat slavery directly and come back as living proof of how Northern avoidance enabled federal support of slavery.[64]

According to the same minister, Jacobs provided evidence "that it is possible for a colored man to have a mind; or to exhibit *great shrewdness*, and *give utterance to forcible thoughts without a mind.*" The minister's statement speaks to a widespread expectation of white antislavery supporters that Black lecturers perform their intellectual abilities in order to refute stereotypes of racial inferiority. Surely Jacobs was ambivalent about being typecast in such a role, even as he was undoubtedly proud of his hard-won education and abilities. In his lecture, Jacobs narrated "a very interesting incident, which took place when he was about nine years old," between James Norcom and himself:

> His master, who was a physician, sent him to carry two or more parcels to as many different places. Through mistake he miscarried one or more of them. On his return, his master inquired into the matter. The lad said he *thought* he had distributed them correctly. His master reproved him sharply for using such language, and said, with a soul-withering look, 'Who gave you a right *to think?*'[65]

Jacobs's scene demonstrates how slaveowners manipulated the line between thinking and unthinking humans to shore up their own power. For Jacobs, one can only buy into racist justifications of slavery if one ignores how slaveowners violently reduce the conditions of possibility for thought for the enslaved. Yet if this scene satisfied abolitionist expectations by giving an eyewitness account of his own experience as a slave, John already focuses attention on what his master said rather than his own suffering. While this incident did not make it into *Despots*, likely because it would have competed too closely with the primal scene in which he is caught between his owner's and his father's commands, it is telling that he locates his dawning recognition of the meaning of slavery in the effort to control his ability to think for himself.

When he wrote his own account of the tour, Jacobs chose a different incident to write Garrison about: a confrontation with a clergyman in the tiny village of Cato. On a Sunday, the "Slave Savior" and John walked eleven miles through the snow to make their appointment, only to find that the little schoolhouse was packed and that many attendees were forced to turn away. Nearby, two churches stood empty. When Walker told the audience that the reason they were forced to "breath[e] each other's breath over and over" in the packed room was because "slavery predominated in the churches of Cato," a local reverend jumped up in defense. He claimed that the churches were unavailable to the speakers not because of what they said, but when they came. By arriving after noon, they had broken the Sabbath. Therefore, "according to the Bible and the principles of Christianity," the reverend concluded that he had "no reason to expect that we would come." "Does that Rev. brother believe it to be a greater sin to travel through the snow to meet an appointment on Sunday, than it would be to tell a wilful lie?"[66] Jacobs asked:

> Let us suppose this charge true—that we are Sabbath breakers. Why should they condemn us for doing the thing that they always have taught us was essential to our salvation—the assembling of ourselves together? I have yet to learn that I have not as good a right to get up, or go to, an anti-slavery meeting on Sunday, as they have to get up, or go to, their meetings. Now, if the sin is in entering the town on Sunday, why do they not rebuke their brethren from the country? They are guilty of the same crime. If because it is an anti-slavery meeting, why do they come to hear, and participate in those meetings?[67]

Combining his training at the Adelphic and the American Anti-Slavery Society, Jacobs dismantles the clergyman's argument, exposing his charge of Sabbath breaking for what it is: a pretense concealing the church's prejudices. As a performance before a largely white audience, the lecture demonstrates Jacobs's chess-like ability to outmaneuver an opponent and score a point (much as in *Despots* where he encounters the clergymen on the train). If this is a dramatic performance, it is only one insofar as he chooses to dramatize his own thinking in action. Instead of using his experience as a slave to make himself into the object of his audience's pity, he uses it to shore up his authority before them.

When Jacobs wrote his next letter to Douglass and the *North Star*, he switched into a different rhetorical mode. At a missionary meeting in Rome, New York, he heard the following resolution discussed: "All that is necessary to make us more successful in making proselytes of the heathen, is more piety." After the missionaries "related some thrilling stories of the people in Bengal," they told a story about a converted "Catholic girl" who received a "Bible" but was made to return it by her priest:

> This they thought was an unpardonable sin. Oh that I could find words to express my indignation! Do they not know that every Bible they have handled since they have been on their mission, has been in part purchased with the blood of the slave? And if they were honest, they would write on the lid of every bible, "The price of the blood and souls of those who are not allowed to read it."[68]

One of the colonizer's ways of maintaining his innocence is to long for the very precolonial past that he has helped destroy. This is what anthropologist Renato Rosaldo has called "imperialist nostalgia."[69] For Jacobs, the Northern missionary similarly evades reckoning with the effects of the proslavery church at home by redirecting his attention toward converting colonized peoples abroad. Yet the rational exposé of hypocrisy, moral blinders, and corruption isn't enough for Jacobs. Just as Douglass had moved to Rochester in search of greater freedom of expression for himself and for abolition, John was working out his own style of righteous invective. This style of Black jeremiad is exclamatory, condemnatory, and damning—and it is an integral part of *Despots*. He writes to Douglass:

> Oh what a happy land of missionaries and slaves, Bibles and hand-cuffs, Bible pedlers and men pedlers, all belonging to the same church! Of all the horrible things that the sun ever shone upon, a baby-stealing, woman-whipping, man-murdering and war-making religion is the most horrible. These men are leaving scenes of suffering here at home, to go to a land where the introduction of them would not for one minute be tolerated.[70]

Rather than simply use reason to expose the irrationality and hypocrisy of his opponents, he lets loose a string of juxtapositions and phrases that resonates sonically and formally with the intensity and power of a curse. John signed his letter, "yours for the truth."

A few weeks later, John reached Rochester, where he met Nell and Douglass before his lecture at Minerva Hall. A young Quaker named Julia Wilbur declared it "an interesting meeting." After recitals of "Be Free, Be Free" and Whittier's "The Branded Hand" before a large audience, Jacobs "gave a slight sketch of his life," the earliest documentation that he had begun developing a narrative of his life. He looked, Wilbur wrote, "as if he <u>might</u> have been a gentleman's servant, smart, active, witty, Good looking. He had usually fared pretty well, but the chains of slavery galled his free spirit."[71] According to Nell, Jacobs "eloquently presented the wrongs of the American slave . . . in a manner and earnestness that carried conviction to the hearts of the audience. He is eminently deserving large and generous audiences."[72]

After two weeks off, the tour began again with twenty-seven dates in thirty days. Their roles became more clear-cut, with Walker cast as the martyr, the white man who had sacrificed himself for the Black, and Jacobs as the object lesson in humanity, the Black man who was as worthy as any man. One editor even declared that they were both "representatives of Jesus of Nazareth."[73] Now in his midthirties, Jacobs was making up for lost time as he crafted his performance abilities. The reserve and decorum he had learned as a servant and steward still helped him navigate white society, but he was shedding this "unassuming" manner in favor of new modes of dramatic expression and new ways to escape from the pull of white abolitionist expectations. In the last two months of the tour, Jacobs and Walker lectured throughout Massachusetts, passing through John's old haunts. In New Bedford, Jacobs visited the studio of Joseph Whiting Stock and commissioned the only surviving image of him (which appears in this volume as the frontispiece and is discussed at length in "John Jacobs at First Sight: Notes on a Frontispiece," following *No Longer Yours*).

Though he had made less than one hundred dollars over the entire trip, he was starting to find in Rochester something closer to freedom. If Douglass preached "sacred self-sovereignty," Jacobs was learning that a core part of that principle consisted of remaining true to his own words, honing their dramatic intensity, and developing new confidence in his own expressive powers.[74]

Signifying Life

Then John Jacobs set out on his own. Now employed by the Massachusetts Anti-Slavery Society as a lecturing agent and as a small part of the One Hundred Conventions movement, his aim was to "agitate in the State the question of Dissolution" from the union and "the question of slavery."[75] At Hopedale, Adin Ballou's utopian nonresistant community, Jacobs gave a speech—that, thanks to convention secretary and "worthy sister" Abby Price, is almost fully preserved and includes an early version of his life story—in which he presented his account "in a modest and unassuming, yet manly and dignified manner." Though Price shifted Jacobs's speech into the third person, after reading *Despots* one can easily imagine Jacobs uttering the following sentences:

He had been around the world as a seaman, and had seen slavery in many countries; but in no other country was slavery so hopeless as in this. Here the slave had not, as a general thing, as in other places, a chance to buy himself. Here you dare teach the slave to read the Bible; in other countries he had the same right that others had. In the Southern States we saw the sects selling each other; but in no other land did we see this done. We needed Missionaries from other countries to teach us the very first principles of Christianity. There were those who thought we had no business to interfere with it, because what the law makes property *is* property; what the law makes right *is* right. Well, upon what right was this law founded? Had he not a *prior* claim to himself? Though he was stolen, was he not his own? They had been robbed, degraded, and for that hated.[76]

In place of slavery, which confined slaves to their bodies by denying them literacy's ability to expand a person's worldview, Jacobs represents himself as a cosmopolitan sailor. Like an anthropologist, he establishes distance from the US to compare its customs and habits with other lands to see how American slavery stacks up. By provincializing the US, he turns the ethnographic gaze against the colonizers themselves, arguing that they need to be *decolonized*. To begin this unlearning, he turns to personal experience:

> He had been a slave. He had seen slavery in all its horror. He knew the slave was not happy in his situation. They were compelled to be false to their true feelings—to appear happy when they were not. They were compelled to say they do not desire freedom when they do. But if there were any who loved servitude, he would open the way for their education, and then if they loved slavery better than liberty, let them enjoy it. He contrasted the situation of the bondman with that of the free laborer at the North. The slave was not allowed to act for himself, or *think* for himself. Subject to the caprice of his master, the slave was exposed to every cruelty.[77]

The Jacobs of this speech is as much the Jacobs of Harriet's *Incidents*, concerned with the vicious effects of slavery on the slave, as it is of his own *Despots*. Harriet's narrative demonstrates how slavery catches slaveowner and slave alike in a vicious circle, such that the enslaved are compelled to become counterfeit persons—laborers against their will, actors of emotions they do not feel, and victims of desires they can scarcely fend off.

In December 1848, John returned to Boston to find Harriet working there as a seamstress for the Willis family. On New Year's Day, he officially moved west to Rochester, en route enrolling Louisa at Hiram Kellogg's Young Ladies' Domestic Seminary in Clinton, New York, one of the only schools that admitted girls of color. On his return to Rochester, he also purchased the Anti-Slavery Reading Room. "He thought of opening an anti-slavery reading room in Rochester," Harriet wrote, "and combining with it the sale of some books and stationery; and he wanted me to unite with him."[78] John also intended to open "a Circulating Library," like that offered by the Adelphic in Boston.[79]

He then embarked on a new lecture tour—this time with Douglass. For five consecutive Sundays, Douglass had been lecturing at Minerva Hall, and on the sixth he gave a final lecture there to kick off the tour. He took as his topic John C. Calhoun's "Address of the Southern Delegates in Congress to their Constituents," which he restyled, "John C. Calhoun and Forty Other Thieves." As Nell wrote in his recap, Douglass occupied a seemingly "presumptuous position . . . a fugitive from slavery sitting in judgment upon Calhoun, the embodiment of that giant crime."[80] Douglass argued that the problem for proslavery politicians like Calhoun was the wording of the "so-called 'slave clauses.'" In distinguishing the original intent and meaning of the clauses from the historical context and legislative intent of its framing, he argued that no "clear recognition of slavery in the United States Constitution" can be found—certainly nothing like what Calhoun presumed. In fact, so ambiguously are the clauses worded, most famously by avoiding the words *slave* and *slavery*, that they might "bear a very different construction; and taken in connection with the preamble of that instrument, the very

opposite of the construction given it by this wily band of slaveholders, and they have just reason to apprehend that such a construction
may yet be placed upon that instrument as shall prove the downfall
of slavery."[81] How different is Douglass's mode of abolition from
the roles assigned ex-slaves by white abolitionists?

Jacobs and Douglass set off on their tour in knee-deep snow. At
their first stop, they each spoke for an hour and a half. "In his usual
calm but feeling manner," Jacobs spoke of the "'foul treachery and
ruinous wrongs' connected with the whole system of slavery." "Listened to with attention and interest throughout," he earned new
subscribers for the *North Star* and sold some of his Anti-Slavery
Reading Room books as well.[82]

The next day, as they rode another ten miles, their hair frosted
over and their ears, noses, and toes half froze. No meeting had been
booked in Mendon, and so they made their way to East Mendon and pleaded for a space to lecture in the Mendon Academy.
Arriving in town often meant meeting with "rebuffs, insults, and
indifference," and searching long and hard for the kindness of
strangers—and an opportunity to warm themselves by a fire. In
the "old slaveholding town" of Bath, an Irish storekeeper "assured us
that this was not our native land, and that we ought to go to Africa.
The impudence of this proposition," Douglass wrote, "shows how
easily the oppressed may be transformed into the oppressor." At one
stop they earned a few more subscribers and were eagerly invited
back. At another, the taverner told them that "'n*****s' were better
off in slavery, and that [they] were only making [the slaves'] condition worse by lecturing against slave-holding." The next morning
he seated them at his table with his white family and boarders for
breakfast. "We found his practice better than his theory," Douglass
quipped. In one town, a pastor greeted them with open arms and
gave them his church for the day; in another, the room was so cold
they had to end early; and in another, "bigotry, apostasy, hypocrisy,
and slander did their utmost to prevent our having a fair hearing
before the people." Despite such obstacles, "Jacobs was unusually

happy . . . and evidently made a deep impression upon the listening hundreds present." "In sixteen days," they had "travelled at an average of twelve miles a day, made some twenty speeches, got twenty subscribers to the *North Star*, and we hope have removed much prejudice against the Anti-Slavery cause."[83]

When Douglass and Jacobs came to Julia Wilbur's hometown of East Avon, it was "the event of the week" for her. In her diary, she describes the great pains she took to brush away locals' "unwillingness" and "fears . . . that people would be abused" in order to secure the Baptist House for the lecture. Thirteen people showed up. Douglass and Jacobs both "spoke well," but their "views were so radical" that several people walked out.[84] When the two stopped at her home for dinner, Wilbur was elated, however. They "appear intelligent on almost any subject & are very agreeable in conversation. They have seen more of the world than people in General, & I suppose make good use of their eyes & ears. They are very gentlemanly & appear at ease in any society." So impressed was she that the young Quaker wrote in her diary, "We consider this visit quite a Chapter in our lives. And the privilege of their acquaintances for such we esteem it to be, as no ordinary occurrence."[85]

They returned to Rochester in March, cutting the tour short. Douglass had a lot weighing on him: not only was he in a war of words with two leading Black newspaper editors, Samuel Ringgold Ward, of the *Impartial Citizen*, and Henry Highland Garnet, of the *Ram's Horn*, but the *North Star* was also in dire financial straits And so Jacobs would have to go it alone. But for the moment, he had something else occupying his attention: his sister had moved to Rochester.

Harriet moved in with Quaker reformers Amy and Isaac Post, who served as a pillar of abolitionism in Rochester.[86] They also opened the eyes of Black abolitionists to the spiritualism that had taken hold in Upstate New York in the 1840s. Harriet took over the Anti-Slavery Reading Room from John. As John wrote in the *North Star*, the office "has been newly stocked with the latest and best works on slavery and other moral questions." Books sold included Douglass's *Narrative*, Walker's *Narrative*, Richard Hildreth's *Despotism in America*, George Bourne's *Slavery Illustrated in Its Effects on Women and Domestic Society*, and Lysander Spooner's *The Unconstitutionality of Slavery*. Julia Wilbur soon met Harriet at the Reading Room, beginning a relationship that would continue in contraband camps, hospitals, and schoolhouses during the Civil War.[87]

On the road again, John met with racism, deceit, and disappointment. When he arrived in a village and asked for a space to lecture, the courthouse was inevitably being painted, a revival meeting was already scheduled, a friend had forgotten to arrange a meeting, or a minister objected to using his church. In the hamlet of Johnson Creek, Jacobs had to pay out of pocket to rent the schoolhouse and make a fire to warm his audience. The going was also excruciating: Jacobs had to travel to one village to set up a meeting, return to the previous village to make his prior appointment, and then walk back to the village to give the lecture he had just set up. On one such occasion, after finding no friends to help him, he was told that no one would show.

A week later, before a "quite Whiggish" audience, he was told that "it was too hard for their wives and families to be obliged to sit and hear [him] tell of the brutality of the slaveholders and their abettors." Jacobs replied:

> Is it right that we should submit to these indignities? Is it easier to bear the infliction [of] the rod than it is to administer it? Where is the wrong of slavery? Is it in our telling you your wickedness, or your continuance in it?

A Whig magistrate then dared John to touch him. He told him that if he lectured at his town, Spencerport, he would meet with "eggs, bricks, and stones." John went anyway. His account of the meeting in the Methodist church is longer and more impassioned than his recap of any other speaking date:

The audience was large, but very disorderly; they hissed like serpents, and stamped their heels like asses. Seeing they were displeased with my remarks I asked to be corrected, if I had given utterance to a single sentence that was not true. The reply was, we have come to hear you talk about slavery. "That, (said I) is the very thing I am doing, if we had no slaveholders we should have no slaves, I am discussing the character of a slaveholder, in the President of the United States. If slavery is a disgrace, upon whom rests the disgrace? . . . Are you not guilty of all that I have accused you? Have I asked you for gold and silver, or have I asked you to take your feet off the necks of three millions of your countrymen, whom you have so long oppressed? for this you threatened to stone me, where is your sympathy? is it with the oppressed or the oppressors? Dare you call yourselves friends to your country, who have elected to the highest office in the gift of the nation, a man in who you could see nothing but blood, rapine, and robbery?—is the battle field the place for men to learn acts of humanity, and have instilled into them the principles of peace? Is the slave mart the place for men to learn to deal justly, love mercy, and walk humbly before God? If these things are true, why am I to be stoned for telling them[?] It may be painful to your ears to hear them, but far more painful to us who are made to endure them. I came among you to speak for the dumb—the crushed and the bleeding slave; I pointed out the new links in their chains that you had forged; and for this act of justice and humanity, you barred your doors against me, and in violation of your law you tried to gag me, because I dared to call Zach. Taylor that old and skilful murderer and cradle plunderer, a disgraced man; but if God spares my life and strength—

You shall have him in Florida with his bloodhounds training,
And in Mexico the veins of his innocent victims draining;
You shall have him ready and rough,
Until you repent and cry—Enough![88]

That night, the hissing crowd refused Jacobs's best efforts to direct them to examine their relationship with slaveholders. If what they wanted was the old humanitarian contract, a safe pedestal from which to look down at the slave in general, as well as the ex-slave before them speaking, they were asked to agree to a revolutionary contract, which bound them to analyze not the slave, the plantation, and the South but those who made this system possible: the politicians upholding a proslavery America, above all President Zachary Taylor, a Whig and owner of 131 slaves. For an audience of uncertain allegiance like this one, such a contract must have been deeply unsettling, since speakers like Jacobs and Douglass expected their audience not only to scrutinize their politicians but to look inwardly as well. In holding a mirror to their audiences' faces, the two men assumed the power to direct them to examine their own complicity with slavery. When the audience hissed at him, they only hurt him enough to make Jacobs double down on his indictment of Taylor and those in the audience who had voted for him. "What a time [John] has had on his last tour," Douglass wrote the Posts, "Will it not dishearten him? I fear it."[89]

John continued to lecture. In May 1849, he spoke at the Fifteenth Anniversary Meeting of the American Anti-Slavery Society. With compromise looming and slave state aggression rising, Jacobs sharply rebuked Thomas Paul Smith, a twenty-two-year-old African American who had fragmented Black Boston by opposing school desegregation.[90] Jacobs took Smith to task for a different issue, however: arguing that Black Americans should join the Free Soil Party in the interest of gradual abolition. Smith "has said the Free Soil party was the child of the Anti-Slavery Society," Jacobs wryly declared. "Now I ask him, would he have us leave our acknowledged high and advanced ground of principle, and go back to be taught by our children?" After Jacobs sat down, Garrison rose to support Jacobs: "Never shall we gain one inch, by compromise, or sacrifice, of the highest moral principle."[91]

The next day, Jacobs declared that he had been a disunionist since long before Garrison started advocating for it; that is, since John Calhoun first preached it in the 1830s, when John encountered him in Washington. He wanted to see a bloodless abolition, without violence. "If any one asked him what must be done to abolish slavery," he answered, "it must cease to be respectable." By making slavery "disreputable," by showing the slaveholder that "he would not be supported by those opposed to his traffic in flesh and blood," Jacobs saw shame as a path to abolition, one that might break apart "the *social* union between Northern men and Southern slave-owners," which was held together by religious hypocrisy.[92] In the process, he gave an updated version of his Hopedale speech, introducing a scene that would make it into *Despots*:

> He had been round Cape Horn, and had never seen anything there to equal the wickedness practiced in the United States. On that coast they worshipped idols, and sold golden Christs; but here they sold Christ himself in the shambles. In returning from a convention in Springfield, he heard a clergyman say, in one of the cars, that he was of the same opinion as Dr. Cox, that the Bible sanctioned slavery. He (the speaker) had not been before aware that Dr. Cox held those sentiments. He took an opportunity of addressing the clergyman, and said to him, "Sir, may I be permitted to ask you a question?" He (the clergyman) did not reply, but looked as if he would condescend to listen. The question he put to him was, "Did he believe there was any meaning in the passage of Scripture in which Christ said: 'Forasmuch as ye have done it to the least of these little ones, ye have done it unto me?'" The clergyman said, of course, there was meaning in it. He (Mr Jacobs) then asked him whether it was lawful for the slaveholders to make chattels of those for whom Christ died. His answer was, that that depended upon the amount of light they possessed. Then said he, (Jacob) [*sic*] in reply, "If they want light, why don't you send some of your missionaries to them?" (Hear, hear) He now asked that assembly why these clergymen ought not to be designated by their true names, as hypocrites, knaves, and robbers. (Cheers)[93]

Chess-like as always, Jacobs positioned the clergyman to make a losing move. By quoting Matthew 25:40, he extracts proof from the clergyman of the church's hypocrisy; not only does the clergyman

hold that African-descended peoples are less capable of enlightenment, but he also can't even be consistent about his racism because
he does not offer religious instruction to a supposedly less enlight-
ened population.

Jacobs continued to lecture throughout the summer, but even
compared with his earlier struggles, he wrote that "at no time
during my laboring in the cause as a lecturer, have I found so few
friends, as on the present occasion." To make matters worse, he had
"had to hire Halls and meeting Houses in most of the places where
I have been." By September, with news of the discovery of gold in
every paper, he was thinking about going to California, since "the
people will not turn out in these citys to here lectures on slavery."[94]
And so in fall 1849, he quit lecturing. In 1848 and 1849 he had been
on the road for at least 450 days. With so much mileage on his feet,
his body, and his psyche, and with the political situation worsening,
he began to consider other possibilities for life.

But he did not leave for California right away. In November, he
opened an oyster saloon in the Waverly Buildings on State Street in
Rochester. "He proposes to cater, in the most admirable manner, to
the taste and appetite of his fellow citizens," Douglass wrote. "Mr.
Jacobs is a most excellent cook, as we can testify."[95] Situated next
to the railroad depot, Jacobs's oyster saloon was in a perfect loca-
tion, but competition with at least five other oyster restaurants was
intense. Soon Jacobs was at war with C. W. Swan's Oyster Depot,
which had also just opened but with far more capital. Swan's ads
claimed that he was the only vendor to carry Amboy oysters, but
on Christmas 1849, he ran a new ad. "This is to caution all those in
the habit of purchasing Oysters that the name of Amboy Oysters
is upon every huxter shop and oyster dealers sign in town, purport-
ing to have for sale Amboy Oysters, which is all a hoax and impo-
sition, as there is not, neither has there been, or will be, any genuine Amboy Oysters to be had, only at my office, under the Bank of
Monroe, Eagle Block."[96] Though other vendors also sold Amboys,
John seized the opportunity to reply. "Men will lie, but oysters cannot," his headline reads:

To all lovers of good OYSTERS, I would recommend a perusal of Mr. C. Swan's notice, headed "more signs than true" and while on your way to the Eagle, stop and look at Jacobs' lot of Oysters, on the corner of State and Buffalo Streets, and judge for yourself who has got out the lying sign, and pass him by. I have but one kind of Oysters, and Mr. S. shall either acknowledge them to be as good Amboy Oysters as he ever saw, and pay up like a man, or allow his name to come before the public as a calumniator. I am receiving my Oysters from Mr. R. Gutman, off Perth Amboy, who writes to me as follows—Mr. Jacobs, Sir—You may rest assured of a good quality of Oysters from me at all times.[97]

The result of Jacobs's challenge is unclear, but his business doesn't seem to have gotten much further off the ground.

During this period, however, Harriet and he had other opportunities, as Nell unfailingly remembered in letters to Amy Post. For it was then that they became Nell's chosen family and that the Posts' house at 36 Sophia Street became a gathering place for the trio, as well as for others in their circle, including Douglass's sister, Charlotte Murray, who held onto her daguerreotype of John long after he left Rochester.

If You Have Not Swords

Nine months later, John Jacobs stood in a crowded City Hall Park in New York City at high noon. Days before, he had been confronted with a terrible choice: betray Garrison's credo—*No Union with Slaveholders!*—or continue to speak in public as a fugitive and risk reenslavement. He chose to speak, despite the fact that the second Fugitive Slave Act had been passed days before, on September 18, 1850. Thousands of Black New Yorkers stood before him, gathered to greet James Hamilton Williams, known to the press as "Hamlet." The Williamsburg resident had gained notoriety as the first New Yorker apprehended under the Fugitive Slave Act. Though he pleaded that his mother was free and he had been born free, the court had ordered that he be transported to Maryland and into slavery.

That evening, Jacobs was part of a crowd of more than fifteen hundred, "two-thirds of those present being women of color," who assembled in Zion Chapel, determined to liberate Hamlet. The organizers styled themselves "the committee of thirteen," perhaps as a jab at the Senate committee that had passed the Fugitive Slave Bill. When John took the podium, he caught fire. Sarah Hallowell Willis wrote to her sister, Amy Post, with a combination of admiration and concern: "His resistant spirit was raised to its highest pitch." With one breath, he extended a "hand of fellowship to his colored brethren." With the next, he told them, "if you have not swords, I say to you, sell your garments and buy one."[98] In a subsequent article, he was described as a fugitive, but he told the world that he was much more:

> If there be any man here tonight who wants to know my name, tell him it is *John S. Jacobs*, of South [*sic*] Carolina, and that I am an American citizen, that I never denied that name, neither did I ever disgrace it. They said that they cannot take us back to the South; but I say, under the present law they can; and now I say unto you, let them only take your dead bodies. (Tremendous cheers.) . . . I would, my friends, advise you to show a front to our tyrants, and arm yourselves; aye, and I would advise the women to have their knives too. I don't advise you to trample on the laws of this State . . . but I advise you to trample on this bill, and I further advise you to let us go on immediately.[99]

Though he had never allowed anyone to buy his freedom and was legally a fugitive slave, he calls himself a citizen. And in calling for violence when necessary, he breaks from Garrisonian principle in favor of Douglass's position that violence is sometimes necessary to assert "moral personhood" and elaborate "a selfhood worthy of entering the public sphere," a position Jacobs may have heard a month before at the famous Cazenovia convention.[100] But such a break was more an admission that Garrison's principle failed to account for the fugitive slave's position, as even Lewis Tappan recognized when he said that "the law gives the freeman of the North no alternative, he must disobey the law," not to flee to Canada, but stand "unmoved and unawed."[101]

Tears ran down James "Hamlet" Williams's face as he greeted the crowd after learning that they had raised eight hundred dollars to redeem him. As one of the thirteen, Jacobs may have felt temporarily vindicated, too, though he knew that for every Hamlet saved, ten others were seized under the new law. Even within the crowd, a racist police officer was working undercover, and he recorded seeing that "between 12 & 1 o'clock p.m. the N***** Hamlet accompanied by a legion of other n*****s (some of a darker colour than himself) came into the Park and after exhibiting himself to the public was carried on the shoulders of several big buck n*****s over in front of the Tribune office."[102]

In the same breath as he celebrated Hamlet's return, John began preparing a third way to remain true to his Garrisonian principles: leaving the country. He was not going to go to a settlement in Canada or sail for England as William and Ellen Craft had done, however, for he had set his eyes on something brighter: the prospect of independence and a break from the hardship of a day-to-day existence. A week later, he was gone. Before sailing, however, he secured Cornelia Willis's promise that she would protect his sister from capture and the "reign of terror to the colored population."[103] John then set out for California—where the law did not apply.

_____

THREE

THE WORLD

MY COUNTRY

If the American flag is to be planted on the altar of freedom, then I am ready to be offered on that altar, if I am wanted; if it must wave over the slave, with his chains and fetters clanking, let me breathe the free air of another land and die a man and not a chattel.

JOHN SWANSON JACOBS, "A Colored American in England" (1861)

Exile

In September 1850, few things glittered for the fugitive slave. With the North no longer safe, passages to freedom suddenly became longer and more perilous, and many long-settled, self-emancipated slaves were forced to uproot their lives. Over the next decade, a migration crisis ensued, with an estimated 5 percent of the African American population choosing expatriation.[1] Many went to Canada, some to Britain, others to Jamaica and Mexico. John Jacobs went to California.

Ushered into the Union by the Compromise of 1850 as a free state, as it had been since Mexico's 1829 abolition of slavery, California's 1849 Constitution declared that "neither slavery, nor involuntary servitude, except for the punishment of crimes, shall ever be tolerated in this State."[2] As a result, California "was a twofold Eldorado . . . and a harbinger of salvation" for "the unfortunate sons of Africa," as a Swiss miner wrote.[3] Alongside the flickering possibility of legal recognition of African Americans as persons, California stood for the idea of taking the dream of reparations into one's own power, of working by hand to become independently wealthy. For Black men like Jacobs who had devoted the past decade to the ideas of elevation and liberation without a dollar to show for it (and in John's case, debts), financial liberation represented a chance to better realize those goals by extracting from the land the value that had been extracted from him.

With his experience on a whaler, Jacobs likely worked his passage to San Francisco. For the next six years, he worked as a miner, first in gold rush California, and then, after California passed the Fugitive Slave Act in 1851, in Australia, which was also undergoing a gold rush. Working on the Pacific rim of empire meant a return to the sea and an eyewitness education in the differences between American and Australian styles of settler colonialism and racial caste. It also meant fighting against new modes of oppression, such as Chinese exclusion and state exploitation of miners.

Jacobs's first sight of San Francisco in spring 1851 must have been overwhelming. When he had sailed past in 1842, San Francisco had been called Yerba Buena, a Mexican-ruled village of 196; by 1851, more than 30,000 people had arrived, and the harbor rivaled only New York in the volume of ships from all parts of the world. To get his bearings, he may have stayed somewhere like the Golden Gate boardinghouse, which catered exclusively to Black sailors and was run by William Mathews, a free Black man from Massachusetts. John surely found letters waiting for him from his sister, who never failed to look for him, and he probably asked after a few people from Rochester and Boston who had arrived before him. As he began to prepare for the mines, he gathered advice from guidebooks, newspapers, and word of mouth, and learned that supplies were cheaper in San Francisco than Sacramento, the last substantial outpost before gold country. Drawing upon his expertise as a steward, he bought provisions and major items: canvas for a tent, blankets, a hammock, mercury for attracting the gold to the bottom of the pan, shovels, hoes, pickaxes, long mining boots, gaiters, and heavy-duty clothing. Some things, such as a frying pan and cooking utensils, he probably already had. Since miners' and sailors' diets were quite similar, he likely bought onions, sugar, hard bread, coffee, tea, butter, flour, lard, salt, molasses, vinegar, bacon, hams, sausages, jerked beef, and lemon juice.[4]

After reaching Sacramento, he learned how to buy a mining claim. Since this was his first one, he probably did what many newcomers did: stake a claim to an unused or abandoned portion near a river and assert squatter's rights. "Full of hope and expectations," he wrote Harriet to tell her that he had "just completed his arrangements to commence his work in the bed of the river."[5] John probably chose a bed digging because "in summer, the miners generally are engaged at what are called the 'wet diggings,' in or beside the beds of rivers."[6] After he selected his claim, he turned down an offer of five hundred dollars for it and set to work. He quickly learned the three major techniques of prospecting: panning, sluicing, and digging.

John's first claim was a bust, and he held off telling Harriet how "burdened with care" it made him. His worries may not have been triggered by anything out of the ordinary, since mining had a steep learning curve, and no amount of expertise could guarantee gold. And in any event, merely finding gold was not enough to keep a miner solvent. He had run into bad luck and had come out poorer than he went in; adding insult to injury, not only had he turned down a generous offer for his claim, but the miners next to him had taken two thousand dollars apiece out of the ground too.

Abandoning his first claim, in October 1851 John moved to Mormon Island, or Natoma, as it was called by the indigenous Nisenan people. "Mormon Island proper," a disappointed miner wrote, "is nothing but a large bar on one side of the river, converted into an island by a narrow canal dug round it for the purpose of draining that portion of the channel. The name, however, has extended itself to the village that has grown up on the neighbouring bank, and which consisted, at that time, of a single street nearly as broad as it was long."[7] Today the town of Mormon Island, which had grown to 2,500 people in 1852, lies submerged by the earthen wing dam that formed Lake Folsom.

Then Joseph arrived to work with his uncle. Not much is known about what he had been doing since he returned to America in 1850 from a whaling cruise. Harriet talked of coming, too, but ultimately stayed out of a sense of obligation to the Willises and because she was plagued by chronic, lifelong mobility problems from her time in the garret. Joseph, John, and three others then staked out a new kind of claim. As Harriet wrote, they "have gone so far under the hills that they work by candle light"; as John told her, "there has been a great many new discoveries where persons never thought of looking for gold and it has given new life to mining."[8] Harriet refers to an emergent technique known as *coyoting*. "In many parts of the Northern mines, but more particularly on the middle fork of the American River [where Mormon Island was], large quantities of gold are being taken from the *coyote* diggings," one author wrote that month:

> A passage is cut into the face of the hill, of sufficient dimensions to admit easily a man with a wheelbarrow. After passing in some distance, a hole is sunk to the bed rock, in many places *from seventy-five to one hundred and fifty feet deep*, the dirt being brought up in buckets, by means of a windlass. The dirt is regularly tested as they go down, and as soon as the level is reached, at which it will pay, the washing commences with a long tom [a sluice box longer than six feet or so]. In many cases, fifteen feet of paying dirt is found, although in some it does not pay, except on the ledge. As soon as one hole is exhausted, it is filled up again and the parties, having extended their tunnels, sink a new one. . . . In many of these tunnels and pits, pumps have to be kept going. . . . Candles are kept burning in them all.[9]

Thus, just as a coyote digs its den deep into a hillside, John and Joseph found themselves boring deep into the earth. This time they were more successful, and John was able to send Harriet one hundred dollars to cover Louisa's schooling and living expenses.

For miners like John and Joseph, success quickly incited white resentment. Although most miners' golden dreams vanished into leaden realities, Black, Chinese, Mexican, Chilean, and indigenous Californians were overwhelmingly targeted for violence. And whereas California had banned slavery, it was lax about passing other laws concerning slavery and arbitrary about enforcing them, a combination that proved explosive. Southern whites were not dissuaded from bringing slaves into the new state, while others impressed Miwoks and Hawaiians for placer mining. Then, in April 1852, the state passed a more extreme version of the Fugitive Slave Law, "which declared that any black person who had migrated to California before it joined the Union either as a fugitive or with a slaveholder was considered property and faced jail or a fine."[10]

In late 1852, John and Joseph packed their bags. They had gone west not to help America accomplish its "manifest destiny" but to escape it. Experience had taught John that America had no special purpose, except, it seemed, to persecute him. So he decided to go to Australia, as far away as possible from the US. "[I] hope John will be lucky in Australia," Nell wrote. "How richly he deserves success."[11] When news of John's departure reached her, Harriet wrote that she hoped that she "may be enable[d] to tell you that my Brother is free"—not because he had approached Sawyer to buy his own free papers but because he had set out to search for freedom in another land.[12]

An Australian Undercommons

John likely worked his way across the Pacific. Because steamships and sailboats bound for Sydney or Melbourne commonly stopped at one or more intermediate ports to resupply, John may have set foot in Honolulu and surveyed the changes a decade had made, or his ship may have dropped anchor in Tahiti, the Navigator Islands,

Norfolk Island, Apia, Tonga, or Vanuatu. The expansion of empire, whaling, and the Pacific gold rushes had strung these islands together into a network of transpacific shipping routes that also gave sailors and passengers glimpses of other cultures and ways of life. John and his nephew arrived in Australia in the spring of 1853 and soon after began preparing to head to the goldfields of Victoria and New South Wales.[13] This time, they found it easier getting ready. They most likely brought some of their equipment with them, and, just as important, their Californian know-how about mining techniques, toolmaking, claim scouting, and gold rush culture. Yet Sydney and Melbourne presented dangers all their own, and John and Joseph had to be vigilant. "Adam Smith settled the question of the 'wealth of nations,'" wrote the Italian miner and anarchist Raffaello Carboni, but "the source of pauperism will be settled in Victoria by any quill-driver, who has the pluck to write the history of public-houses in the towns, and sly grog sellers on the gold-fields."[14] Prudent and careful as always, John would fare better than his nephew would.

Even on the other side of the world, John may have found old friends and acquaintances. William Gustavus Allen, editor of the *National Watchman*, and Joseph Hall Putnam, a Boston friend of Jacobs and Nell, were only two of the hundreds of African Americans who opted to leave California for Australia in search of wealth and rights. He had not left American politics and culture behind entirely either. *Uncle Tom's Cabin* was serialized in multiple newspapers, and the *Empire* was regularly publishing antislavery articles about America. Fiercely antislavery newspapers could even be found at the mines themselves.

It is unclear where John and Joseph established their claim, but there is a "John Jacobs" among the 5,000 miners who signed the Bendigo petition in mid-1853.[15] The petition is commonly said to mark the start of years of agitation for the right to vote and democratic reform, as well as protests against unjust regulations, excessive mining license fees, and brutal law enforcement by the colonial government. The protests culminated in a battle that is now memorialized as the birthplace of Australian democracy: Ballarat. On December 3, 1854, the troops of the Fortieth and Twelfth Regiments stormed a stockade at Eureka that 120 multicultural miners had hastily erected in the middle of the gold mining area. In just twenty minutes, the disciplined police soldiers, who outnumbered the miners three to one, killed as many as 60 miners. "So cowardly despotic rule as this will be an everlasting disgrace to the Bloodthirsty wretches who caused it," an American miner named Thomas Pierson wrote, "and the day I think is not far distant when the people will assent and maintain their rights here in spite of all the minions of despotism."[16]

Of the thirteen rebels singled out to be tried for high treason at Victoria's Supreme Court in February 1855, two were "men of colour": James McFie Campbell, from Jamaica, and John Joseph, a "powerfully built" African American from Baltimore or New York. Joseph was one of many Americans involved in the Eureka incident, but "whereas the other United States citizens arrested for their involvement received the full assistance and support of the United States Consul and the local American community, Joseph received none. He was not recognized as a fellow citizen, and later accounts of Eureka written by Americans . . . make no mention of him." The first man to be tried, he was acquitted "because they were tried by a jury of their peers, drawn from a community that by and large sympathised with the miners' grievances and had little respect for the autocratic style of government that prevailed in Victoria."[17] Joseph was carried through the streets in celebration when he left the courtroom.

From long experience, John Jacobs knew how to read between the lines of the coverage of the event, and it is even possible that he had been involved in the miners' rights protests of the previous two years. In his eyewitness account, Pierson framed the event as many Anglo-Americans did: as a repetition of the American Revolutionary War. Yet just as these accounts erased the involvement of people like John Joseph and Joseph Campbell, the Black experience of America undermined this analogy. "They remember the blood that had just been spilt by their fathers about some tea, a little paper, and such-like things, which the more they were contrasted with the wrongs of the slave, the more insignificant they grew," John writes.[18] Despotism continued to thrive in America long after the British were thrown out.

It lived within Australia too. Several weeks later, an African American man writing under the pseudonym "Homo" published a letter to the Melbourne *Argus*: "I crave the privilege of uttering through the columns of your paper, one word of entreaty to the Legislature of this colony to hesitate long before passing an enactment oppressive to the Chinese, or to any other class of men in this country." "I feel too deeply to write with proper calmness," he wrote. "I have myself been subject to just such injustice":

> I am a colored man, and through the operation of such laws as are now proposed to be enacted against the Chinese, I have for years been knocked about from pillar to post in the United States,— having been obliged to leave a Southern State for no crime—for no alleged *fault*, except that I was a "free n*****."[19]

In Illinois, he wrote, he was forced to leave the state in thirty days because of a racist immigration law targeting people of African descent. In California, he enjoyed some success, but a party of ruffians took advantage of the fact that Black and native people were barred from giving testimony in court and robbed his house. "I then took ship for Australia and when I landed here believed that at last I had reached a free country," the author writes, with the keen sense of justice found in fugitive slave narratives such as John Jacobs's, as one editor was quick to observe. "Homo . . . deserves to be classed with such distinguished 'free n*****s' as Frederick Douglass, the Rev. Dr. Pennington, Wells Brown, Henson, and Garnet, all of whom have been numbered amongst the 'chattels personal' of the slave holders, and in their day have worn the galling fetters of the bondman on the plantations in America, where it is said 'all men are born free and equal!'"[20] Before the letter appeared, Jacobs had been successful enough that he left the mines for Paramatta, near Sydney. Like "Homo," he was highly motivated to make a different narrative of liberation visible, one that did not fly under the miners' adopted slogan of "no taxation without representation." Against such tea party notions, he must have recalled the mottos of radical abolition: "No Union with Slaveholders" and "My Country the World, and My Countrymen All Mankind."

The week of the "Homo" letter, John walked into the *Empire*'s office. Founded by Henry Parkes, who would serve as premier five times and be called "the father of Australian federation," the daily paper took a strong stand against slavery and published material that included an excerpt from William Wells Brown's *Clotel*, Ralph Waldo Emerson's 1855 lecture on slavery, and letters to the editor on the Anthony Burns fugitive slave case in Boston. It is not surprising, then, that they would have a "correct copy" of the US Constitution and Richard Hildreth's *History of the United States*. Jacobs probably surmised as much and asked for the texts as a ploy to start a conversation.

When Jacobs returned several weeks later with his manuscript, he gave it a new title: "United States *Despots*." Partly a nod to Hildreth's *Despotism in America* (1842), which the Jacobs siblings had sold at the Anti-Slavery Reading Room, it also may allude to the concurrent rise of anti-Chinese sentiment in Australia. In particular, the governor of Victoria Charles Hotham actively subscribed to a theory of "oriental despotism" that labeled the Chinese as heathens averse to Christian morality and was used to justify anti-Chinese legislation. Jacobs's experience in the transpacific world dramatically transformed and deepened his abolitionist views, allowing him to draw connections between America and the world and imagine transnational solidarity with migrant labor forces from what we would today call the Global South. From John's anticolonial point of view, the real despot was Hotham, not the Chinese.

How *Despots* was received by the Australian public is unknown.

Though transatlantic slave narratives were sold in some bookstores, and though antislavery texts were excerpted in newspapers, nothing like Jacobs's autobiography had been published in Australia before. Jacobs told the editors that he was planning on leaving Australia, and characteristically, he was true to his word. He knew that Australia was not where his roots were and that mining was not to be his career. Harriet, he also knew, had been in agony, having not heard from him for three years: no one, not even Amy Post, was as close to her as her brother, who knew her whole story and more, and who used to "mingle his tears with [hers]" when she came to him, her "spirits . . . grieved and mortified."[21] To remain in Australia meant permanent separation from Harriet, who had written that Australia was not a place where she could "possibly go"— presumably because of her chronic mobility disability.[22] And so, some months after publishing *Despots*, he set sail for London.

As John was heading to sea, Harriet was reading a letter he had written when he had returned to Sydney from the mines. Having not heard from him for so long, she was positively ecstatic. So concerned had she been about John and her son's fates that she had hired a medium to try to contact them. "I have had a letter from my Brother and Son just as the spirits told me it would be even the very Language was in the letter he beged to be remembered to you and Mr Post saying that he would write to him and settle as soon as Joseph returned from the mines where he was settling some business for him my letter was five Months coming written last Febhruary."[23] John could finally settle his old debts.

John and Harriet's lives were converging at last, even if the Atlantic was still going to be between them, since John was resolved never to return to the US while slavery still existed. As ever, old obstacles endured and new ones cropped up: Harriet's chronic pain flared up again; she found time to write her autobiography scarce between her responsibilities to the Willis children and the need to hide her writing from Nathaniel Parker Willis, who was sympathetic to slavery; and she found it hard to make connections with the right abolitionists. For his part, John had to work his way to

England first, meaning he was compelled to move at the speed of and in the direction of a global trade route—through the Indian Ocean, across the Red Sea, and down around the Cape of Good Hope, stopping at trading ports on the way.

In turning away from the goldfields, John abandoned the miner's dream of digging out of financial dependence forever. He also left something else: Joseph. It is impossible to say why Joseph stayed behind. Perhaps he had fallen into bad company. Perhaps he had grown so accustomed to passing (he "was so entirely white that he always passed for a white man") that he decided to leave his past behind.[24] Perhaps he simply decided at twenty-eight to seek his own fortune. Or perhaps illness so disabled him that he was unable to travel. Whatever the case, Joseph's letters to John and Harriet petered out, and they never heard from him again. Nearly a decade later, Harriet would receive a letter written in a strange hand, which claimed that Joseph's right arm was so disabled by rheumatism that he was unable to write. The author claimed that Joseph needed four hundred dollars in gold for a passage home; Harriet sent the money, but Joseph never appeared. A later search in Melbourne came up empty.[25] Joseph was likely dead.[26] He had gone to the other side of the world never to come back—just like his namesake, Joseph Horniblow, just like Jack Cotton, just like so many men in the family. Harriet did not know how right she was when she had written about "the anxiety the two Joseph[s] had given their parents."[27]

Foreign Correspondent

After a yearlong voyage, John arrived in England in August 1857. He immediately headed for an institution that would serve as his home for the next five years: the Sailors' Home. Part of a worldwide network of charitable institutions, the London Sailors' Home charged a small fee for a roof and a spartan room, lessons in moral improvement, and a place designed to avoid booze, brothels, and exploitation by boardinghouse keepers and kidnappers. If moral instruction may have rankled some of its lodgers, others, like Joseph Conrad, recalled it as a "friendly place" for seamen, built with some "regard for the independence of the men who sought its shelter ashore, and with no ulterior aims behind that effective friendliness."[28] In London, John became a career mariner. Over the next fifteen years, he worked more than thirty voyages as a steward or cook on ships transporting goods to and from England: sugar from St. Kitts, oranges from the Black Sea, cotton from Egypt and India. He even helped complete the transatlantic telegraph line and sail a gunboat to Bangkok as a gift for the new King of Siam. On average, he spent about ten months at sea and two in London.

At the same time, he resumed his work as an abolitionist in several ways. First, he began in earnest to help Harriet publish her autobiography. And not long after he arrived, he probably told her too about his plans to republish *Despots*, for soon after, Harriet and John began working together to find a publisher for their narratives. Though their correspondence is woefully incomplete, it seems significant that it was only when John moved to London that Harriet concluded that her best chance to publish *Incidents* would be in England. "I have been thinking," Harriet wrote in June 1857, "that I would so like to go away and sell my Book—I could then secure a copywright—to sell it both here and in England—and by identifying myself with—it I might do something for the Antislavry Cause—to do this I would have to get letters of introduction from some of the leading Abolitionist of this Country to those of the Old."[29] The strongest transatlantic abolitionist bond they forged in their efforts to publish their stories would be their own.

Second, he got to know the leading Garrisonian activists in London. A few months after arriving, John found time to dine with George Thompson, the legendary activist who had helped abolish slavery in the British empire in the 1830s. On Christmas Eve, Thompson wrote to his daughter, Amelia Chesson, about his meeting with Jacobs:

> Jacobs is a "good fellow." I have as much confidence as I have ever had in any colored refugee who has come to our shores. He

is modest, disinterested, and I believe truthful honest and with a deep concern for his brethren in bonds. Teach [granddaughter] May to prize her amber beads—teach her to abhor the prejudices that work ruin and slavery of soul and body to millions of Gods children like Mr Jacob [*sic*]—teach her by precept and example to honor all men and to reverence the moral image of her maker whether it be stamped upon the soul of a black man or a white one. Woe to the United States! Clouds of wrath are gathering which, ere long, will burst upon that guilty nation.[30]

A few months later, Jacobs wrote a "letter on the coolie trade" and brought it to the *Star*, the radical newspaper that Thompson's son-in-law, Frederick William Chesson, edited. By virtue of his time in the Pacific and in the Caribbean, he had witnessed the trade in Chinese indentured servants. His letter is lost, though perhaps the "J. S. C." who wrote a letter to the *Evening Star* is actually "J. S. J." That letter describes taking passage from Shantou to Havana and witnessing the deaths of 332 indentured servants from suicide, poison, flogging, fever, scurvy, and "frightful disease." "I cannot fill up your valuable space with the details of cruelty I have witnessed on board coolie ships," the author writes, "but suffice it to say the horrors of the African slave trade never exceeded that of the so-called 'Coolie Free Emigration.'"[31] Whether this is indeed Jacobs's letter, the one he did submit to Chesson marked the beginning of a long relationship between the two men. They soon attended plays and cricket matches, took tea, and met each other's families. And whenever John returned from the Black Sea or the Ottoman empire or Brazil, he always brought gifts for the Chessons' children.

In summer 1859, they became close antislavery allies as well, after Chesson and Thompson founded the London Emancipation Committee (later known as the London Emancipation Society). Jacobs was elected as a founding member of the British Garrisonian group, who counted among their members expatriate African Americans including William and Ellen Craft, John Sella Martin, and Sarah Parker Remond, as well as Thompson, Chesson, and John Stuart Mill.[32] As one author describes it, "Gatherings held by this organization were often held at Exeter Hall in the Strand, though they also occurred in working-class parts of London, such as Lambeth, where pro-Union sympathizers tended to be found in greater numbers than in more affluent areas of the city."[33] A rival of the moderate British and Foreign Anti-Slavery Society, the London Emancipation Committee held regular meetings, staged debates, and published tracts. In 1860, for example, meetings concerned the "current state of affairs in America" and the "American Crisis and Slavery"; Thompson and Douglass debated over the Constitution's relationship to slavery; and William Craft told his life story, which he and Ellen published the following year as *Running a Thousand Miles for Freedom*.

Jacobs's letter to the *Star* provides a glimpse into how he contributed to the committee's objectives not simply as a board member but as a sailor. For his career in the merchant marines made him the committee's most valued foreign correspondent in the tumultuous years leading up to US emancipation. By working the trade routes between England and the Caribbean, Egypt, the Black Sea, and South America, he supplied the society's members with direct intelligence about England's shifting attitudes toward American slavery. This is the third way that he resumed his abolitionist work: as a sailor. On committee pamphlets, Jacobs's address is listed next to his name as "Wells Street, London Docks." He was the abolitionists' eyes and ears on the world.

As John built up a network in London, Harriet was building hers in New England. It is highly likely that the siblings were executing a coordinated, multipronged plan to publish *Incidents in the Life of a Slave Girl* and republish *Despots* around this time. Accompanied by Nell, Harriet paid Maria Weston Chapman and Deborah Weston a visit at Chapman's home in Weymouth, Massachusetts, in fall 1857, where she "secured [Chapman's] interest in her forthcoming Book and anything she can do towards perfecting it in matter or manner."[34] A month later, Nell wrote to Amy Post that Harriet's "book is probably suspended" but immediately added that John "would like her [Harriet] and Louisa to cross the Atlantic" and then, cryptically, wrote that John will be visiting the US soon "but only for a brief business (even this is confidential)."[35] Clearly, John was interested in helping Harriet find a publisher in Britain, but what business was he planning on conducting in the US? Did he want to republish *Despots*? Did he have leads that might help Harriet? Whatever his wishes for his own narrative may have been, it seems that John was primarily concerned with helping his sister by this point.[36] Six months later, Harriet convinced the Willises to allow her to sail to England, even if she had to accept the indignity of traveling as Moses Grinnell's "maid."

After stepping off the *Persia* in Liverpool bearing letters of introduction from Chapman, she took the train to London to see her brother, who was not due to depart on the *Admiral Kanaris* for Constantinople and the Black Sea for a couple weeks.[37] Seven years had passed since they had last seen each other. Did they allow themselves time for reunion? Did they cry over Joseph? John helped introduce Harriet to the Chessons, and she called upon them nine times in the span of two months—for tea, dinner, with the family to see George Thompson, and with Amelia Chesson to the Crystal Palace to see Madame Grisi perform the aria "Casta Diva."[38] As Harriet and the Chessons became closer, she divulged more of her personal history and gave her manuscript to them to read.

Harriet then went to Dublin to see the *Anti-Slavery Advocate* editors Richard Davis Webb and Hannah Waring Webb "to try & publish an account of her own experiences of slavery & of her escape from it." She was sorely disappointed, as Hannah found the manuscript "raw & high flown—difficult to mend & unfit for publication. We consulted & considered a good deal & got opinion from sundry capable [judges], which resulted in the conviction that she could not advantageously dispose of her manuscript to a London bookseller, at least in its present condition."[39]

Harriet would be disappointed in John, too, for her hopes of inducing him to return to the US that autumn failed; instead, John signed back on board the *Admiral Kanaris* and then the *Leopard*, a steamer plying the Baltic trade between London and St. Petersburg. After his sister returned to the US, John's relationship with Frederick Chesson deepened, and they would often spend their evenings together. Chesson dined at the Sailors' Home with John, and more often John would come to the Chessons' house and the two men would hit the town. At this time, they went to see the "famous but wicked *Judge and Jury*," which Fred described as a "strange mixture of ribaldry and pathos."[40] John continued to bring presents from his voyages to the Chessons: Turkish slippers and attar of roses for Amelia, Turkish pipes and a fez for Fred, tortoises for the children.

In summer 1859, as John joined the London Emancipation Committee, Harriet gathered up her courage and brought her manuscript to a Boston firm, Phillips and Sampson, but they would not accept it without an introduction by either Harriet Beecher Stowe or Nathaniel Parker Willis. Stowe gave Jacobs "the clinch" again, rejecting her a second time, and Willis, as a slavery apologist, was hardly an option. A year later, with Amy Post's introduction in hand, she submitted the manuscript to Thayer & Eldridge, who accepted it on the condition that she approach Lydia Maria Child. After "trembl[ing] at the thought of approaching another Sattellite of so great magnitude," she set up a meeting with Child at the Anti-slavery Office. Fortunately, the author of *Hobomok* turned out to be a "whole souled Woman" and the two women "found the way to each other's hearts."[41] Unlike the Webbs, Child was not daunted by the manuscript, even if it "involve[d] the reading of a good many M.S. pages, and the writing of a good many," because "to help the slave is about all my life is good for now."[42]

Child's work on the manuscript is today the best-known example of the heavy hand of the white abolitionist editor. She replaced the final chapter on John Brown with one on the death of the Jacobses' grandmother, transposed sentences and pages, "so as to bring the story into continuous order," and prompted Harriet to elaborate on "the outrages committed on the colored people in Nat Turner's time." At the same time, she "put the savage cruelties into one chapter, entitled 'Neighboring Planters,' in order that those who shrink from 'supping upon horrors,' might omit them, without interrupting the thread of the story." While Harriet had once written of "identifying [her]self with" her book" to "do something for the Antislavry Cause," she learned that the contract and the copyright for her book were secured in Child's own name—not for malicious purposes but because it was decided for Harriet that, "under the circumstances," her name could not be used.[43] Child helped secure a circulation of two thousand copies, one thousand of which Wendell Phillips agreed to take on, and four hundred for Harriet to sell herself. When Thayer & Eldridge went bankrupt, Phillips stepped in to secure funding to buy the stereotype plates and proceed with printing.

When John learned that her narrative was due to be published in November 1860, he decided that he would try to republish his autobiography; he may even have been trying for some time. He knew that Chesson was invested in putting the voice of the enslaved in service of abolition of all kinds, from slavery to the "coolie" trade to cruelty against indigenous groups. And with his involvement in the London Emancipation Committee, he had the opportunity to meet other editors, including Harper Twelvetrees, and to speak with authors such as the Crafts. He had probably realized that he had a new opportunity to give his narrative a wider audience, and he had certainly shared *Despots* with Chesson and perhaps others. When he arrived back in England in October, he learned that an opportunity had arisen to publish the narrative in a magazine called the *Leisure Hour*, a middlebrow Victorian magazine published by the Religious Tract Society that carried the subtitle *A Family Journal of Instruction and Recreation*. How this news sat with Jacobs is up to the reader's imagination, but he did not have much time to decide, because he was due to board a new ship, the *Pilot Fish*, bound for Rio de Janeiro.

The voyage left on December 17, 1860, and, as always, John Jacobs worked as a steward. The crew all boarded the ship at the Princess dock in Liverpool. Immediately, the voyage got off to a rocky start. A sailor came aft to the mates' cabin to complain about the quality of the beef; when the captain defended it, the sailor became incensed. The next day a piece of beef was found hanging from a handspike with a chalk message underneath: "This guts all for seven mariners." It was a warning for the captain and for the other sailors who refused to back the man in his complaint. The captain's way of resolving things was simply to tell John to give the men another piece of meat.

In February 1861, when they reached Rio, a seaman began to feel unwell and went to the hospital. The next day, three more men went. A few days after that, the first man died. For the next month, yellow fever raged on the boat, and almost everyone on board was taken ill. John recovered after five days, but two more men died.[44] When the *Pilot Fish* returned to England in mid-May with a cargo of rosewood, how did John react to discovering that his defiant narrative had been censored, rewritten, and published under the sanitized title "A True Tale of Slavery"?[45] His autobiography had begun appearing in weekly installments in the *Leisure Hour* two weeks after *Incidents* was put on sale at the Anti-Slavery Office in Boston. At about half the word count, the 1861 version is censored, rearranged, and reworded. The legal critique is cut and the text is recomposed as a relatively standard autobiographical slave narrative. Pseudonyms are used in lieu of real names, and the names of Washington politicians are stricken altogether, as is any mention of them gambling.

With the recovery of *Despots*, we can now compare two versions of a single slave narrative to see the effects of white abolitionist editing on a Black text. Furthermore, just as the editors of the *Leisure Hour* removed the fire-breathing oratory of *Despots*, it is quite likely that Lydia Maria Child struck from *Incidents* much of the rhetoric of protest that Harriet was using up through the *Dred Scott* decision of March 1857, when she wrote "I see nothing for the Black Man—to look forward to but to forget his old Motto—and learn a new one his long patient hope—must be might—and Strength—Liberty— an[d] Death."[46] With this language, so reminiscent of the protest rhetoric she and John had learned from Douglass, we get a hint at the more radical language that Child excised. This is also apparent from Harriet's preface to *Incidents*, in which she declares that she has written her autobiography *not* "to excite sympathy for my own sufferings" but to arouse in women "a realizing sense of . . . how deep, and dark, and foul is that pit of abominations" called slavery."[47]

It is a testament to both John and Harriet that they were able to publish their autobiographies at all. Composed over the span of thirteen years, these narratives were likely written to be read together. Published in America, Australia, and Great Britain, these are global slave narratives that offer new opportunities to expand our understanding of abolition and allied modes of protest against slavery and other systems of exploitation.

Two months after shots were fired on Fort Sumter to begin the American Civil War on April 12, 1861, Harriet was in New York City carrying two letters from John. The first took his sister to task; the second took his former country to task. John's "scolding lines" berated his sister for not sending her book to "different people in England," which Harriet was reluctant to do because she was in debt and because she was not eager to "give it a circulation there before I tried to turn it to some account," presumably because she did not want to publicize the story of her drinking of "the cup of sin, and shame, and misery" unless she had to.[48] Rather than give up or reflexively reject her brother's advice, Harriet sent a copy of her book to Chesson, then followed up to inform him that she had just shipped the stereotype plates to him. The UK edition of *Incidents* was retitled *The Deeper Wrong; or, Incidents in the Life of a Slave Girl, Written By Herself.*

John's second letter was addressed to Amy Post's husband, Isaac. Harriet sent it to the *National Anti-Slavery Standard*, where it was published as "A Colored American in England" (see appendix 1). Introduced now as "a brother of 'Linda,' the fugitive slave," John apologized for his long silence, which, he wrote, "does not characterize the language of my heart." He wrote of the "disturbed state of the Union," and adopted an oracular pose, declaring that "those who have long sown chains and fetters will reap blood and carnage. Their troubles have begun; God only knows where they will end." He concluded by saying that he does "not think of leaving London at present," but "shall wait to see what course the North intends to pursue. If the American flag is to be planted on the altar of freedom, then I am ready to be offered on that altar, if I am wanted; if it must wave over the slave, with his chains and fetters clanking, let me breathe the free air of another land and die a man and not a chattel." John was not coming back to America, and not anytime soon, it turned out.

The night before writing his letter, he had gone to hear Thompson speak. Thompson had spoken on the subject of slavery and cotton, trying, Jacobs recalled, "to convince the people of this country of the great mistake they had made in not encouraging the cultivation of cotton in their colonies, and to explain the true cause of the slaveholders seceding from the Union."[49] Not long before, Thompson had written a letter to Garrison for the *Liberator* in which he stated that he "endeavoured to make [himself] master of the constitutional argument, in relation to the doctrine of States rights and secession," and concluded that "the present struggle *must* end in the downfall of slavery."[50] In a "lengthy speech" given at Leeds and London, he spelled out "the origin of the secession movement in America and its material influence on the cotton trade of this country." The cause of the war was "simply and solely slavery."[51]

A few days after his letter appeared, Jacobs signed aboard the *Queen Victoria*, which was bound for Alexandria, as Egypt promised to supply British mills with the cotton that they had previously imported from the American South. Before departing, Jacobs visited Thompson, and although what they talked about is unknown, their interests and positions suggest just how much they had to discuss regarding the US Constitution and Britain's role in boycotting Southern cotton and thereby influencing the outcome of the war. Whether Jacobs had the luxury to choose his next ship based on where it was going and what it was going to pick up, it seems that at the outset of the war he had a role to play as a correspondent and participant-observer who could best serve the cause by collecting information for the London Emancipation Committee on his voyages.

Then, disaster struck. Three weeks after leaving Liverpool on his second voyage on the ship, one of the engines broke down, setting the ship off course. In the middle of the night, in a "heavy sea," the wind veered to the northwest, and at 4:00 a.m. the ship ran aground seventy-three miles west of Alexandria. Water poured into the engine room; by daylight it was underwater. The thirty-three crew members and the captain and his mates made for shore, rowing for Alexandria. They made it as far as a place the British called "Arab's Tower," better known to Egyptians as the tomb of Osiris. There, the men "were obliged to provide themselves with arms on account of the hostile feeling displayed by some Arab tribes."[52] Three days later, the HMS *Pelican*, which had been docked in Alexandria to attend the Prince of Wales's royal visit, came to rescue them.[53] In Alexandria, John probably needed several days to recover and to regain his bearings, as he had to find his way back to London by himself. En route, he sent Amelia Chesson an account of his "wreck . . . and fortunate escape" (see figure 3.1).[54]

Somehow John's next voyage wound up being even more disastrous. Less than a month after returning to London, he signed aboard a Liverpool vessel called the *Lloyds* as a cook in late April 1862. A large screw steamer just launched by the firm of Pile, Spence & Co., the *Lloyds* was reputedly bound "for Havana and any of the West India Islands, North or South America, or any port or ports in America, to be discharged in the United Kingdom."[55] While crossing the Atlantic, however, Jacobs noticed that among the cargo of salt, coffee, sulfur, and bar iron were a series of suspiciously long, thin wooden boxes—exactly the right size for rifles. When it was announced the ship was making an unplanned stop in the Bahamas, John's misgivings increased. Upon entering the harbor at Nassau, the captain told the crew that he aimed to "run the blockade before Charleston and offered three months' pay extra to such as would remain with the ship." The entire crew refused the captain's offer, but most ultimately accepted when he upped the amount to twenty pounds, or one hundred dollars. The only person who continued to refuse was John, who demanded that he be sent home to London,

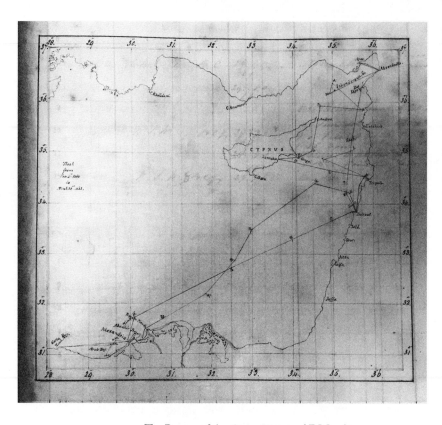

FIGURE 3.1. The Rescue of the *Queen Victoria*. ADM 53/8511.
Courtesy of The National Archives, Kew.

as he was fully aware of Charleston's reputation for imprisoning
and enslaving free sailors of color. Jacobs's stance infuriated the
captain, who made "various efforts . . . to indure Jacobs either to
go to Charleston or to settle and sign a satisfaction."[56] When John
refused again, the captain brought John before a Nassau police
court on charges of desertion. And so, as the Civil War raged, John
Jacobs found himself having to represent himself in court against a
pro-Confederate captain in a pro-Confederate British colonial city
that owed its financial boom almost entirely to the fact that it had
become the major entrepôt for funneling goods to and from the
Confederacy. In four years, the value of Nassau's trade, "valued at
less than £400,000 in 1860," would soar "to more than £10,000,000

in 1864."[57] "The law was all on the side of Jacobs," the *New York Independent* reported, "but the public sentiment of Nassau was so strongly against him, and in favor of the unlawful and contraband trade with the Rebels that he might just as well have looked for snakes in Ireland as justice or sympathy in New Providence."[58]

Jacobs argued his case brilliantly, employing the debating skills he had learned in the Adelphic and before hostile audiences on the lecture circuit, aboard ships, and in foreign ports. Before the police magistrate, he called out the captain and Pile, Spence & Co. for violating the UK's neutrality agreement. Captain Smith denied "under oath that he had had any idea of running the blockade—asserted that he was going to Halifax, and that he had never in any manner mooted the subject of going to Charleston either to Jacobs or any of his crew." Ultimately, Jacobs was able to obtain a discharge by demonstrating that the ship had deviated from its original itinerary by stopping in Nassau. According to the *Independent*, "The *Lloyds* finally sailed without making any provision for sending Jacobs home, and he could get no satisfaction from the consignees." John was once again stranded. After being prevented by the magistrate from reporting the incident to the British consul, he boarded the *Emma Tuttle* for New York City. By complete accident, he was going to be able to see his sister. He also made a point to call on one of his oldest allies, Sydney Howard Gay, at the *Independent* office to tell him how things stood with the pro-Confederate ships of Liverpool, and how he had, once again, become a newsworthy case. His self-reported case was published on May 29, 1862.[59] "The Blockade ran him in to New York," Harriet wrote, and "he was here three days."[60] The *Lloyds* returned from Charleston to Liverpool with 1,775 bales of cotton.[61]

Languages of the Heart

When John returned home, he stayed in the Sailors' Home for the last time. As news of the Union army's practice of "liberating" slaves and President Abraham Lincoln's proposed "slave emancipation" spread, John was preparing to get married.[62] When the couple walked into St. Barnabas church two months later, John was forty-seven and a lifelong bachelor, and Eleanor Aspland was twenty-nine, British, white, mother of a boy and a girl, and a recent widow.[63] Eleanor's parents consented to the marriage and appeared as witnesses at the church. On the marriage certificate, John signed his full name: John Swanson Jacobs. This is the only extant document with his middle name, and there is no indication where it came from. John listed his address as Rosoman Street in Clerkenwell, a working-class neighborhood known for printers, prisons, and sailors, and indeed he lived a few doors down from the *Clerkenwell News* and the Working Men's Club. Harriet wrote Amy Post with mixed feelings: "I must tell you some news my Brother is married. . . . I hope to see him when we have a free Country I would rather he had married here but he must be the judge of his own happiness."[64]

If Harriet worried that John's marriage would keep him in England after Emancipation, she was not wrong. Yet it is hard to say whether it was his marriage that kept him in London or his career as a sailor. Whatever the case, his marriage conformed to his work: over the next four years, he was on shore for no more than two weeks at a time between voyages, and sometimes as little as two days. Never at a loss for work, over the next four years he worked more than eleven voyages, shipping goods to London from such ports as Malta, Odessa, Constantinople, and Smyrna.

After American emancipation and after the Civil War had ended, John did not return home. Instead, he went to court, unsuccessfully suing the *Brenda* for unpaid wages.[65] Soon after, on May 27, 1866, Eleanor gave birth to their only son and John's only biological child: Joseph Ramsey Jacobs. Within a month, John was at sea again, this time on the *Medway*, one of three British ships charged with completing the transatlantic telegraph cable that would allow for near instantaneous communication between North America and Europe. If the voyage symbolized progress for many Anglo-Americans, for John it may have reminded him of other, less immediate forms of communication, like that memorialized in his son's name, which kept alive the memory of Joseph Horniblow; of Harriet's son, Joseph; and of their uncle, Mark Ramsey. Not a month after returning to London, John departed again on the *Far East*, bound for India.

When he arrived in Kolkata in March 1867, he left the ship, as he had told Chesson he was planning to do. What he did in India for the next four months is unknown. His voyage back on the *King Arthur* took more than a year. While he was at sea, Harriet and Louisa took the RMS *Cuba* to Liverpool to begin a fund-raising tour for the Freedmen's movement, and particularly for hospitals for sick and infirm ex-slaves, especially emancipated Black women and orphaned children. They had moved to Savannah, Georgia, after the war to work for the Freedmen's Bureau; Louisa ran the Lincoln Free School and Harriet ran a hospital. In 1868, they spent eight months in England and Scotland, as Harriet promoted the sale of *Incidents* at soirées and other "philanthropic *conversaziones*" put together by female aristocrats and influential Quakers, "for the purpose of calling attention to the mission of a coloured lady named Mrs. Harriet Jacobs."[66] When John returned home at the end of June 1868, Harriet had just the third opportunity in eighteen years to see him. He spent an unprecedented seven weeks ashore with his American and British families. Harriet surely took to heart her two-year-old nephew, named after her lost son and their lost uncle. Were John and Harriet able to communicate all that had happened to them? Did Harriet get along with John's wife, who would later list all of her children, Joseph Ramsey included, as white on the census roll? Did they talk about their autobiographies? And what did they think now that the tables had turned, that Harriet now enjoyed a transatlantic reputation as an abolitionist and John was an anonymous member of a migrant labor force?

Whatever else they talked about, the siblings must have made time to talk about the prospects of John returning to the US. Harriet and Louisa's trip to England marked their final fund-raising effort; they were not going back to Georgia but were returning to Boston. When they returned, they took over a Cambridge boardinghouse for Harvard students and faculty. John also kept hearing that old friends from the London Emancipation Society were packing their bags and returning home. The Crafts called on Frederick Chesson to say goodbye, as he found out when he paid a visit to say goodbye himself a few days later. He was not returning to America just yet, however. In fact, he was going to circumnavigate the planet again, in what would prove to be his last voyage as a sailor. John goes "to Siam," Chesson wrote in his diary, "and will be absent the best part for a year.—He sails in a gunboat (which is also a sort of yacht) ordered for the new King of Siam."[67] The British government had built the *Lotus*, lining it with teak and outfitting it luxuriously for the new king, Chulalongkorn. The boat had problems from the start: eight days out, a gale blew away its steering apparatus; the boat was weighted incorrectly and was underpowered to boot. With such a long voyage ahead, the crew mutinied and successfully demanded that the ship be brought back to Plymouth. It then took five long months for the ship to make it to Bangkok, whereupon the king changed its name to the *Regent*.[68] Having read the most famous antislavery novel of them all, *Uncle Tom's Cabin*, did the young ruler recognize John as an American man of color and invite him to talk about his experiences as a slave? Imagine the words of a former American slave in the court of *The King and I* (minus Anna Leonowens's and Rodgers and Hammerstein's orientalism). Did the old words of abolition retain their power? Or were they now hollow, an empty performance to satisfy a king's curiosity about Stowe's novel? In the last entry he would make about his longtime friend, Chesson wrote that "Jacobs is one of the best coloured men I have ever met, almost too good."[69]

For twenty years and more, John Jacobs had been on the move. He had found his way home from the other side of the world countless times. Through courage, intelligence, and patience, he had walked away from slavery and social death and forged life after life—mariner, abolitionist, miner, husband, father. Some of these lives are undocumented, and what documents do survive tell us only the barest of facts: that John Jacobs existed, that he worked, that he moved, that he breathed. If these facts tell us more about where John was, his autobiography exists to remind us of who he was and serves as a call to imagine this man into the world. When John Jacobs returned from Thailand in late 1870 or early 1871, he had made up his mind. He was going to return to America.

EPILOGUE

Afterlives

Body Down

You won't have an easy time finding John Swanson Jacobs in the Jacobs family plot in Mount Auburn Cemetery in Cambridge, Massachusetts, for no tombstone marks his grave. Head down Clethra Path and you'll know you're at lot 4389 when you arrive at Harriet and Louisa's marble headstones. Washed, reset, repointed, and polished, the headstones stand as a material testament to Harriet's ascendance into the inner sanctum of the African American canon, a status that has made the site one of the most visited memorials in a Greek Revival cemetery that keeps torches burning for Charles Sumner and Oliver Wendell Holmes, Winslow Homer and Margaret Fuller, Robert Creeley and Stanley Cavell. Less illustrious figures such as Harrison Gray Otis, who as a lawyer played a small role in reenslaving Athena Knox and her family, are also buried there.

To find John's grave, you need to look harder. Skirt the edges of the family plot until you light upon a slight depression in the corner made by a four-by-eight-inch stone. Push away the leaves of grass and discover a single word: "BROTHER."

What is a gravestone with no name?

What is a memorial with no memory?

John Jacobs has become a stranger to the world, just as he is

FIGURE 4.1. John Jacobs's Grave, Mount Auburn Cemetery, Cambridge, Massachusetts. Photograph by Jonathan D. S. Schroeder.

a stranger in his own grave. Not long ago his grave marker had sunk beneath the earth completely. The burial and resurfacing of John Jacobs's grave marker is an apt symbol for his disappearance from historical memory—and the work that remains to be done to resurrect him. Yet in 1873, when William Lloyd Garrison spoke at John's funeral, he spoke beside a monument that stood high on its pedestal, proclaiming a name that had stood for radical abolition and much more. As the monument crumbled and collapsed, Louisa tried to repair it before her own death in 1917 but failed to find the money. After the monument was damaged beyond all repair, a single stone survived—"BROTHER"—which was reset as a "flush lawn marker" in 1957 (see figure 4.1).[1] In his eulogy, Garrison may have recalled the letters that John gave him to read before audiences in America and Scotland, which revealed the incredible story of his sister and the outrageous efforts of her "owners" to reenslave her. Or he may have remembered when John held watch over Boston Harbor for an entire night in a heroic bid to rescue a fugitive slave who was due to be shipped back to "hopeless bondage" in New Orleans.[2]

In his final hours, John recalled how he had "revered [Garrison] as the forerunner, the awakening power of freedom in the colored race."[3] On December 19, 1873, he died unexpectedly after "an illness of a few days"; he left no will, and his cause of death is unknown. Soon after, Louisa wrote to Garrison to invite him to come speak at Jacobs's funeral; it is on account of this letter that we know any details of John's death. And yet if this letter surfaces a critical moment of John's existence that would otherwise remain unknown, it reproduces the biases of archival preservation. After all, Louisa cherry-picked this detail from John's final hours to persuade Garrison to speak at the funeral, not because it represented the most important part of her uncle's final hours; and if Garrison had not donated his own papers to the Boston Public Library, which now forms the cornerstone of its massive Anti-Slavery Collection, we would likely not know about the letter at all. Cited without critical framing, this letter reproduces these biases by centering Garrison and reproducing the power that he amassed in his lifetime; more perilously, it risks convincing us that Garrison is *all* John talked about in his final hours, rather than leading us to the recognition that this is *all we know* of his final hours. Because archives did not collect their papers, we can only imagine how other funeral attendees, including Harriet and Louisa, Eleanor and their children and old friends such as William Cooper Nell, remembered John. A few years later, Garrison wrote of John as a person who had taken refuge under the British flag, "in every situation leading an upright life, exhibiting a manly spirit, and commanding the respect of all who know him."[4] And yet Garrison knew not the half of it; he knew nothing of what Jacobs had lived through as a sailor, miner, and Black citizen of the world. The republication of John Jacobs's autobiography begins to tell this untold story.

It is hard to say why John returned to America at the beginning of 1873. When shots were first heard over Fort Sumter, he had vowed never to return to America so long as its flag flew over "the slave, with his chains and fetters clanking." So why did he wait so long—ten years—to return? Was his body breaking down after multiple decades at sea? Had he waited for Harriet to start a home after her own decade of constant travel, teaching, and fundraising for freepersons of color? Had his London antislavery friends turned toward other causes? Did his family refuse to leave England? Though such questions proliferate without immediate answers, posing them brings us closer to the fabric of Jacobs's lifeworld, a world that would otherwise be foreclosed by the Scylla of archival erasure and the Charybdis of uniform standards for historical evidence.

In his final voyage, John crossed the Atlantic for his sister, Harriet, whom he had been missing for twenty-three years. They kept missing each other for reasons beyond their control. The only paying jobs available to John as a Black man required him to be hypermobile and prevented him from establishing a home in any normative sense. As a Black woman, Harriet found that her opportunities were precisely the opposite: *hypo*mobile, domestic jobs confining her to work in a white family's home. In this respect, the siblings sought out humanitarian work not just to develop their intellectual and political talents but also to find relief from the grinding knowledge that they had no choice but to sacrifice so much of their freedom of movement for their economic survival. Even in this space of relative freedom, which gave them the partial autonomy of choosing to march for a cause, and of taking charge of that cause to achieve forms of autonomy undreamed of by white Americans— even here their lives had simply not synced up. When John was an abolitionist, Harriet was a live-in housekeeper and nurse; when Harriet was an abolitionist, John was a sailor. And so they found solace in writing to each other.

Around 1869, Harriet capped her years of travel by taking the Atlantic Navigation Company to court in one of the first civil rights suits in the US (verdict unknown; the New York judicial archives have "misplaced" the case file). She was finally ready to start her own home—for herself and her daughter, Louisa, if not for her long-lost son, Joseph. She quit her job with the New England Woman's Club, which represented not a break from women's rights so much as from the club's elite white women founders—including her friend and former employer Cornelia Grinnell Willis. And so she moved to Cambridge, Massachusetts.

Together with Louisa, Harriet opened a boardinghouse for Harvard University students and faculty, an occupation that would sustain her until her death in 1897. For the first time, she was her own boss, even if her home was not entirely hers. When she heard that John was coming home, she contacted his old friend from the Adelphic Union Library Association, Edward B. Lawton. Building on the fact that she had convinced his daughter, Sarah, to move to Alexandria, Virginia, in 1861 to help set up the Jacobs school for formerly enslaved children, Harriet asked the family for a place for John to stay until he got settled. And so John moved into the crowded house of Eliza Lawton and eight of her children in Cambridge.

Not long after, Eleanor and the children arrived, and the family moved into a triple-decker row house on Brewer Street.[5] Harriet had met John's white wife, Eleanor Aspland, once before and likely greeted her with mixed feelings. And yet Harriet's long-cherished fantasy was actually playing out, and so she did her best to knit John's and her families together.

Harriet had also become friendly with fellow former North Carolina slave Mary Walker, who had spent the entirety of the 1850s trying to rescue her children and had also become a boardinghouse proprietor. John would never meet Mary, however, for she died just as Harriet was in the process of moving her boardinghouse to 127 Mount Auburn Street, which backed onto Walker's boardinghouse on Brattle Street and which Walker's daughter, Agnes Burgwyn, subsequently ran.[6] He did have a chance to meet many of the lodgers at both dwellings, including Harvard mathematician-philosopher-raconteur Chauncy Wright, Henry

Adams and his brother Charles Francis Adams, and visitors such as a young Henry James.[7] In Cambridge at large, John found that many of his old friends had become local leaders, including former Adelphic members Joshua Bowen Smith and Patrick H. and John T. Raymond. Black abolitionists William Wells Brown, John Milton Clarke, and Lunsford Lane, all of whom had published their own slave narratives, also made Cambridge home. John may have joined the Bethel African Methodist Episcopal Church, which opened its doors that year.

Just as John was settling into his house with his family, he fell ill. After a lifetime of separation, he died six days before Christmas, two months before he would have turned fifty-nine. He was initially buried in Mary Walker's recently vacated plot in the public Cambridge Cemetery, since "at that time, burial in a friend's lot, if death was unexpected and no lot had been previously purchased, was not uncommon."[8] Two years later, Louisa had him reburied in a plot she bought for their family in the adjacent Mount Auburn Cemetery. She bought land with space for four graves. Today, the fourth site, which was presumably for her brother, Joseph, sits empty. Eleanor is buried in Cambridge Cemetery.

Spirit High

When John died, Eleanor was forty-one. She stayed in America, never remarrying, occasionally taking on boarders to help ends meet, and dying in 1903 of uric acid poisoning and cerebral congestion. Her son from her first marriage, William Herbert, became a watchmaker and jeweler but continued to live at home in Somerville, Massachusetts, with his mother.[9] Daughter Eleanor became a compositor, got married, and moved to Michigan. Joseph Ramsey Jacobs became a foreman for a stained glass company and later a "statistical clerk." He married Hallie Brown in 1891, and they had no children. They moved several times in and around Boston before settling in Winthrop, on the north side of Boston Harbor. When the census takers knocked on his door, he identified as white, a status he adopted not only because he could but also because his mother had raised him that way. Indeed, when they first came to America, Eleanor's children were listed as white and John's birthplace is listed as "England." When Joseph died in 1961, the Jacobs name died with him.

Harriet and John's half brother, Elijah Knox Jr., had been born free in Hertford County, North Carolina, in 1824 and moved to New Bedford, Massachusetts, in the 1860s. In New Bedford, his descendants flourished: in 1903, his son had the highest score on the civil service exam, settled into a job at the post office, and married a woman named Estella. They had five children. Whereas the two daughters were steered toward vocational training, the three sons were sent to college. William Knox Jr. earned his PhD in chemistry in 1935 from the Massachusetts Institute of Technology. Lawrence Knox also went into chemistry, receiving his doctorate from Harvard in 1940. During the war, both of them worked on the Manhattan Project, with William appointed head of the all-white Corrosion Section and Larry researching radiation.[10] After the war, William moved to Rochester, New York, to work at Eastman Kodak and patented two dozen processes for coating compositions and wetting agents. Clinton Knox received a PhD from Harvard in European history and subsequently set his sights on diplomacy. In 1957, he became the first African American secretary to NATO, and in the following decades was appointed ambassador to Dahomey (Benin) and Haiti. The Knox family are the closest living relatives of Harriet and John.

Yet the most important legacies are not found in bloodlines, but in lines of belonging that dissolve conflicts, ease tensions, and help old words and actions retain their power. If these meanings are constantly receding from us, John Swanson Jacobs's *The United States Governed by Six Hundred Thousand Despots* is a bolt of lightning that scorches the earth across time and space.

John Jacobs is dead.
In the words of Arthur Jafa:

body down, spirit high

body down, spirit high

body down, spirit high

spirit high

spirit high

spirit high

light

light

light[11]

JOHN JACOBS AT FIRST SIGHT

Notes on a Frontispiece

John Swanson Jacobs's author portrait never graced his autobiography. Neither did his name. When *Despots* was published, it was said to be written "by a fugitive slave." In making John Jacobs's words visible again by republishing his lost autobiography, this volume also seeks to make John Jacobs visible again. Chief among the ways of making a person visible is biography, the act of giving words to a life. But there is also another way, which we might call *iconobiography*—giving an image to a life. When I began this project, there were no images of John Jacobs. The frontispiece to this volume may be the first. In these notes, I explain how I came upon the painting, how I came to identify the sitter as Jacobs, how he used the charged and contested visual space of the author portrait to represent the process of self-liberation, and why, as a white editor, I decided to reproduce the painting as a frontispiece. Rediscovered in the early 1970s at an antique sale on Cape Cod, this portrait has been known only under titles that emphasize its anonymity— *Portrait of a Seated Mulatto Man in ¾ Profile* and *The Man Holding the Liberator*. In the 1980s, the painter was identified, but the sitter remains unknown. To prove the identity of a person from a portrait when no other image survives for comparison is extremely difficult.[1] Writing about this effort is important because it makes explicit questions that are at the heart of this volume. Can John Jacobs be given an identity as an individual? Is he more than the series of collective identities given him by historical archives, which categorize him by occupation and status: slave, abolitionist, sailor, miner, resident, husband, passenger? To see what place there might be for him in the world today, it is necessary to understand how he represented himself to the world.

Archival success stories are rarely straightforward, and this one is no exception. In 2017–18, I'd just discovered that John and Harriet's great-grandparents and their five children had escaped to New Bedford in the 1790s, in a bid for freedom that was ultimately thwarted by their owner's family. As I drove back and forth between Boston, New Bedford, Providence, and Raleigh to piece together the event, I kept returning to the work of Kathryn Grover, who has done as much as anyone to document New England Black history and culture, particularly in New Bedford, a city that is extremely proud of its abolitionist history.

When Grover learned that I was researching the life of Harriet Jacobs's brother, she told me of a painting that she'd included in a 1991 exhibition at the New Bedford Whaling Museum that she thought might be of John. The painting had been loaned from the now-defunct Balch Institute of Ethnic Studies, and by the time I began looking, it was believed to be lost. I figured out that the Balch had merged with the Historical Society of Pennsylvania (HSP) in 2002, and, after emailing them, a curator named Sarah Heim sent me scans of their folder on the painting, which included my first view: a low-resolution, grainy photocopy of a photocopy of a photo of the painting.[2] The loss of quality of an image between copies is known as "generation loss," and this great-grandchild of the original was a mess. And yet from out of the completely opaque background, a face was visible—calm, composed, half smiling.

In one letter in the HSP folder, a scholar named Juliette Tomlinson writes in 1986–87 of her research on the painting. Tomlinson was invited to examine the painting because she was the foremost and quite possibly only expert in the world on a prolific nineteenth-century portrait painter named Joseph Whiting Stock, and because the painting shared so many similarities with Stock's work, especially the uncanny perspectives that give Stock's paintings their gothic, folk qualities and make them desirable at auction. When she came to Philadelphia, she verified the artist as Stock.

In the same folder, a Balch curator named Betty Louchheim wrote to the editor of *American Heritage* magazine about reproducing the painting for their 1992 "Winter Art Show" issue. In the letter, she listed four possible sitters: William Wells Brown, Nathan Johnson, Richard Johnson, and Jeremiah Burke Sanderson. It's not a bad list, though the New Bedford agent of the *Liberator*, Richard Johnson, was sixty-eight in 1848 and obviously too old, and the New Bedford agent of the *North Star*, Nathan Johnson, was fifty-five. Brown is a good choice, since he was lecturing in Massachusetts in April 1848, was the highest-paid agent of William Lloyd Garrison's Massachusetts Anti-Slavery Society that year, and was also light-skinned. However, Brown did not lecture in New Bedford that month, and in any event, Brown does not have a beard in surviving images and has a widow's peak in most images.[3] Sanderson is arguably the best candidate of the four: thirty-seven, light-skinned, longtime New Bedford resident and abolitionist. In one of two surviving portraits, he wears his beard similarly, but his head is longer, he has a high forehead, he's balding, and his eyebrows are thinner.

Because the folder on Tomlinson's visit only documents the HSP's side of things, I couldn't tell what research she had conducted on the sitter. Fortunately, I discovered that her research files on Stock are preserved in the Frick Museum's Art Reference Library, including a folder on the painting. What that folder contained, however, would remain a mystery for several years. The Frick Library was moving buildings. And the COVID-19 pandemic had begun. As happened many times during 2020–21, my answer was in a box that no one could touch, and so I was forced to set my search aside.

In September 2021, my partner and I were walking back to a remote cabin in the Maine woods after foraging mushrooms when I found a stray bar of reception and compulsively checked my email. Long after I'd given up on sending "just checking in" emails, there it was: an email from the Frick with a paperclip icon next to it. As the PDF and JPEGs downloaded at dial-up speed, I held my breath. When I clicked on the first image, I saw a scan of the photo of the painting. High-res! But still black-and-white. I was one step closer to finding the painting, however, which I had learned was most likely in the off-site storage of the African American Museum in Philadelphia (AAMP), which had received a donation of all the Balch and HSP's African American–related materials after the merger. Faced with another dead end, I looked more closely at the new image, which revealed much more of the background. The sitter is in a black jacket and tie, his hand grasps an April 1848 copy of the *Liberator*, his arm rests on an armchair, and he is posed against a background with a velvet curtain tied back by a tassel—most likely one of several props the artist kept in his studio to help portray his male sitters as cultivated, successful professionals and tradesmen.

Tomlinson's Frick file turned out to hold a document that would prove indispensable for identifying the painting—Betty Louchheim's "Search for the artist and the sitter of 'The Man Holding the Liberator.'"[4] In 1986–87, it turned out that Louchheim had made an expansive search, contacting an entire roster of institutions and experts, from John Hope Franklin to Benjamin Quarles, the Schomburg Center to the National Portrait Gallery, and the Tuskegee Institute to Bowdoin College. Yet Louchheim's correspondence with Tomlinson in the dossier also makes clear that the pair did not know very much about African American history, art, or culture. "I really can't suggest who the subject of the portrait might be," Tomlinson writes Louchheim. "You mentioned there was a large negro colony in New Bedford at that time so it could be anyone." The two corresponded regularly in the months before Tomlinson's visit to Philly, and in another letter Louchheim found it impossible to rule out Frederick Douglass as the sitter, despite his status as the most photographed person of the nineteenth century.

From the responses she received, Louchheim compiled a list of nine possible sitters: Henry Bibb, William Wells Brown, Frederick Douglass, Richard T. Greener, John Jones, "Leisendorff [*sic*] of San Francisco," William Cooper Nell, Charles Lenox Remond, and William Whipper. The list is, for the most part, preposterous: Greener was four years old in 1848, Whipper forty-four and heavyset; Bibb was a Liberty Party supporter and called an "enemy" of the *Liberator*; Jones lived in Chicago and William Leidesdorff in San Francisco; and Remond was skinny, dark-complexioned, and balding. Douglass had already begun the *North Star*, which signaled his break from Garrisonianism, and he kept his hair "natural" in the style of Alexandre Dumas, in contrast to the sitter here, whose hair is parted and, though unstraightened, neatly coiffed. Sidney Kaplan, scholar of African American culture and history, astutely suggested Nell, but it is unlikely that Nell was in New Bedford in April 1848, the date of the newspaper in the sitter's hands, because he, too, had moved to Rochester the previous winter and published articles in the *North Star* on April 7, 14, and 21. And Brown, as mentioned before, although a lecturing agent for the Massachusetts Anti-Slavery Society, was lecturing elsewhere in Massachusetts that month.

John Jacobs was also on the payroll of the Massachusetts Anti-Slavery Society that year as a lecturing agent. And unlike Brown, he had strong ties to New Bedford, having escaped there in 1839 and worked on the *Frances Henrietta* for the next four years on a whaling voyage. In April 1848, after two days of lecturing in Nantucket,

Jacobs and Jonathan Walker sailed for New Bedford, most likely on the morning steamship, *Massachusetts*. Entering New Bedford, the thirty-sixth destination on a grueling interstate tour, Jacobs returned to the city that had given him some of the protections, employment, and community that make home and personhood possible. He saw the whalers and sailors and the candle- and rope-works that he and his great-grandfather, Jack Cotton, had known well, a life he would resume eight years later when he left Australia and became a full-time mariner. In New Bedford were old friends, an escape from the "mobocratic" spirit of small-town racists, and a reprieve from living in close quarters with the inflexible and severe Walker. And Boston and a visit to his sister and his niece and nephew were on deck.

The hilly cobblestone streets of New Bedford's downtown provided many aids to memory: the African Methodist Episcopal Zion Church where Douglass had begun preaching, William Howland's free produce store, and William C. Taber's bookstore, where Jacobs had probably bought the primers that he had used to teach himself to read while in the Pacific. With each lecture that he gave, it became more and more likely that one day Taber might sell *his* book; and even if they didn't, Jacobs could also take matters into his own hands in Rochester and perhaps even sell his own autobiography one day (not long after, he would buy the Anti-Slavery Reading Room). Did he then walk off the street into Stock's studio?[5] When he entered, he found the artist sitting in a wheelchair, a recent invention that a Boston doctor had built especially for Stock, who had been paralyzed as a boy after an oxcart had fallen on him. Jacobs, who had seen the frontispieces to Douglass's and Brown's narratives, had schooled himself in Nell's transcendentalist philosophy of elevation, and had just moved to Rochester to join Douglass's new, Black-run antislavery machine, knew full well the importance of such portraits. "How was a person," Marcus Wood asks, "who had been legally and economically designated as outside humanity, while a slave, to present himself or herself before a free white readership in America or Europe, or to their smaller audience of fellow free blacks?"[6] So perhaps Jacobs, too, wanted a picture that showcased the talent and potential he had worked hard to cultivate and the dignity and respect he had worked just as hard to earn after he had escaped lifelong bondage.

The case that John Jacobs is the sitter in this painting is a strong one. All evidence points to him. Yet the case is not conclusive. After all, how can one recognize someone based on words alone? Are these the same "bright intelligent eyes" that looked out at the *Empire* editors in Sydney seven years later? Is this the person described as "a man of colour, whose complexion would be hardly noticeable among the average specimens of the English face?" Who "looks as if he might have been a gentleman's servant, smart, active, witty, good looking . . . at ease in any society," as the Quaker Julia Wilbur wrote? Is it possible to reach across time and say that this person bears a family resemblance to Harriet Jacobs, whose only formal portrait was taken nearly five decades later, in 1894, when she was eighty-one, but who was similarly light-skinned and whose smile seems just like the sitter's? Or is this simply someone from New Bedford such as Jeremiah Burke Sanderson, who was also involved in antislavery politics? Even after ruling out the options based on the portraits of African American abolitionists that do survive, the best one can do is make an educated guess. So let's hope that this is a picture of John Jacobs.

If it is, the story gets even better. A few months after I received the Frick files, I hired a research assistant in Philadelphia and asked her to pay a visit to the AAMP and see what she could turn up. Dejay Duckett, the museum's vice president of Curatorial Services, found the painting right away—it wasn't off-site at all, but in the main vault! A few days later, I received high-res, DSLR color photographs, which revealed a wealth of new detail about the painting. A laurel pattern on the curtain, tied by a tassel to a column, were most likely props of Stock's to communicate Jacobs's command of classical learning (think of the pride of place that Douglass gives *The Columbian Orator* in his *Narrative*).[7] A few days later, I took the train down and saw the painting for myself, if only to be in the presence of an object that I had been seeking for so long.

Identifying an image of a person who exists only in words is a riddle with no obvious answer. So too with this biography. Archives can silence individuals even when they preserve records about them, in ways that say more about how institutions failed people like John Jacobs than about John Jacobs himself. In institutional records, the borders of John Jacobs's identity become amorphous, because Jacobs is treated as a member of a group, a type, a representative of a collective. My decision to include this painting as the "face" of this autobiography and the face of John Jacobs is most certainly about giving John Jacobs an identity for today. But it is also about recognizing that the work of constructing Jacobs's life often can only draw the rough outlines of his world instead of clearly delineating his "identity." The obstacles that archives present, because they were asymmetrically constructed to privilege the powerful, mean that sometimes the best we can do in reconstructing the identity of John Jacobs is to recover his collective identity, which may explain something about who he was as an individual but also says a lot about what he shared with other people who shared his lot in life. Perhaps the subject of this painting is Sanderson. Or perhaps it is someone else who also checks the seven or eight boxes I've used to make the case for Jacobs. Whoever it is, this is someone who chose not to be defined negatively as a nonindividual, a member of a mass body subject to exploitation, racism, and other harms, but someone who saw themselves as belonging to a collective who wanted to make the world a more just, more equitable place—by fighting for rights, dignity, citizenship, and a place in the world.

This is a painting of a remarkable Black man. Based on available evidence, I believe it is of John Jacobs and that this is the portrait he would have liked to include in his autobiography. John Jacobs was a Black citizen of the world who lived as a slave in North Carolina, an abolitionist in New England, and a sailor in every port of call in the world, from the first time he sailed out of New Bedford to his last major voyage, from London to Bangkok. Jacobs was also the author of not one but two autobiographical slave narratives. If this is truly John Jacobs, this painting represents one of his greatest achievements. "Negroes can never have impartial portraits at the hands of white artists," Douglass wrote soon after Jacobs had his portrait painted. "It seems to us next to impossible for white men to take likenesses of black men, without most grossly exaggerating their distinctive features."[8] And yet somehow Jacobs managed to convince a hostile world to recognize him as he wanted to be seen.

Giving up his country and his career proved costly: he never received the recognition that often accompanied the publication of stand-alone, hardcover versions of other slave narratives. No transatlantic cosmopolitan like William Wells Brown and Henry "Box" Brown, he could no longer expect the fame that his book's circulation in print might have brought. To escape from American injustice and to stay true to his own principles, antislavery and otherwise, he had put himself in circulation instead. As a member of a global labor force, Jacobs pulled off a miracle by getting his narrative published at all; that he did more in an Australian newspaper than what many of his peers were able to do in the transatlantic world is just as incredible. Because he never received recognition in his lifetime, it is only now that we can begin to appreciate how he crafted a revolutionary new contract between Black narrator and white reader and an impersonal style that testifies to the lengths he had traveled. Had his life gone in another direction, he would today be mentioned in a select group of Black abolitionists that includes Henry Bibb, Ellen and William Craft, Douglass, Henry Highland Garnet, Solomon Northrup, James Pennington, Maria Stewart, and, of course, his sister.

My decision to include this portrait as the frontispiece is ultimately about giving John Jacobs the space and access he did not have for huge periods of his life. In reproducing this central convention of the antebellum slave narrative, I do not mean to indicate that I am trying to reproduce *all* of its trappings, for the genre was hierarchically constructed, placing white abolitionist editors above Black authors. I take it as my responsibility to describe that hierarchy and dismantle it. Giving John Jacobs his frontispiece is about giving him an autonomous space to demonstrate his self-fashioning, in both his visual and verbal representation. The other parts of this volume seek to avoid the white envelope / Black message structure as well in different ways; their goal is not to provide John Jacobs with a certificate of good character so that skeptical/racist white readers can trust he is telling the truth. Rather, they seek to describe how John Jacobs pioneered a new style of slave narrative that can properly be called the "global slave narrative," and to show that he lived a life that is even more incredible than his autobiography. Instead of intervening in the reader's judgment of Jacobs, the paraliterary parts of this volume elaborate on why his text and life *matter*.

LIST OF EMENDATIONS

This list enumerates changes that I, as editor, have made in the copy-text. I have tried to remain maximally faithful to the narrative. However, because the editors of the *Empire* added punctuation and new spellings to John Jacobs's narrative, I have corrected obvious typographical errors, inconsistent spelling, and inferred misreadings of John Jacobs's original manuscript. While John Jacobs spelled several surnames differently than they appear on written records, including Hanablue (Horniblow), Moumon (Moorman), Carbaras (Cabarrus), and Carnes (Cairns), I have chosen to preserve his spellings (except in cases where his spelling closely resembles the written version).

PAGE(S)	*EMPIRE* READING	COPY-TEXT READING
3	History of the United States	*History of the United States*
3	History	*History*
5	Hannablue	Hanablue
5	James R. Norcom	James A. Norcom
7	Hannablue	Hanablue
8	Moss	Mass
8	begged to leave to	begged leave to
9	Act	Fact

PAGE(S)	*EMPIRE* READING	COPY-TEXT READING
15, 29	Collings	Collins
15, 69	slave-holder	slaveholder
15	Of	Off
19	christian	Christian
8, 20	anti-christian	anti-Christian
25–26	Cofield	Coffield
31	than	that
36	Bosman	Bozman
40	lfe	life
42	Sawyers's	Sawyer's
42	crosed	crossed
42	of	off
45	"cure." Though	"cure," though
45	city	City
46	gentlemen,	gentlemen.
47	to——— and	to ——— and
47	call	Call
48	Custom house	Custom House
48	Astor House Hotel	Astor House hotel
51	df	of
51	Frances Henrietta	*Frances Henrietta*
53	Casper	Caspar
54	her,	her.
55	Go you and seize him;	"Go you and seize him;"
57	History of the United States	*History of the United States*
58	an	and
68	on	of
73	peace.	peace?

APPENDIX I

Writings by John Swanson Jacobs

1. John S. Jacobs to Sydney Howard Gay, September 7, 1845
2. John S. Jacobs to Sydney Howard Gay, June 4, 1846
3. John S. Jacobs to William Lloyd Garrison, February 27, 1848
4. John S. Jacobs to Frederick Douglass, March 3, 1848
5. "Antislavery Office and Reading Room," March 23, 1849
6. John S. Jacobs to Frederick Douglass, April 20, 1849
7. John S. Jacobs to Frederick Douglass, May 4, 1849
8. John S. Jacobs to Zenas Brockett, [September 6, 1849?]
9. "Men Will Lie, but Oysters Cannot," January 9, 1850
10. "A Colored American in England," June 29, 1861

In this and the following appendix, I have chosen not to use *sic* to point out deviations from conventional spelling, ungrammatical constructions, and unexpected language in the original source documents. Spelling and grammar were less standardized in the nineteenth century, and to flag these instances would needlessly distract the reader.

Boston Mass Sep 7th 1845

Friend Gay

there is a friend of mine with you whose case I would like to have known he is a young man from edenton NC his mother is free I belive she bought her time previous to his birth but not withstanding he is to be held as a slave untill he is 28 years of age how this is I will not attempt to explane the young man is of age let him speak for him self I have written to you because I knew no one else upon whom I could depend for prompt attention to the case I have several letters that he sent me when the hand of oppression bore heavily upon him but he seames to have forgoten those times and thinks of returning again to the house of bondage he is now about 27 years of age I wrote him a letter on the 5 and advised him to go and see friend Hopper* I expect an answer from it to morrow Joseph Jacobs in the ramblers office† will give you any information respecting him that you may wish I hope that the legality of the case will be tested

Yours in the cause of liberty
J. S. Jacobs
No 36 grove St boston

ALS; Sydney Howard Gay Papers, Rare Books & Manuscript Library, Columbia University‡

---

* Isaac Tatem Hopper (1771–1852), a Quaker reformer, moved from Philadelphia to New York City in 1829, in the wake of the controversy that split the Society of Friends into "'Orthodox' and 'Hicksites.' . . . In 1841 he became an agent for the American Anti-Slavery Society and subsequently was disowned by the Friends for his abolitionism." *HJFP*, 1:44.

† The *Rambler* newspaper was located at 138 Nassau Street in New York City.

‡ ALS stands for "autograph letter signed."

Chelsea Mass June 4 1846

Friend Gay,

they have let the cat out of the bag and I thort that I would tell you that it proved to be a devel in disguise my sister received a very affectionate letter lass week from her young mistress—Mrs. Mesmore she writes of her having married and also of having heared that my sister had gone to England she has been waiting the arrival of Mr W* and now reminds my sister of her former love and in that affectionat manner so peculiar to this no soul Nation she want to know if she wont come home that she had never consented for her Father to sell her <u>becaus</u> she did not wish her to be the slave of any one but her self who had alwais lovd her and been kind to her—in deed it seems to me that the old Dr letter to the New York blood hounds and the young Dr† letter to my sister with the one received last week would pusel all of the pill makers in the city, to get them in to a shape sutable to our taste let me give you an extract from all of them

the old Dr writes his to New York to be put in to the hands of the smartest polease officer in the city offering $100 rewards for her and after having discribed her as minutely as possible he sais that he dont wish to sell her at any price he wants to get her to make ensample of her for the good of the institution

the young Dr writes as if he had Just come from a camp meeting, his hole head is full of love the purest of the Delilah kind he is a fraid that she is not happy and comfortable away from all of her friends and relations and after assuring her that the family still entertain the most friendly feelings to wards her he then begs her to write him where she is that he might restore her to her former happiness (hell)

the letter that was written by Mesmore as you know was

---

* Nathaniel Parker Willis.

† John Norcom (1802–56), son of Dr. James Norcom (1778–1850).

acompleat forgery and in addition to that it was as black er falshood as ever escaped the bottomless pit he said that a northern gentleman wished to buy her and that the Norcom family would have nothing to do with her when in fait he then intended and since has married in the Norcom family the newly made Mrs Mesmore wants her to return home or buy herself but as my sister has not the means to buy her self and finds these cold regons more healthy than the suny South they will have to love each other at a distance the sweetest love that can exist betweene master and Slave I dont know this mr Mesmore the New York men ketchers has run him in to Edenton since the baby stealers run me out but to Judge him by his letters I should say that he was equil to 15 grains of epecuane* mixed in a like warm water but poor fellow he has paid dear for his wife has been shot mobed and emprisoned but for the want of time I must leave this interesting family may the Lord have mursey up on them

yours in behalf of the oppressed the world over

John S. Jacobs

ALS; Sydney Howard Gay Papers, Rare Books & Manuscript Library, Columbia University

* Ipecacuanha, a homeopathic medicine made from the roots and rhizomes of *Cephaelis Ipecacuanha*, a shrub native to Brazil and parts of South America. Ipecac syrup was used to induce vomiting.

Incidents in Western New York

Cato, (Four Corners,) N.Y., Feb. 27th, 1848

Dear Garrison:

Jonathan Walker and myself had an appointment to this town for the Lord's day, and our notice was a week in advance of us. On Saturday night, we spoke to the people at H[annibal]. The next day we walked 11 miles through the snow, with our bag of books on our backs, and no dinner, to meet the appointment at Cato. The time came—the bell rang, and we went with the friends to a schoolhouse; while there were two churches in this place empty. The room was soon crowded, and the people coming and going who could not enter. J. W. told the people that they were sitting there, breathing each other's breath over and over, because slavery predominated in the churches of Cato. After he had closed his remarks, the Rev. Mr. Hurbert rose to defend his craft. The Presbyterian church, he said, had heard of Mr. W's coming, and had enquired of several persons to know who Mr. Walker was, but none of his friends could tell him. He asked some of the most thorough abolitionists in the church to tell him what they intended to do with J. W. and J. S. J.; and they thought, as no one knew them, they had better go into the schoolhouse, lest they should do, as some others had done, who, he said, had preached infidelity. But his main objection was, that inasmuch as we did not arrive in the place at noon, according to the Bible and the principles of Christianity, he had no reason to expect that we would come. What means this? Does that Rev. brother believe it to be a greater sin to travel through the snow to meet an appointment on Sunday, than it would be to tell a wilful lie? If this is not what he means, no one but himself understood what he meant to convey to the minds of the people.

Mr. Walker charged him of accusing us of Sabbath breaking, which charge he did not deny. Let us suppose this charge true—that we are Sabbath breakers. Why should they condemn us for doing the thing that they always have taught us was essential to our salvation—the assembling of ourselves together?* I have yet to learn that I have not as good a right to get up, or go to, an anti-slavery meeting on Sunday, as they have to get up, or go to, their meetings. Now, if the sin is in entering the town on Sunday, why do they not rebuke their brethren from the country? They are guilty of the same crime. If because it is an anti-slavery meeting, why do they come to hear, and participate in those meetings?

Yours,

J. S. JACOBS

Liberator, March 31, 1848

---

* Hebrews 10:23–25: "Let us hold fast the profession of our faith without waver-ing; for he is faithful that promised; and let us consider one another to provoke unto love and to good works: not forsaking the assembling of ourselves together, as the manner of some is, but exhorting one another: and as much the more, as ye see the day approaching."

A Little More Piety

Rochester, March 3, 1848

Dear Douglass: — A few days ago, I attended a Missionary Meeting in Rome, N.Y., where a resolution was discussed, in substance, like this: "All that is necessary to make us more successful in making proselytes of the heathen, is more piety."

My business there was to get a notice of an Anti-Slavery meeting read; but I was told that they could not read it. They related some thrilling stories of the people in Bengal. One story that pleased the missionaries very much was, that some one, some where, at some time or other, gave a Catholic girl a Bible, which she read with much pleasure, until her priest became acquainted with the fact, who made her carry it back.* This they thought was an unpardonable sin. Oh that I could find words to express my indignation! Do they not know that every Bible they have handled since they have been on their mission, has been in part purchased with the blood of the slave? And if they were honest, they would write on the lid of every bible, "The price of the blood and souls of those who are not allowed to read it."

Oh what a happy land of missionaries and slaves, Bibles and handcuffs, Bible pedlers and men pedlers, all belonging to the same church! Of all the horrible things that the sun ever shone upon, a baby-stealing, woman-whipping, man-murdering and war-making religion is the most horrible. These men are leaving scenes of suffering here at home, to go to a land where the introduction of them would not for one minute be tolerated. One of the speakers asked his hearers to read the 12th chapter of Rev.† He might with great

---

* "For the laity, Catholics favored a mediated relationship to the scriptures, and thus to God, while Protestants thought all believers could have a direct relationship with God through the Bible." *HJFP*, 1:95.

† "The twelfth chapter of Revelation, concerned mainly with the theme of persecution, presents a vision of a pregnant woman pursued by a many-headed dragon

propriety have said the 18th. "I heard another voice from Heaven, saying, Come out of her, my people, that ye be not partakers of her sins, and that ye receive not of her plagues; for her sins have reached unto heaven, and God hath remembered her iniquities, for trading in slaves and the souls of men."* Let us suppose those missionaries' wives and children were now clanking their chains in India. Would they tell us that they had business of greater importance than their deliverance from whips, and chains, and slavery, to attend to? Would they hail the man that held them as a good Christian and a brother?

Yours for the truth,
JOHN S. JACOBS

North Star, March 3, 1848

---

that would eat the infant after its birth. The child is born and taken up to God, while the woman flees. . . . The speaker, by referring to this chapter, was encouraging the missionaries to endure the persecution they faced in their work, which they believed to be the work of Satan." *HJFP*, 1:95–96.
* Revelation 18:4–5, 13.

Rochester, March 23, 1849

Antislavery office and Reading Room,

No. 25 Buffalo St. Rochester, opposite the Arcade.

This office has been newly stocked with the latest and best works on slavery and other moral questions. Among them are the Young Abolitionist—Poverty its illegal causes and legal cure—The Power of Kindness—The Branded Hand—History of the Mexican war—Theodore Parker's Sermon on J. Q. Adams—d[itt]o on the Mexican war—d[itt]o his letters to the People of the United States—The Church as it is or the Forlorn hope of Slavery—Despotism in America, and Archy Moore.

I intend to have in connection with [the] office a Circulating Library, as soon as I can get a sufficient number of useful and instructive books of a moral and scientific character.

JOHN S. JACOBS

North Star, March 23, 1849

Rochester, April 20, 1849

Communications.

AN ANTI-SLAVERY TOUR

Frederic Douglass:—I feel it due to those laboring in other depart-
ments of the antislavery cause to report my experiences as a lecturer.
I left Rochester* Sunday March 18th. Monday the 19th, I spoke at
the Universalist Church in Clarendon, to a small but attentive audience. Tuesday the 20th, I went to Southbarr, at evening I attended
a religious meeting held in the School House, where I conversed
with Mr Gaston the Presbyterian Minister, who told me there was
a revival of religion in progress at the Centre, and for himself he was
opposed to the introduction of the subject of Slavery, Peace, Temperance, or anything calculated to draw off their minds from the
importance of getting religion. I told him should they have it sea-
soned with a little humanity it would do them no harm; he admitted
it would do them no harm, but still refused to give me a hearing.

I then said to him, Mr. Gaston suppose some one should pass
through this town, and steal and carry off two or three children, and
their mothers with aching hearts and streaming eyes should send
their petition to your church asking the prayers of the righteous
which avail much, in behalf of the restoration of their children to
their fond arms, would you treat their petition as you have treated
the cause of the slaves? He then declared that he would object to
the offering a prayer at those meetings, for the deliverance of three
millions of his countrymen from chains and slavery.

There was a Mr. O. T. Burns present, who agreed with Mr. Gaston. Mr. Burns said he had lived in Kentucky, and knew that we said
some hard things of slaveholders that they did not deserve; he said
they were kind and hospitable. What he meant was this—they stole

* All towns listed are in New York state.

pigs and ducks from their slaves, and stuffed him with them! Here I am at a loss, I do not know which is the most valueless Mr. Burns' idea of hospitality or Mr. Gaston's religion; the one will admit of robbing the poor to feed the rich—the other of heathenizing, and stealing men, women, and children for the glory of God, and good of souls.

Wednesday the 21st, I went to Pinebill, and from there to Oakfield. Here, too, they were holding protracted meetings. The cause of bleeding humanity finds but few friends at protracted meetings and revivals of religion. They are all so busy in trying to save that invisible and undefined part of man called the soul, that they will see his body, the image of God, trampled in the dust unheeded.

Thursday the 22nd, I returned to Southbar and made arrangements for a meeting to be held at the School House, on Friday Evening the 23rd, which was well attended. Saturday the 24th, I went to Albion, the friends (if there be any of them, and I sought dilligently for them) had made no arrangements for a meeting. The Court House, the only public building that is not barred against the cause of the oppressed, had been newly painted. A deacon of the Presbyterian church tried to get the vestry of the Methodist church, but Mr. Mehay the minister objected to my having it. The deacon told me I would find friends and an antislavery church at Eagle Harbour. That is more than the deacon can say of his church, or that I can say of the people of Albion.

Sunday the 25th, in the absence of the Wesleyan minister of Eagle Harbor, I spoke to a few friends of the cause that had assembled for morning worship. The streets were so muddy that the people could only get to the Meeting House in wagons.

Monday the 26th, I went to West Gaines, but finding no arrangements had been made for a meeting, I did not attempt to get up one, judging from the appearance of things it would be labor lost.

Tuesday and Wednesday, the 27th and 28th, I lectured at Johnson's Creek. My first lecture was in the School house. After much entreaty, and fifty cents in cash, which was afterwards made up to me, I got them to allow me the privilege of opening the doors of their church, and making a fire for them, that they might sit there comfortably, while I spoke for the dumb. How long people will content themselves to sit in a little school house to hear such lectures is for them to say. The idea of a church being dedicated to God, that bars its doors against humanity, is absurd. "God is not mocked, is not this the fast that I have chosen to loose the bands of wickedness, and let the oppressed go free, and that ye break every yoke?"*

Thursday and Friday, the 29th and 30th, I lectured in Lockport; the meeting was slimly attended, though I do not regret having gone there. At Dr. T's house I saw an old man fifty-one years of age, who had just made his escape from the prison-house of American slavery. There were many things connected with his case that refreshed my mind, making me feel more thankful for my own freedom, and more anxious for others.

Saturday the 31st, I lectured in the Universalist church at Ridgway Corners. After the meeting I made an appointment for Sunday afternoon, and then went to Lindonville to make arrangements for one or more meetings there, but I could not find a man in the village to lend a helping hand. I left these, who had told me I could not get the people to come out and went to the Presbyterian church and saw the trustees, who told me I could have the church for two evenings. I carried my notices to the churches, for Sunday and Monday evenings, then left for the Corners, to my afternoon appointment; the meeting was well attended. I returned to Lindonville, and to the astonishment of those inactive abolitionists whose doctrine is "they are joined to idols let them alone,"† I had a full house; after the lecture, I invited the little children that had heard me to come again and bring their little friends. I lent them some little books to take home with them. Monday the 2nd, this evening

---

* Galatians 6:7: "Be not deceived; God is not mocked: for whatsoever a man soweth, that shall also he reap." Isaiah 58:6: "Is not this the fast that I have chosen? To loose the bands of wickedness, to undo the heavy burdens, and to let the oppressed go free, and that ye break every yoke?"
† Hosea 4:17: "Ephraim is joined to idols: let him alone."

must have been one of deep interest to all present. I had acted some-what imprudently, in walking six or eight miles to get up a meeting for the next day, and returned quite fatigued and feverish, brought on by abstinence and disease. I entered the house at a very early hour; those little girls were there singing an antislavery song. The change was so great I soon felt like another man, knowing I was among friends, though they were small ones, I got them to open the meeting with an antislavery song, their choice was "I am an aboli-tionist, I glory in the name,"* &c, their fathers and mothers must have felt the force of those words as they fell from the lips of their children. I told those little girls how little slaves were treated, I was heard with apparent interest.

Tuesday, April 3rd, I had a meeting in the vestry of the Method-ist church, in Medina. Old Zack† has got many friends there; dea-con Cook, and brother Snell made quite a speech in his defence, he was afraid I should injure the cause by calling them thieves and rob-bers and Taylor whigs pro-slavery; I hope the time is not far distant, when pick-pockets will shun such men.

Thursday the 5th, I went to Gaines, West Gaines, and Albion, but could not get up a meeting in either place. Saturday the 7th, I lectured at the Wesleyan chapel, Eagle Harbor, the audience was quite disorderly, being in part made up of some boatmen, whose highest idea of manliness seemed to be disturbance. Sunday the 8th, I lectured at the Baptist church in Holley to a large audience. Here the arrangements had been made by our friend Morgan, and the Presbyterian minister kindly waived his evening meeting, that I might have a full house; the meeting went off well.

At no time during my laboring in the cause as a lecturer, have I found so few friends, as on the present occasion. In some of these

* Written in 1841 by William Lloyd Garrison, "Song of the Abolitionist" was reti-tled "I Am an Abolitionist" in William Wells Brown's *The Anti-Slavery Harp: A Collection of Songs* (Boston: Bela Marsh, 1848).
† Zachary Taylor (1784–1850), twelfth president of the United States, owner of 131 slaves, and general in the Mexican-American War.

towns, it has been more than a year since the slaves of this land have had any one to tell of their wrongs.

Your fellow laborer in the cause of humanity,
JOHN S. JACOBS

North Star, April 20, 1849

Rochester, May 4, 1849

Friend Douglass:—As the question is frequently asked us why we do not go where slavery exists, and lecture there on the subject, and we are as frequently told, that the people at the North are all abolitionists, I will give you the character of some of them as illustrated a few nights ago in Spencerport.* Sunday April 15th, I lectured to a large audience in the Presbyterian church at Adams Basin, the meeting was opened with a prayer from Mr. Ball. Monday, 16th, I spoke at the Methodist church on the Lyle road, in the town of Gates. The audience was not very large, but evidently quite Whiggish. An old man, a worthy member of the church to which he belongs, but would not be in a Christian church or decent society, said it was too hard for their wives and families to be obliged to sit and hear me tell of the brutality of the slaveholders and their abettors.

Is it right that we should submit to these indignities? Is it easier to bear the infliction [of] the rod than it is to administer it? Where is the wrong of slavery? Is it in our telling you your wickedness, or your continuance in it?

A Mr. Coaser, a Whig magistrate placed old Zack [Taylor] behind General Washington, then dared me to touch him. Failing to draw out others to his assistance, he told me that eggs, bricks, and stones should be my reward, if I dared to give utterance to such sentiments in Spencerport as I had uttered there. Tuesday, 17th, I lectured to a large audience of manly persons, in the brick School House on the Lyle road.

Wednesday, 18th, I went to my appointment at Spencerport. The meeting was held in the Methodist church. The audience was large, but very disorderly: they hissed like serpents, and stamped their heels like asses. Seeing they were displeased with my remarks I asked to be corrected, if I had given utterance to a single sentence that was not true. The reply was, we have come to hear you talk about slavery.

* All towns listed are in New York state.

"That, (said I) is the very thing I am doing, if we had no slaveholders we should have no slaves, I am discussing the character of a slaveholder, in the President of the United States. If slavery is a disgrace, upon whom rests the disgrace? Do you make slaveholders more honorable by having them to rule over you, or do you make yourselves less honorable in choosing them? You may call good evil, and evil good, but they will ever remain the same. That which God and humanity have cursed, let no man call good. Is it a crime for me to love my country? Have I shown bitterness of feeling in speaking to you? Are you not guilty of all that I have accused you? Have I asked you for gold and silver, or have I asked you to take your feet off the necks of three millions of your countrymen, whom you have so long oppressed? for this you threatened to stone me, where is your sympathy? is it with the oppressed or the oppressors? Dare you call yourselves friends to your country, who have elected to the highest office in the gift of the nation, a man in whom you could see nothing but blood, rapine, and robbery?—is the battle field the place for men to learn acts of humanity, and have instilled into them the principles of peace? Is the slave mart the place for men to learn to deal justly, love mercy, and walk humbly before God? If these things are true, why am I to be stoned for telling them[?] It may be painful to your ears to hear them, but far more painful to us who are made to endure them. I came among you to speak for the dumb—the crushed and the bleeding slave; I pointed out the new links in their chains that you had forged; and for this act of justice and humanity, you barred your doors against me, and in violation of your law you tried to gag me, because I dared to call Zach. Taylor that old and skilful murderer and cradle plunderer, a disgraced man; but if God spares my life and strength—

You shall have him in Florida with his bloodhounds training,*
And in Mexico the veins of his innocent victims draining;

* "Taylor had used bloodhounds to track down Native Americans during the Second Seminole War (1835–1842), and abolitionists often suggested that the animals were used to trail runaway slaves as well." *HJFP*, 1:151.

You shall have him ready and rough,
Until you repent and cry—Enough!*

Thursday, 17th, being unable to obtain a house in Spencerport to lecture in, I went to Ogden. Here I stopped with an aged lady, whose heart was larger than her fortune. On learning that I had a horse, she enquired of her daughter how much money there was in her purse. She answered "five shillings." "It is enough, let him take his horse to the Tavern to be fed," she replied. I thanked her, and told her my mission was not to rob widow's houses, and for a pretence make long prayers, but to cry out against these wrongs. In the evening, I spoke in the School House to a small audience, the General's friends did not pay me a visit.

JOHN S. JACOBS

North Star, May 4, 1849

---

* This verse is most likely Jacobs's own composition.

[Fonda, NY, September 6, 1849?]

Friend Venoas* [. . .]:

I promised to give you a sketch of my tour. My first stop was at Fort Plain [New York]. I could get no place to speak in there. The Minister of the Presbyterian Church said that he had put his foot upon all such subjects—here I stoped at a rum Hotel. When the bell rang for breakfast I went in with the rest of the boarders. At dinner I done the same but the boarders rose from the table and left the room. I told them that if I was the cause of their leaving, they could return. By this time a female rum seller, the Land Lord's wife I suppose, came in the bar room and with a look full of meaning she asked me if I eat with white folkes. I told her I did. Well said she we are not Abolitionist here. I said mam that has nothing to do with the case in hand. I am a boarder, was not that bell for them to go into to their dinner; yes said the Landlord but you should have known your place. I told him that the table was my place at dinner. But your place as a colored man is to wait until the other boarders are don. Sir I will not conform to the acts of colored. Nor white men. Unless they are just and equal but I will drop this story. I have lectured 3 times in Troy and one in Albany at the expense of $7 or $8 I received no incoragement to go to the Spring. I am to lecture here

---

* "'Venoas' was the way Eleanor Franz, who originally published this letter, transcribed the name Zenas, although she had found the letter in Brockett's correspondence. Excised here is her parenthetical remark: 'not spelling of Zenas' name.' Zenas Brockett (1806–83) married Candace Salisbury (1807–75) in 1832. They lived on a farm two miles from the village of Brockett's Bridge, part of the town of Manheim, N.Y. Their home was a stop on the Underground Railroad, and Zenas regularly donated time and money to the abolitionist cause; the Brocketts' circle included Gerrit Smith, John Brown, and Frederick Douglass." *HJFP*, 1:168. The Brocketts were also longtime friends of Louisa Jacobs, who would stay at their home during the summers through the 1880s. See Mary Maillard, ed., *Whispers of Cruel Wrongs: The Correspondence of Louisa Jacobs and Her Circle, 1879–1911* (Madison: University of Wisconsin Press, 2020).

to night in the Methodist church and tomorrow night at Ames. I have no appointment beyond that—the people will not turn out in these citys to here lectures on slavery, I am not sure but that I will go out West as soon as I returne home. The people are less active in this state now. Than they were two years ago. I have had to hire Halls and meeting Houses in most of the places where I have been

Pleas excuse my hast I am afraid my letter will be too late for the mail give my love to Lou tell her I will write her soon to Clinton,* my regards to all

[J. S. J.]

Little Falls (NY) Evening Times, May 29, 1953

---

* John had sent Harriet's daughter, Louisa Jacobs, to school at Hiram Kellogg's Young Ladies' Domestic Seminary in Clinton, New York, one of the only schools that admitted girls of color.

Rochester, January 9, 1850

MEN WILL LIE, BUT OYSTERS CANNOT—To all lovers of good OYSTERS, I would recommend a perusal of Mr. C. Swan's notice, headed "more signs than true," and while on your way to the Eagle, stop and look at Jacobs' lot of Oysters, on the corner of State and Buffalo Streets, and judge for yourself who has put out the lying sign, and pass him by. I have but one kind of Oysters, and Mr. S. shall either acknowledge them to be as good Amboy Oysters as he ever saw, and pay up like a man, or allow his name to come before the public as a calumniator. I am receiving my Oysters from Mr. R. Gutman, off Perth Amboy, who writes to me as follows—Mr. Jacobs, Sir—You may rest assured of a good quality of Oysters from me at all times.

I would like to have you compare them with other Oysters, as I cannot all times tell what the quality of an oyster is while in a frozen state. I will take back Oysters at any time, within twenty-four hours, from the time of sale, with pleasure, if they are not of the very best kind.

☞ Persons wanting large quantities, will please give me a few days notice.

JOHN S. JACOBS
No 3 Waverly Block
AGENT, corner of State and Buffalo sts.   Jan8 ltd

Rochester (NY) Daily Democrat, January 9, 1850

London, June 29, 1861

A Colored American in England

The writer of the letter from which we present the following extract is a brother of "Linda,"* the fugitive slave, whose remarkably interesting life, written by herself, and revised by Mrs. Child,† was lately reviewed in our columns. The letter was addressed to our friend, Isaac Post, of Rochester.

London, June 5th, 1861.

My Dear Friend: I hope you will not judge me by my long silence. Believe me, it does not characterize the language of my heart. I do not like much to deal with words, but with actions. You and your family have shown yourselves friends to me and mine, and not to me only, but to my oppressed brethren, for whose sake I hope our Father and our God will reward you all. You that have believed in the promise, and obeyed his word, are beginning to see the moving of His hand to execute judgment and bestow mercy. Those who have long sown chains and fetters will reap blood and carnage. Their troubles have begun; God only knows where they will end. The excitement in London is daily increasing, but the greater portion of the people seem to be ignorant of the character of the slaveholder and of the cause of the disturbed state of the Union, and still more so with regard to the best means of abolishing slavery. Yesterday I read the views of one man who believed it best to let the old slaves work out the freedom of their children, and when they have died off, then let the children be free, and there would be an end to the evil.

* In the 1860s and 1870s, the shorthand way of referring to *Incidents in the Life of a Slave Girl* was to call it *Linda*, after Harriet Jacobs's pseudonym in the narrative, Linda Brent.
† Lydia Maria Child.

This reminded me of the story of the poor-house, which I will not repeat. Last night I heard our tried and true friend, George Thompson, who tried to convince the people of this country of the great mistake they had made in not encouraging the cultivation of cotton in their colonies, and to explain the true cause of the slaveholders seceding from the Union.* I am sorry to say, that with all the blood and guilt on the slaveholders' souls, there are Englishmen here that dare express sympathy for them. I hope it is their ignorance, and not the want of humanity. I do not think of leaving London at present. I shall wait to see what course the North intends to pursue. If the American flag is to be planted on the altar of freedom, then I am ready to be offered on that altar, if I am wanted; if it must wave over the slave, with his chains and fetters clanking, let me breathe the free air of another land, and die a man and not a chattel.

With dear remembrances of old friends,

I am yours, truly,
JOHN S. JACOBS

National Anti-Slavery Standard, June 29, 1861

---

* On Thompson's speech, see p. 172.

APPENDIX 2

Writings on John Swanson Jacobs

Boston, October, 1845
☞ We rejoice to perceive under what favorable circumstances the
Adelphic Union Association* will commence their Ninth Annual
Course of Lectures, and earnestly call upon all our colored citizens
(for whose special benefit these Lectures are to be delivered) immediately to supply themselves with tickets, which, it will be seen, are
placed at a very trifling sum. Our anti-slavery friends should also
try to sustain the course by their presence.

ADELPHIC UNION LIBRARY ASSOCIATION.

The Introductory to the Ninth Annual Course of Lectures before
this Association will be delivered at Ritchie Hall, on Tuesday evening, November 11th, by REV. WILLIAM E. CHANNING, of New-York.

Arrangements have been made for Lectures on succeeding Tuesday evenings, from the following gentlemen, viz:

Rev. John T. Sargent,	J. V. C. Smith, M.D.,
" Theodore Parker,	Henry B. Stanton, Esq.,
" E. H. Chapin,	James McCune Smith, M.D.,
Wendell Phillips, Esq.,	of New-York,
S. P. Andrews, Esq.,	Wm. Lloyd Garrison,
Thomas Paul,	Edward Young, Esq.,
Henry Clapp, Jr.	

Tickets at 75 cents each, admitting a Gentleman and Lady may
be obtained at the Bookstore of B. H. Greene, 124 Washington-
street, and at No. 25 and 7 Cornhill, as also of the Committee.

* On the Adelphic, see pp. 126–29.

WILLIAM C. NELL,

EDWARD B. LAWTON,

CHRISTOPHER R. WEEDEN,

CHARLES A. BATTISTE,

THOMAS COLE,   } *Lecture Committee.*

JOHN S. JACOBS,

HENRY WEEDEN,

ALFRED G. HOWARD,

Exercises to commence precisely at 7½ o'clock.

Liberator, October 31, 1845

The Old Reflector

Utica, Wednesday, Jan. 26, 1848
For the Christian Contributor.
"The Branded Hand"

Norway, N. Y., Jan. 14, 1848.
[. . .] Mr. Jacobs will give them the proof, that it is possible for a colored man to have a mind; or to exhibit *great shrewdness*, and *give utterance to forcible thoughts without a mind*. He gave, when here, a very interesting incident, which took place when he was about nine years old. His master, who was a physician,* sent him to carry two or more parcels to as many different places. Through mistake he miscarried one or more of them. On his return, his master inquired into the matter. The lad said he *thought* he had distributed them correctly. His master reproved him sharply for using such language, and said, with a soul-withering look, "Who gave you a right *to think?*"

Mr. J. says it is impossible for him to describe his feelings at that moment. He felt degraded under a system of wrong which would not admit his right of thinking.

Oh if slavery would be content with overworking, starving, lacerating, maiming, branding and killing the *body*, it might be endured. But when, not satisfied with such wrongs, it engages in the more diabolical work, of maiming, bruising and annihilating *mind*, and putting its manacles upon *thought*, it is enough to call from earthly and heavenly intelligences, one common shriek of abhorrence. God speed the man with the "branded hand," and his fellow-laborer in the righteous cause of the poor slave!

Yours truly,
F. PRESCOTT

* Dr. James Norcom (1778–1850).

[. . .]

The addresses of Capt. Walker and Mr. Jacobs were listened to with deep solemnity and the tenderest sympathy both for them as victims of the slave power and for the millions who are yet groaning in American slavery.—When they spoke of the slaveholders, it was more in pity than in anger. And who does not pity the sinner who is seen to commit sin with greediness and urge his steps onward the righteous and inevitable death of the impenitent?

Christian Contributor, January 26, 1848

Rochester, March 26, 1848

Mar. 26th . . . This evening attended Anti S[lavery] meeting at M[inerva] Hall to hear Jn. S. Jacobs & Jonᵃ. Walker. It was a very interesting meeting. Jacobs gave a slight sketch of his life & he looks as if he might have been a gentleman's servant, smart, active, witty, good looking. He had usually fared pretty well, but the chains of slavery galled his free spirit. At 8 yrs. of age he saw the inconsistency of it & determined to be free.

Walker gave a short account of his sufferings & exhibited his Branded hand to those who wished to see it. G.W. Clarke sung "A man's a man for a that" & "Whittier's address to Walker on his return to Mass." Whoever heard that singing I think can never forget the "Branded Hand."

It was very beautiful indeed, both in sentiment & execution.

There was a very large audience, which spoke well for the cause of Anti Slavery in R[ochester]. One yr. since such a meeting could not be seen in Rochester, I am sure there must be a growing interest in the cause.

JWLD

Rochester, March 31, 1848

Communications

JONATHAN WALKER AND JOHN S. JACOBS

On Sunday evening, March 26th, Minerva hall* was crowded (even beyond the sanguine expectation of friends) by an audience who seemed eager to learn of the American Inquisition, from those whose personal experience could defy refutation.

Jonathan Walker, be it known, was accused and found guilty of "attempting the escape of a few of his fellow beings from bondage, to which they were subjected for no cause over which they or their ancestors had any control, but because they were of the weaker party, and had not the power to assert their rights among men." For this crime he had been imprisoned at Florida eleven months—subjected to the pillory—a heavy fine—and branding in the hand with the letters "S. S.," meaning *slave stealer*, but which have received their appropriate interpretation of *slave saviour*.

Captain Walker's narrative† excited an intense interest among the audience, many of whom could scarce conceal their surprise and indignation in view of the facts;—a citizen of the American Republic thus inhumanly tortured, for endeavoring to rescue seven men from a far worse bondage than was ever dreamed of by our

---

* Rochester's Minerva Hall "occupied two upper stories of the Minerva Block" and was "erected late in 1844 on south east corner of Main & South St. Paul streets. Dimensions: 99ft. long, 48 ft. wide, 21ft. high. Seating capacity 2000. Lighted by two tiers of windows the upper tier to be used for ventilation." *Rochester (NY) Daily Democrat*, December 6, 1844. Minerva Hall burned down in 1858.

† Jonathan Walker, *Trial and Imprisonment of Jonathan Walker, at Pensacola, Florida, for Aiding Slaves to Escape from Bondage, with an Appendix, Containing a Sketch of His Life* (Boston: Anti-Slavery Office, 1845).

revolutionary fathers, who, in consequence of a three penny tax on tea, waged a seven years' war with the mother country.

John S. Jacobs eloquently presented the wrongs of the American slave, and though his own sufferings were far from being as grievous as the majority in the Southern prison house, yet he could testify that slavery, disguised in any form, was indeed a bitter draught. His experience and observation were narrated in a manner and earnestness which carried conviction to the hearts of his audience, and in summing up his reasons for hating slavery, and every influence supporting the infernal system North or South, the "sea of upturned faces" gave a concurrent expression, "We too hate slavery."

Friend Jacobs is a young man, who made good his flight from bondage seven years since, and is now nobly doing his part to diffuse information on the subject of slavery and the means of its abolition. He is eminently deserving large and generous audiences. His soul is interested in the subject. His devotion to the cause, and his integrity of character, are well known and esteemed among the friends of the slave in Boston and vicinity.

In September, 1846, the city of Boston was the scene of an exciting battle for liberty.* A slave had escaped from New Orleans in a merchant vessel, and landed on the soil of Massachusetts, supposed by him, as by many others also, to be sacred to man and his God-given rights. He was hunted like a partridge on the mountain, secured and sent back to hopeless bondage. The friends of freedom put forth their power to save him, but the wicked slaveholder, aided

---

* "The Second Edition of the [Boston] Chronotype of Thursday morning states that a fugitive slave arrived in the brig Ottoman on Tuesday from New Orleans. When the fact was known, the Captain landed him on Spectacle Island [in Boston Harbor], to be detained till the next vessel sailed, that he might be returned to his owners.—While on the Island he took advantage of his keepers, took their boat and set sail for South Boston. He was pursued and captured on South Boston Bridge, accused of stealing a pocket-book, and borne off in a boat down the harbor, where they are now in waiting for the sailing of the Niagara to-day, and intend putting him on board. Four boats with proper writs were out all night, and thus far their search has been in vain." "A Fugitive Slave," *New York Daily Tribune*, September 12, 1846.

by *Northern men—Boston men*, triumphed. In the struggle to save this flying victim from the "peculiar domestic institution," many men performed wonders; but none among them was more zealous or more executive than John S. Jacobs. For one whole dark night, (after vainly seeking for help in his chosen plan of rescue,) he was watching on the islands in the harbor, hoping to secure freedom to his brother. None the less praiseworthy was his effort or those of others, because not crowned with success.

This, and many other deeds under my own observation, in the cause of the panting fugitive, justify me in a grateful acknowledgement to his merit. It may not be amiss here to add, that the abduction of this man from Boston was the occasion of the largest meeting ever held in Faneuil Hall, the old cradle of Liberty, and which was presided over by the lamented John Q. Adams.*

John S. Jacobs (as will be seen by a notice in another column) proposes a series of meetings in Massachusetts. All who love liberty and hate slavery, will be interested and rewarded by an attendance.

The exercises at Minerva Hall were interspersed with several Anti-Slavery effusions by Geo. W. Clarke, the liberty vocalist.† The song, "Be Free, Be Free," and "Whittier's Branded Hand," seemed to inspire the audience with the true sentiment of freedom.—The allusions to "*that Branded Hand*," as appropriately expressed by the vocalist, pointing repeatedly to Captain Walker, was not without its influence upon the meeting, at the close of which many gratified their curiosity, and deepened their horror of slavery, by an inspection of the "branded hand."—W. C. N.

North Star, March 31, 1848.

* John Quincy Adams died on February 23, 1848.
† "Be Free, O Man, Be Free" was published in antislavery and temperance vocalist George W. Clark's *The Liberty Minstrel* (New York: Leavitt & Alden, 1845), 134.

Little Falls, NY, April 14, 1848

THE BRANDED HAND

Capt. Walker and his companion, Mr. Jacobs, arrived here [Little Falls, NY] on Saturday from the westward, on their way to Massachusetts, and addressed a small audience that evening at Alexander's Hall. Our citizens were duly apprised by handbills, of these victims of the Slave Power; but such is the deadly paralysis of the public heart and conscience in this latitude—as well among the various religious sects as throughout the ranks of the political parties—that only 15 or 20 adults were present, out of a population of 3,500. Of the *seven* clergymen of our village, a single one attended—during part of the exercises. (Collection taken, 56 cents! room rent, $1.)

—We are impressed with the conviction that those upright and amiable persons—Messrs. Walker and Jacobs—are, in a striking and appropriate sense, the representatives of Jesus of Nazareth. The one is emphatically, as was his Divine Master, "despised and rejected of men,"* though ardently engaged in promoting their welfare; while the other is an earnest and diligent laborer, and has been a severe personal sufferer, in behalf of fallen and wretched Humanity. Did Christ show his nail-marked hand to doubting Thomas? Even so, doth Jonathan Walker exhibit his Branded Hand to satisfy all doubters of his identity.

And the treatment these brethren receive from the great mass of professed religionists at Little Falls is not dissimilar to that awarded to the humble carpenter's son of Nazareth, by the pious priests and Pharisees of Judea!—*Herkimer Freeman.*

Liberator, April 14, 1848

---

* Isaiah 53:3.

Milford, Massachusetts, August 5, 1848
The Anti-Slavery Convention appointed to be held in Milford, met
on Sunday morning, July 30, in Washington Hall, a capacious, pleasant room in the new, quiet, well-ordered Temperance House in that
village. The prompt attendance in the morning indicated a full house
through the day, and inspired the friends of Freedom with the hope
that the good cause would have, through the influence of the meeting, a new impetus.

The Convention was organized by appointing E. D. Draper, one
of the slaves' truest friends, to the chair, and A. H. Price Secretary.
A portion of Scripture was read by Adin Ballou, a prayer offered by
Samuel May Jr., a spirited song, "Come join the Abolitionists," was
sung by a large portion of the audience, and a committee of three
appointed to draft resolutions, consisting of Oliver Johnson, Adin
Ballou, and S. May Jr.*

While the Committee were preparing Resolutions, John S. Jacobs
came forward, and in a modest and unassuming, yet manly and dignified manner, proceeded to address the audience. He spoke of his condition as a slave, of his insuppressible love of freedom, of his escape

---

* "Ebenezer D. Draper (1813–87), [was] an abolitionist, advocate of temperance
and nonresistance, and businessman. . . . He and his wife, Anna Thwing . . . were
original members of the Hopedale Fraternal Community" (*HJFP*, 1:115). Abby
Hills Price (1814–72) was a leading member of the Hopedale community, an
abolitionist, and a women's rights activist. Adin Ballou founded Hopedale "as a
cooperative religious community devoted to the principles of Practical Christianity and nonresistance" (*HJFP*, 1:106). Samuel May Jr. (1810–99), was an abolitionist, Underground Railroad operator, pastor of the Leicester Unitarian Church
(1835–46), pacificist, and supporter of the women's rights movement. "Come Join
the Abolitionists" was printed in numerous abolitionist song collections, including George W. Clark's *The Liberty Minstrel*, Brown's *The Anti-Slavery Harp*, and
Anti-Slavery Songs: A Selection from the Best Anti-Slavery Authors (Salem, OH:
I. Trescott, 1849). Oliver Johnson (1809–89), was an abolitionist, women's rights
advocate, journalist, and cofounder of the New England Anti-Slavery Society;
he served as editor of the *Christian Soldier, New York Tribune*, and *Anti-Slavery
Bugle* and often guest-edited the *Liberator.*

from bondage, and then with much feeling alluded to the imprisonment of the three men* in Washington City, for helping men to escape
from a bondage that had been so galling to him. And he remarked,
there are those being assembled to what they suppose the worship of
God, by the bells sounding around us, who are ready to sanction that
act, to blame abolitionists for endeavoring to wake up the public mind
to the wickedness of their imprisonment. He thought theirs could
not be Christian worship, for it was *Christian* to feel for *all*. He said
there were those who supposed the abolitionists were doing a great
deal to render the slaves unhappy! Does it make them unhappy to tell
them that we *know* what they most bitterly *feel*—that we pity them,
deprived as they are of *all* their rights? He had been a slave. He had
seen slavery in all its horror. He knew the slave was not happy in his
situation. They were compelled to be false to their true feelings—to
appear happy when they were not. They were compelled to say they
do not desire freedom when they do. But if there were any who loved
servitude, he would open the way for their education, and then if they
loved slavery better than liberty, let them enjoy it. He contrasted the
situation of the bondman with that of the free laborer at the North.
The slave was not allowed to act for himself, or *think* for himself. Subject to the caprice of his master, the slave was exposed to every cruelty.
Here he related a story of a man who was tortured with hot irons to
compel him tell what he had done with jewelry he was supposed to
have stolen. He believed if the churches would take a decided stand
against slavery, it would soon fall; but if they would not, he asked that
they do not throw obstacles in the way of those who are doing all they
can for its destruction. He had been around the world as a seaman,
and had seen slavery in many countries; but in no other country was
slavery so hopeless as in this. Here the slave had not, as a general thing,
as in other places, a chance to buy himself. Here you dare teach the
slave to read the Bible; in other countries he had the same right that

* In April 1848, Daniel Drayton, Captain Edward Sayres, and Chester English
attempted to help seventy-seven fugitive slaves escape from Washington, DC, on
a New Jersey schooner, the *Pearl*. Citizens of Georgetown put together a volun-
teer party and captured the *Pearl* off the coast of Maryland. See "The Abscond-
ing Slaves," *New York Commercial Advertiser*, April 20, 1848.

others had. In the Southern States we saw the sects selling each other; but in no other land did we see this done. We needed Missionaries from other countries to teach us the very first principles of Christianity. There were those who thought we had no business to interfere with it, because what the law makes property *is* property; what the law makes right *is* right. Well, upon what right was this law founded? Had he not a *prior* claim to himself? Though he was stolen, was he not his own? They had been robbed, degraded, and for that hated.

If there were any there who were ready to vote for the regularly nominated candidates, he charged such with the guilt of sanctioning the cool, deliberate murders of slavery. Again, there were those who began to see that we have had enough of this guilty already; who were talking about leaving the parties to which they were attached, and who were ready to form a new organization, under the same slavery-sanctioning Constitution. Such would do but little towards relieving the three millions oppressed, until they took the high moral ground of *"No union with slaveholders."*

He called upon the different sects to unite as *one* in opposing the wrongs of the land, and they would soon fall. When he came on here he expected to find that the churches were all engaged in anti-slavery; that the ministers were all preaching against it, and he was greatly surprised to find the contrary to be true. He alluded to the idea that were slavery abolished they would all come flocking to the North. He said they would choose to stay where they were. They had every inducement to stay—the climate, the associations, the graves of their kindred. But he said as others could speak better than himself, he would close his remarks. [. . .]

Evening Session.

After a song, John S. Jacobs first addressed the meeting, alluding again to the condition of the slave, to the fact that he was liable at any moment to be seized and dragged back again. He said he might think it would not be permitted; but he could not help it so long as the whole North was allowed to be the hunting-ground of slavery.

Non-Resistant and Practical Christian, August 5, 1848.

East Avon, NY, February 18, 1849

Feby. 18th, Sunday

The past week has been a very busy one. The fine sleighing has given us a charm for visiting & receiving visitors. The weather has been remarkably cold, but still we have had some very pleasant days. But the event of the week was the Anti Slavery M[eeting] at East Avon, attended by F. Douglass & Jno. S. Jacobs. It was not until some unwillingness was manifested, & some fears expressed that people would be abused that we were able to obtain the Baptist House for them. A notice was pretty extensively circulated, but after all, the Sexton was the only representative of the village of E. Avon. Two gentlemen, not villagers, were present & the rest, 11 in number, went from Rush. It was cold & tedious weather, but I had supposed that there was more curiosity if nothing else among the people than there seemed to be.

Some few had heard of Douglass, but others knew not that there was such a person.

He supposed that there would but few attend the P.M. [evening lecture], but still we expected more, for all that we knew that A[von] was so behind the times in every Good work. Both ministers gave out notice as far as they could & did all that we could expect of them.

But in the evening there was a greater turn out than we expected. Jacobs & Douglass both spoke well, & to those accustomed to hearing A.S. [antislavery] Lectures it was all intelligible. But their views were so radical in the estimation of some who had scarcely before bestowed a thought on the subject, & as there was no time for explanations, many, I presume misunderstood them, some left before the meeting closed & of course such will misrepresent their views. They failed not to denounce the American Church & Clergy, between which & Christianity they made a broad distinction. So some will call them "Infidel" of course. Douglass sometimes treats serious subjects with too much levity, which is all the objection I can make to his Lectures.

On their way to A[von] they called & took dinner with us & we had a very pleasant visit with them. They appear intelligent on almost any subject & are very agreeable in conversation. They have seen more of the world than people in general, & I suppose make good use of their eyes & ears. They are very gentlemanly & appear at ease in any society.

Indeed, we consider this visit quite a Chapter in our lives. And the privilege of their acquaintances, for such we esteem it to be, as no ordinary occurrence, notwithstanding those about us may think we are disgraced.

JWLD

Rochester, NY, March 9, 1849

Editorial Correspondence

A brief account of the events, labors and impressions connected with the lecturing tour of the last two weeks, may not be uninteresting to the readers of the *North Star*. It is in the lecturing field that the Anti-slavery operator comes in contact with the patient, and has the most abundant opportunities for measuring the pulse, and fully acquainting himself with the nature and extent of the disease which he seeks to remove. Here the malignant spirit of slavery is constantly developing itself to public view, so that he must be a dull and slothful observer who fails to read new lessons of Anti-Slavery wisdom from such an experience. Shut up in the narrow limits of the editorial sanctum, poring over books and newspapers, may be a good place to learn the more subtle forms which the pro-slavery demon assumes, but the lecturing field is the stage upon which to get a more vigorous idea of the monster. Throwing aside the mantle of learning and refinement, disdaining all logic and philosophy, he shows himself in all his huge ugliness. Here you may find the raw material of pro-slavery, unadorned by the gilded accompaniments which the dark spirit assumes in the press and the pulpit. You get here the real "barroom" bluster—"tar and feathers"—"ride him out on a rail"—"ought to be hung"—the "*niggers*" ought to be sent out of the country— they are only fit for slavery, &c. The utterance of these and kindred expressions indicates the depth and meanness of the prejudice with which the colored Anti-Slavery lecturer has to meet when he goes forth to plead the slave's cause. But this is not the only view to be taken of the lecturing field. We meet not only the roughest forms of pro-slavery in the country but the most thorough and whole-souled Abolitionists, to commune with whom, is worth all the labors, and even the insults to which the Anti-Slavery advocate is subjected.

But to the journal. Monday, Feb. 12th.—A chilly day, much snow on the ground, and more falling. Left Rochester for Henrietta the place of our first appointment, in company with John S. Jacobs. We were kindly received and entertained at the house of James Sperry, who, though sympathizing with the Liberty League, (or party,) has no scruples against doing what he can to promote the Anti-Slavery cause, by giving aid and comfort to a disunionist and an old organizationist. Our meeting was held in the Congregational Church, the doors of which, I believe, are always open to the cause of freedom and humanity. Considering the piercing coldness of the night, and the sparseness of the population, the audience was large, numbering from a hundred and fifty to a hundred and seventy-five. Friend Jacobs spoke first, in his usual calm but feeling manner, with respect to the "foul treachery and ruinous wrongs" connected with the whole system of slavery. His remarks were listened to with attention and interest throughout, and we hope they will prove to be good seed sown in good ground. When he had concluded, I followed, and made use of my hour and a half to the best of my ability. At the close of the meeting, several subscribers to the *North Star* were received, and friend Jacobs succeeded in selling a few Anti-Slavery publications.

Tuesday, Feb. 13th—Mendon.—Travelled ten miles to this place. Stopped on our way at the house of our Anti-Slavery friend, Campbell,* and after being "warmed and fed," had a refreshing conversation on the hopeful aspects of the cause. We proceeded to our appointment. On arriving at the place where we supposed the meeting would be held, we found that no meeting had been appointed.— The friend upon whom we had mostly depended to give notice and make arrangements for the meeting, having been dangerously ill for a long time, and was now only convalescent, could not attend

---

* Most likely Calvin Campbell of East Henrietta, NY, who paid a dollar to the *North Star* in 1849 and was appointed a committee member of the Western New York Anti-Slavery Society. "Receipts," *North Star*, September 14, 1849; "Fifth Annual Meeting of the Western N. Y. Anti-Slavery Society," *North Star*, December 29, 1848.

to it. Baulked here, we proceeded to East Mendon, and after much running to and fro, finally succeeded in getting the consent of the trustees to use the Academy, in which to hold a meeting that evening. The notice was limited, and the meeting small, but good was evidently done.—Friend Jacobs and myself were hospitably entertained (strange to say) by a person who voted for General [Zachary] Taylor; and though we by no means spared the old "bloodhound," nor the inconsistency and sinfulness of voting for such a man, there was no abridgement of hospitality on that account. It is very strange that professed Christian men, of so much moral feeling and apparent discernment, can be fooled into an error so palpable and gross as that of supporting a manstealer and bloody warrior for the Presidency of the United States. Yet so it is; and it is a mournful fact, revealing a deplorable amount of perverseness of moral sentiment yet to be removed.

Wednesday, Feb. 14th—Rush.—We came here this morning. The weather was biting cold, our hair below our hats covered with frost, and our old horse, though warmed by rapid travelling, was yet partly covered with frost. With ears, nose and toes nearly frozen, we gladly accepted the kind hospitality of our friends, the Halleck family, about a mile from Rush: and when thawed; did not regret our journey, for we found here choice persons, who know how to appreciate the hardships, rebuffs, insults, and indifference with which the humble advocates of the Anti-Slavery cause have to contend. Our meeting in Rush was held in the Baptist Church, and was well attended, in spite of a protracted meeting which the Methodists were holding in the village. Here too we got several subscribers to the *North Star*. We were earnestly invited to visit Rush again.

Thursday, Feb. [1]5th—Avon.—The weather was colder this day than yesterday, and the lofty snow-banks on the windward of the road, poured upon our "devoted heads" a constant storm of stinging snow, most of the way from Rush to Avon. Two meetings were appointed here—afternoon and evening. About a baker's dozen assembled in the Baptist vestry in the afternoon, and were addressed by friend Jacobs and myself. The audience was very respectable in the evening, but very little impression was made upon them.—There was not Anti-Slavery enough in town to give a lecturer on slavery a night's lodging. There is a plenty of piety and Whiggery here, but no hospitality or Anti-Slavery. We went to the tavern, and after being told by the keeper that "niggers" were better off in slavery, and that we were only making their condition worse by lecturing against slave-holding, and that we ought to mind our own business, &c., &c, we went to bed. "Up and dressed" in the morning, we were called to the table to breakfast, and to our surprise, our landlord seated us at the table with his white family and boarders, making no distinction. We found his practice better than his theory.

Friday, Feb. 16th—Lima.—There was no meeting appointed in this place. We called upon several abolitionists, all of whom seemed glad to see us, and expressed a wish that we should visit Lima again, as well as a willingness to get us up a meeting, but nothing could be done at this time. There were religious meetings in progress, an interesting time *just now*, and so the claims of humanity were postponed. Here I parted with friend Jacobs, and went to Rochester, for the purpose of getting some hand-bills printed, so that we might not be wholly dependant upon "luke-warm" friends to get up meetings for us.

Saturday, Feb. 17th—West Bloomfield.—The weather was cold—very cold, but friends were warm and intelligent. Our meeting was held in the Christian Church. The attendance was small, perhaps not more than seventy persons present, yet the meeting was a most effective one, and a deep interest was excited. A revival was in progress here, and some efforts had been made to keep persons from attending the abolition meeting, on the ground that such meetings are injurious to the cause of religion. When will men learn that religion without righteousness is worthless?

Sunday, Feb. 18th—Canandaigua.—Here meetings had been appointed for us—forenoon, afternoon and evening. We were unable to reach there in time for the forenoon meeting, and the time was occupied, we were told, in listening to a sermon from Rev. Mr. Whitney, the minister of the church in which we were expected to speak. On reaching the meeting-house, we found it densely crowded, and many were standing on the outside, unable to gain admission. The sight was heart-cheering. We were there in time to see the congregation leaving, and thus to assure them of our presence in the afternoon. At two o'clock the house was densely crowded, with a most respectable and intelligent audience.—It was a pleasure to speak to such persons. The meeting in the evening was even more densely packed than that in the afternoon.—Both were highly satisfactory to the hearts of humble laborers in the cause of human freedom. Our readers will be disposed to marvel at the fact, that a Christian church could be thrown open on the Sabbath day, with the sanction and encouragement of a Christian minister, for the purpose of hearing the cause of the slave pleaded by two unlearned and despised fugitive slaves, for it is a marvellous fact, demanding explanation. The Rev. Mr. Whitney, the gentleman whose pulpit we occupied, was not long since the favored pastor of the large Baptist church in Canandaigua, and probably would have remained such until now but for his devotion to God and humanity. He saw the sufferings of the American bondman, the deep responsibility of the church and the ministry for slavery, their cold and heartless indifference toward the Anti-Slavery cause, and unable to keep silence, or to preach abstract righteousness longer, he opened his mouth for the dumb, and poured upon the unwilling ears of his pious congregation a fiery stream of Anti-Slavery truth. His church could not stand it. His reasoning of "righteousness and of judgment to come," was painful to them, and they would not bear it. They counselled among themselves how to destroy him, and finally succeeded in getting a majority against him, and ejecting him from the pulpit. But in doing this, they drove off with him some of the purest and best of the flock, and they stand by him until now, receiving the pure word from his lips, in all the plainness and directness of apostolic preaching. These friends of human freedom and Christian purity, though worshipping in a comparatively small room, are nevertheless a broad light to the whole town, and form a most striking contrast with the grim old orthodox churches surrounding them, that

in all the essentials of the Christian religion are as hollow and hyp-
ocritical as were the Scribes and Pharisees. Like them, they "tithe
of mint anise and cummin, and omit the weightier matters of the
law—judgment and mercy."*

On Monday, the 19th, we went to Rushville. Here we held two
meetings in the Baptist Church, afternoon and evening.—Owing
to the extreme coldness of the weather, and the impossibility of
warming the house, we found it necessary to close our meeting
at a much earlier hour than we should have done in more favorable circumstances.—The evening meeting was largely attended—
several subscribers to the *North Star* were received, and we felt compensated for our labors.

From Rushville we proceeded to Penn Yan, on the 20th February. Here bigotry, apostacy, hypocrisy and slander did their utmost
to prevent our having a fair hearing before the people. In addition to the oily-tongued Hawley, once an abolitionist of the real
Garrison stamp—then a "Union" preacher at Groton, Massachusetts—an Anti-Slavery lecturing agent—then a Christian Baptist in
New Bedford—next a Millerite—now an orthodox Congregational
preacher in Penn Yan, seeking to unite the professedly Anti-Slavery
church† (into whose pulpit he insinuated himself on the strength of
his Anti-Slavery professions) with the old pro-slavery Presbyterian
Church from which it seceded years ago, on the ground of its pro-
slavery—there had been one person in Penn Yan, if possible, more
treacherous and detestable—a recreant *black man*, by the name of
Duffin,‡ who, we suppose, [to] gain the favor of a few canting

---

* "Woe unto you, scribes and Pharisees, hypocrites! For ye pay tithe of mint and
anise and cumin, and have omitted the weightier *matters* of the law, judgment,
mercy, and faith: these ought yet to have done, and not to leave the other undone."
Matthew 23:23.

† At the time, Silas Hawley was reverend of the Free Congregational Church on
Main and Chapel Streets and a member of the Liberty Party. Douglass writes
about Hawley elsewhere; see "Retrograde," *Pennsylvania Freeman*, June 1, 1848.

‡ "James W. Duffin (1814–74), a leading black abolitionist, suffragist, and temperance advocate from western New York, served as secretary of the Geneva Colored
Anti-Slavery Society, vice president of the Delevan Union Temperance Society,

hypocrites, lent his *thick tongue* to reviling and slandering us. This same creature has been as [*obliterated*] to our face as a summer's morn, and has repeatedly offered his services to get subscribers for the *North Star*. Oh, the pink of deception!

We however had a good meeting in Penn Yan. The spacious court-house was crowded to its [ut]most capacity, with a most attentive audience. John S. Jacobs was unusually happy [on] this occasion, and evidently made a deep impression upon the listening hundreds present. We enjoyed the privilege of freeing [our] mind, and after us, our friend Mr. [E. M. R.] Glenn of the Liberty party, addressed the meeting. Thus all the efforts made to crush and to prevent us from having the ear of the people failed. The wisdom of the crafty was confounded, and the counsels of the ungodly brought to nought. During our stay in Penn Yan, we enjoyed the hospitality of our friend, J[acob] F. Platt and family, a dear circle, whose kindness and devotion to the Anti-Slavery cause and the elevation of the oppressed with whom they are classed, gives them a high place in our esteem and affection.

Prattsburgh, Feb. 21st.—The moral and religious epidemic which had made such havoc among the old friends of the Anti-Slavery cause in Penn Yan, had come here also.—"Old Zachism" and revivalism had transformed some of our old friends into enemies, and they were widely defaming us as an infidel and a wicked man, that neither feared God nor regarded man—a heretic of the worst stamp. The Rev. Mr. Smith, who even consented to pray at a meeting where I spoke less than a year ago, had now, from his pulpit, solemnly warned his timid flock against attending our meeting, lest they should imbibe the dangerous and damning heresies with which I stood accused. But all this did not prevent a large attendance. Indeed, it may have led many to come who in other circumstances would have staid away. Rev. Mr. Smith took a singular line

and was named to the New York State Council of the Colored People. In 1839, he became an advocate of political abolition, which opposed the Garrisonian moral suasion of Douglass." *HJFP*, 1:138.

of logic to prove me an infidel. He read in his pulpit an article from the Oberlin Evangelist, which gave disjointed extracts from an article written by William Lloyd Garrison, on the Bible, and pronounced him an infidel. The premises being assumed, he stated that Mr. Garrison is the President of the American Anti-Slavery Society, and Frederick Douglass is an agent for that Society: therefore, Frederick Douglass is an infidel. This sophistry and malignity needs only to be stated, to have the one and the other fully appreciated. The meeting was held in the vestry of the Baptist Church where, but for a few rowdies, we should have had a good meeting. A poor, ignorant and drunken young colored man, of the name of Williams, and a young man known by the name of *Sam Hotchkins,**did what they could to make a disturbance in the meeting. The former being drunk, and not seeming to know what he was about, I led him out of the meeting, to which, unlike young "Sam," he did not return. A short history of this poppinjay defender of slavery may throw some light upon his conduct in this instance. First, then he is a son of the somewhat noted Dr. Hotchkins, author of the "History of Western New York," by whom he was educated after the most rigid form of the orthodox faith, and is now a member, in "good and regular standing," in the orthodox church in Prattsburgh. Having a wandering turn of mind, he sought to improve his fortunes by going into business in that Sodom of America, the city of New York. Here Sam *"failed."* But not disposed to "give it up so," he went to New Orleans, and has evidently made himself fully acquainted with the *manners and morals* of that sink of slaveholding iniquity. In his reply to us, he boasted himself acquainted with General Taylor—knew him to be a kind master—had been upon General Taylor's plantation— knew that the marriage relation was respected—(how could Sam know this?)—said that General Taylor was scrupulously careful of the religious rights of his slaves, so much so, that he paid a large sum annually to support a minister of the gospel on his plantation

---

* "Samuel Hotchkin was the son of Rebecca and John Harvey Hotchkin (1781–1851), the minister of the Prattsburgh Presbyterian Church." *HJFP*, 1:139.

to preach to his "niggers." He expressed the wish that General Taylor had a larger number of slaves than he already possessed, for he believed they would be better off as the *servants* of Gen. Taylor than with many other masters. While "Sam" was cruising about in the neighborhood of New Orleans, he so far ingratiated himself into the good will (taking Sam's story to be true) of "old Zack," that the old man-stealer made him a present of a highly-finished *dagger*, which Sam now shows his simple brothers and sisters of the church with a sort of pious delight, accompanying it with astonishing tales of his wonderful exploits *when down South*, so that *Sam* is really looked up to by some good people in Prattsburgh as a most extraordinary *"youth."* Since the election, *Sam* says but little about politics, and is turning his attention to religion. As an evidence of this, he declared that I ought to be *"tarred and feathered"* for coming there during a revival of religion. This son of the church is a fair specimen and representative of his pro-slavery mother. Moulded by our slave-holding religion, receiving it fresh from the lips of his Reverend father, it is not strange that we find him playing the ruffian towards colored persons, and defending slavery in the name of the church. Such examples of contempt for the children of a common Father, brothers of a common family, as he displayed on the occasion of our meeting in Prattsburgh, are abundant in the church of this country, and prove that church to be the bulwark of American slavery.

Feb. 22d—Bath, Steuben County.—This is a dark corner of the State of New York, with respect to the subject of American slavery.—It is an old slaveholding town, and the effects of the system may be easily traced on the inhabitants, both white and colored. The churches here are all closed against a consideration of the subject, and the ministers of religion are dumb. A distinguished member of the Methodist Church was asked if he did not intend to hear us lecture on slavery. *"No! I don't believe God Almighty ever made niggers to teach white persons,"* was his pious and gentlemanly reply. An Irish store-keeper of some note, although he had yet the Irish brogue of his native country on his tongue, assured us that this was not our native land, and that we ought to go to Africa. The impudence of this proposition is the more conspicuous considering the source from which it emanates, and shows how easily the oppressed may be transformed into the oppressor. Irishmen in England are usually spoken of with contempt, as the most degraded and shiftless people of all her Majesty's subjects; but plant them in America, and they at once assume all the airs of aristocratic superiority.—Whatever native Americans may take upon themselves to propose with respect to our removal from this, the land of our birth and our fathers, to a strange land, it does seem that a sense of common modesty ought to forbid men newly imported into this country from taking any part in our expatriation. We are in no wise tinctured with prejudice against the Irish people, and welcome them to our shores with all the cordial good will with which we would welcome any strangers; and further hold their right to come here and reside to be as good as that of the first colonists who came to this country; yet we protest against the insolence of those who have not even "*got quit*" of the pin-feathers of Ireland, when they coolly join with our oppressors and urge us to leave this country, for what they are pleased to call the land which the Almighty has set apart for us. But to the meetings. We held three. Two were well attended, and we hope did something towards dispelling the pro-slavery gloom which overshadows the place. While in Bath, we shared the hospitality of our esteemed friend, E. L. Platt. The aid rendered us by friend Platt and his kind family, shall not soon be forgotten.

Saturday, Feb. 24th, we held a meeting in Branchport, twenty-six miles from Bath; and the snow having melted, we had hard walking to get to our appointment. The meeting here was highly satisfactory. There were but few in attendance, but such as were, seemed to be of an honest and genteel stamp, free from the coarse temper of persons with whom we too often meet in country villages. We were kindly welcomed at the home of Col. Henry, one of the few who combines with an orthodox faith a Christian life.

Sunday, Feb. 25th, in Rushville. Our meeting this evening was held in the Methodist Church. Considering the state of the roads, and the inclemency of the weather, the attendance was large. The meeting was not held in vain. Some were well pleased—others were greatly displeased. One sister thought it very improper for us to talk about the sins of Methodists while in a Methodist Church; but we presume she was not in a state of mind to hear with complacency anything with respect to the sins of Methodist Churches anywhere; so that did not disturb us.

Monday, Feb. 26th.—We held a meeting at Hopewell, in the Wesleyan meeting-house. The attendance was large, and the people seemed quite interested. The Wesleyan Methodist meeting-houses are generally open for Anti-Slavery meetings, and in this respect they form an exception to other churches.

Tuesday, Feb. 27th.—We attended and spoke at the Anti-Slavery Fair in Canandaigua, remarks with respect to which will be found in another column of this number of the *North Star*. In sixteen days, we have travelled at an average of twelve miles a day, made some twenty speeches, got twenty subscribers to the *North Star*, and we hope have removed much prejudice against the Anti-Slavery cause.—F.D.

North Star, March 9, 1849

March 16, 1849

The friends of abolition in Rushville met the 19th inst., according to appointment, to consider the case of those in bondage, and to listen to an address upon the subject by Frederick Douglass, the well-known defender of his race, and the fearless opponent of slavery in all its forms. The manner in which he introduced the subject in the commencement of the meeting, rendered it obvious to the pro-slavery part of the audience, that there was originality and genius yet among the long-despised race. The introduction was very edifying; as were also the remarks of John S. Jacobs, who, in a touching style, gave a brief detail of his sufferings while a slave. The manner of recital was such as to convince all that he was one of those who, by some strange interferance of Providence, had escaped from the hands of the taskmaster.

In progress of the meeting, some remarks made in defence of the Constitution called out an elderly gentleman, formerly from Maryland, who, from early associations probably, entertained a fondness for the chattel system. He had a most unsuccessful labor, as far as his argument was concerned, and a newly fledged limb of the law came to the rescue. Not being able to maintain what his pro-slavery friend had asserted, he finally left for documents which he evidently needed, but which, when procured, proved to be the *esse* of what Mr. Douglass had asserted. The honorable gentleman left the floor, evidently feeling very much as the smaller animal did when he had the honor of contending with a lion, being vanquished, consoled himself with the reflection that it was by a lion. The interruption was uncalled for, and the audience none the wiser for it, save that it paved the way for some interesting remarks from Mr. Douglass in regard to the Constitution.—None of the pro-slavery gentlemen present seemed willing to enter the field of debate, but chose the Indian mode of warfare, keeping up an occasional grumbling, in order to draw the attention of the audience, or to disconcert the speaker.

To deliver the meeting from any odium that may be attached to it, I will say, that the influential, well-bred part of the community held their peace, and probably were the means of restoring others who felt disposed to do differently.

In the evening the audience was again addressed upon the subject of slavery; but the size of the room, and some circumstances attendant upon warming it, rendered the place so intensely cold, that it was impossible for the crowd to remain quiet, or for the speaker to proceed with any degree of comfort. Many had come from a distance, with the expectation of hearing an eloquent harangue, and could not understand why a comfortable place could not have been procured. Mr. Douglass addressed the meeting, and was succeeded by Mr. Jacobs, who being unable to proceed on account of the confusion, retired; and Mr. Douglass took the stand, and for several minutes poured forth a strain of eloquence enough to warm an iceberg. Every one seemed to forget himself, and to listen with increasing interest. The sin of holding the image of Christ in bondage, and of selling the human form, appeared more appalling than ever, and the character of those who legalize the sin, seemed to lose the cloak that has so long hung over it, and the cloven foot of the semblance of justice to display itself. The intensity of the cold rendered it impossible for Mr. Douglass to proceed, and the meeting closed with many regrets that it should have been a failure in part.

Since I wrote the above, we have again been favored with an address from Messrs. Douglass and Jacobs, and under the most favorable circumstances. The chapel was very kindly offered, and the happy combination of light and warmth betrayed the generous spirit of those who, if not abolitionists, in general, are willing that others should speak their sentiments upon the subject. The house was crowded to overflowing, and the care taken by the sexton to see that all were properly seated, and that every corner was sufficiently illuminated, prevented all confusion and disturbance of any kind. The auditory were silent and attentive, and not one dissenting voice was heard during the meeting. It being Sabbath evening, Mr. Jacobs opened the meeting with prayer, and made some very befitting remarks in regard to the time and object of meeting there. Mr. Douglass succeeded him, and by a chain of argument, both brilliant and profound, left the laws and religion of the South in a very perilous position; the sympathies of all were enlisted, and their judgment appealed to. The speaker, in my estimation, emphatically possesses the power ascribed to George Thompson by William L. Garrison—the faculty of thinking on his legs in an incredible manner.* The moment he rises, a perfect "crowd of thoughts," in the language of Byron, seems to surround him; an intense feeling calls up all the resources of his mind; and the love of kindred and freedom seems to rouse every energy. That a good effect was produced by his efforts is very evident. If we could occasionally have an abolition lecture of like character, it is doubtful whether there would be so much indifference upon the subject as there now exists.

E. E.
Rushville, March 5, 1849

North Star, March 16, 1849

---

* "He had the faculty of 'thinking on his legs' faster than any other speaker I had ever heard. But it was not his quickness of perception, nor his fluency of speech, nor his brilliancy of retort, upon which he placed reliance. He felt that the cause which he espoused was invincible, inasmuch as it was based on the rock of TRUTH, supported by the pillars of JUSTICE and MERCY, and patronized by GOD." William Lloyd Garrison, *Lectures of George Thompson* (Boston: Isaac Knapp, 1836), ix–x.

New York City, May 11, 1849
The Anniversaries
AMERICAN ANTI-SLAVERY SOCIETY
Third Day.

Mr. Jacobs, a colored man, of Massachusetts, next addressed the meeting. He said he was a dis-unionist. When the chairman [William Lloyd Garrison] first advocated the separation of the North and South, as the quickest way to overthrow slavery, that was not then new to him, for he was a dis-unionist ever since J. C. Calhoun first preached it.* He wanted to see the abolition of slavery carried without the shedding of blood; and he wished for justice to the slaveholder, as well as the slave. He asked them, would they send him back to the South, if they were required to do so? They would answer no. But if they did not go with their muskets, and blow out the brains of every slave who refused to return, he held they were, in point of fact, dis-unionists. He would now tell them something of a reverend gentleman. A slaveholder, named Skinner,† who was a skinner in every sense of the word, was in the habit of coming every year, to visit his brother, Rev. Dr. Skinner,‡ who, if he mistook not, lived at 160 Green[e] street; and yet the baby-stealing, women-whipping tyrant never received a rebuke from his reverend brother, at whose table he sat. He (the speaker) had a sister owned by this Skinner. She escaped from him; and, rather than go back, she lived for years in a place four feet high. Skinner offered $100 reward for her recovery—not that he wanted her for his services, but that he might make an example of her. So anxious was the old doctor on the subject, that he had a free

---

* John Calhoun began advocating for disunion in the 1830s.
† Jacobs is referring to James Norcom.
‡ Norcom's relative has not been identified.

woman arrested, and put in jail in her stead; and sent a message to his brother that he had secured the runaway. But it was found, on inquiry, that he was mistaken, and the woman was released from prison. There was a time when the fugitive slave could not stand upon any spot of American soil, and be free; but thank God, that was no longer the case, and they had now many cities of refuge. He had always felt that if the friends of the slave only did their duty, the bondage would be put an end to; for if the slaveholder only saw that he would not be supported by those opposed to his traffic in flesh and blood, he would have to give it up. He had no feeling against slaveholders, for his grandmother had taught him to love them as well as any other of God's creatures; but he did not love their cruelty and injustice. If any one asked him what must be done to abolish slavery, his answer was, that it must cease to be respectable. They must make it disreputable, and then the slaveholders would be ashamed of it. In reference to the church question, his opinion was, that they had too much religion in this country. If they had less of religion, and more of Christianity, it would be all for the better. What did the board of missions* say in Massachusetts? Why, that they would preserve a strict neutrality on all exciting subjects, and that they could not meddle with any civil institution. When they made that statement, they knew it was false; for when they preached against idols, was not that calculated to produce excitement? What the hypocrates really meant, though they had not the courage to say so, was that they would not interfere with slavery; and it was well known that they privately accused Christ and his apostles of sanctioning that institution. In this, they were guilty of falsehood. He had been round Cape Horn, and had never seen anything there to equal the wickedness practiced in the United States. On that coast they worshipped idols, and sold golden Christs; but here they sold Christ himself in the shambles. In returning from a convention in

---

* The American Board of Commissioners for Foreign Missions was founded in 1810 by Williams College graduates and became the largest and most important of American missionary organizations. For more information, see p. 8.

Springfield, he heard a clergyman say, in one of the cars, that he was of the same opinion as Dr. Cox,* that the Bible sanctioned slavery. He (the speaker) had not been before aware that Dr. Cox held those sentiments. He took an opportunity of addressing the clergyman, and said to him, "Sir, may I be permitted to ask you a question?" He (the clergyman) did not reply, but looked as if he would condescend to listen. The question he put to him was, "Did he believe there was any meaning in the passage of Scripture in which Christ said: 'Forasmuch as ye have done it to the least of these little ones, ye have done it unto me?'"† The clergyman said, of course, there was meaning in it. He (Mr. Jacobs) then asked him whether it was lawful for the slaveholders to make chattels of those for whom Christ died. His answer was, that that depended upon the amount of light they possessed. Then said he, (Jacobs) in reply, "If they want light, why don't you send some of your missionaries to them?" (Hear, hear) He now asked that assembly why these clergymen ought not to be designated by their true names, as hypocrites, knaves, and robbers. (Cheers)

New York Herald, May 11, 1849

---

* Samuel H. Cox (1793–1880), American Presbyterian minister and abolitionist from Brooklyn.
† Matthew 25:40.

Rochester, November 2, 1849

Our friend John S. Jacobs has opened a spacious oyster saloon at No. 3 State Street, Waverly buildings, where he proposes to cater, in the most admirable manner, to the taste and appetite of his fellow citizens. Mr. Jacobs is a most excellent cook, as we can testify; and we have no doubt that he will give perfect satisfaction to all who may be disposed to patronize him in his gastronomic art.—F.D.

North Star, November 2, 1849

New York City, October 24, 1850

[. . .] John S. Jacobs, a fugitive, then came forward* and spoke nearly as follows:—He said he came here to-night to give some advice, and to extend the hand of fellowship to his colored brethren. He said: My colored brethren, if you have not swords, I say to you, sell your garments and buy one. He regretted that he was not here in time to hear the resolutions read, to know if they were strong enough. If there be any man here tonight who wants to know my name, tell him it is John S. Jacobs, of South [*sic*] Carolina, and that I am an American citizen, that I never denied that name, neither did I ever disgrace it. They said that they cannot take us back to the South; but I say, under the present law they can; and now I say unto you, let them only take your dead bodies. (Tremendous cheers.) This is no time, my friends, to laugh; let us go to the house of mourning, and see the dead body of the wife of Hamlet, and her surviving infants. Well, I would rather see her body dragged to the stake than see her dragged back again into Slavery. I would, my friends, advise you to show a front to our tyrants, and arm yourselves; aye, and I would advise the women to have their knives too. But I don't advise you to trample on the laws of this State, but [advise you to trample on the laws of this State, but]† I advise you to trample on this bill, and I further advise you to let us go on immediately, and act like men. He then advised the colored race to lay aside their religious and political feelings or anything that may tend to separate them, and suggested that a registry should be commenced with the name of every slave, his owner, and all other particulars, that they might tend to give him every assistance; and concluded by advising the fugitives not to suffer themselves to be taken.

North Star, October 24, 1850

---

* On Jacobs's contribution to the redemption of James "Hamlet" Hamilton, see pp. 150–52.
† Typo in original.

New York City, July 28, 1862
John F. [*sic*] Jacobs, a very intelligent colored man, formerly a slave in
North Carolina, but recently for several years a resident of England,
called at our office the other day, and related facts showing that Brit-
ish vessels are still engaged in running our blockade, and that the
British officials in the Bahamas are, if possible, more inimical to our
Union than are the same class of people at home. Mr. Jacobs's story
is a straightforward one, and is substantially as follows: He shipped
as cook on board the steamship *Lloyds*, at London, on the 1st of
May last "for Havana and any of the West India Islands, North or
South America, or any port or ports in America, to be discharged
in the United Kingdom." On the 29th of May the *Lloyds* landed at
Nassau, N. P., one of the Bahama Islands, when the captain (Smith)
announced to his crew that he designed to run the blockade before
Charleston, and offered three months pay extra to such as would
remain with the ship; but all refused and demanded £20 ($100),
which, after much haggling, was agreed to by Capt. Smith. Jacobs
refused to go to Charleston at any price whatever, and demanded,
what was his undoubted right, that he be sent home to London.
After various efforts on the part of Capt. Smith to indure Jacobs
either to go to Charleston or to settle and sign a satisfaction, he
attempted coercion. He had Jacobs taken before a police magistrate
to answer the charge of having deserted the ship. Before this august
court, Capt. Smith, according to the statement of Jacobs, denied
under oath that he had had any idea of running the blockade—
asserted that he was going to Halifax, and that he had never in any
manner mooted the subject of going to Charleston either to Jacobs
or any of his crew. The Magistrate was about sending Jacobs back
to the ship, when the latter called the Court's attention to the fact
that the ship had cleared for Havana, and other places mentioned,
and had no business to be at Nassau. The Magistrate thereupon said
to Capt. Smith, that since (as shown by Jacobs) he had broken his
articles by coming to Nassau before landing at Havana, he could

not feel justified in sending the prisoner back to the ship, which he seemed very much to regret. The law was all on the side of Jacobs, but the public sentiment of Nassau was so strongly against him, and in favor of the unlawful and contraband trade with the Rebels that he might just as well have looked for snakes in Ireland as justice or sympathy in New Providence. The *Lloyds* finally sailed without making any provision for sending Jacobs home, and he could get no satisfaction from the consignees.* The Police Magistrate, Mr. E. B. A. Taylor, even refused to give him a certificate relating the facts to the British Consul at this port. He finally obtained a passage to New-York in the *E. Tuttle*, Capt. Withmore. The *Lloyds*, which is a steamer of over 700 tuns, had a cargo of salt, coffee, sulphur, bar iron, and long, small cases, supposed to contain arms—all intended for Halifax no doubt; particularly as the ship cleared for Havana and landed at Nassau.

New York Independent, July 28, 1862

* For Jacobs's escape from the *Lloyds*, see pp. 173–75.

ACKNOWLEDGMENTS

Since 2016, I've had to learn skills that literary scholars do not ordinarily possess. When I found John Jacobs's autobiography, I sensed
its significance right away; the problem was I had no idea how to
bring it back into the world. I was fortunate, however, that Jean
Fagan Yellin had already performed careful and capacious research
on Harriet Jacobs and her family: I owe an incalculable debt to her
and wish she were here to read this book. At the very start, Caleb
Smith's advice was indispensable. I am also grateful to Ed Baptist,
David Blight, Daphne Brooks, Pier Gabrielle Foreman, Kathryn
Grover, Lisa Lowe, and Manisha Sinha for dispensing wisdom and
patiently listening to me.

Because much of this book was written during the COVID-19
pandemic, I am incredibly grateful for what archivists, librarians,
and curators did to make research possible. Elizabeth Bouvier at the
Massachusetts State Archives located the case file that expanded
the Jacobs family tree by three generations. John Nann at the Yale
University Law Library helped me parse the court systems and
the fugitive slave clause and law. Vann Evans at the North Carolina State Archives and Rick Stattler at the Rhode Island Historical Society located important correspondence concerning the case.
Harold Colson shared McClanahan family records. Dejay Duckett
and Renee Altergott located the portrait of John Jacobs in the African American Museum in Philadelphia. Susan Chore of the Frick

Art Reference Library digitized the case file on the portrait. In the early pandemic, Nan Wolverton and Scott Casper kept the torch of intellectual life burning at the American Antiquarian Society. Later, Karin Wulf, Kimberly Nusco, and Valerie Andrews made the John Carter Brown Library a space for scholarly community when community seemed impossible.

Five fellowships—from the National Endowment for the Humanities, the American Antiquarian Society, the John Carter Brown Library, the Historical Society of Pennsylvania, and the Huntington Library—made this project possible by giving me the time and ability to research, write, and track down leads on the many paths that John Jacobs followed and the many places he lived. For Jacobs in New Bedford and on the *Frances Henrietta*, I am indebted to Lee Blake, Michael Dyer, Mark Procnik, Donna Selvaggio, and Timothy Dale Walker. For Jacobs in Australia, I am thankful to Kaye Vernon. Thanks to Samuel Moriarty for help researching Jacobs in Britain and at sea. And for the end of his life in Cambridge, I am indebted to Stephen Pinkerton and Sydney Nathans. Thanks to Thomas Constantinesco, J. Michelle Coghlan, Nicholas Gaskill, Janet Neary, Lloyd Pratt, and Cécile Roudeau for opportunities to workshop parts of the book. Thanks to Marcus Rediker and Ezra Greenspan for teaching me about writing from below (biography and otherwise). Renee Altergott, Juan Gallardo, Aidan Goddu, Chris McKay, Samuel Moriarty, Claire Stephens, and Kaye Vernon provided invaluable research assistance. I also thank Lesley Knox, for her enthusiasm for this project and help in uncovering the genealogy of the Knox-Jacobs family.

A special thank you to Lauren Berlant and Bill Brown for their mentorship, which has played an outsize role in shaping how I think and write.

To my parents, who taught me to be who I want to be.

Much love to Congress Avenue and to the birds.

And to Sheida, who betters worlds and whom I love unconditionally. 🐦

ABBREVIATIONS

BPL   Boston Public Library.

DAC   Diaries of Amelia Chesson. Raymond English Anti-Slavery Collection, John Rylands Research Institute and Library, University of Manchester (UK).

DFWC   Diaries of Frederick William Chesson. 16 vols. Raymond English Anti-Slavery Collection, John Rylands Research Institute and Library, University of Manchester (UK).

HJAL   Jean Fagan Yellin. *Harriet Jacobs: A Life*. New York: Civitas, 2004.

HJFP   *Harriet Jacobs Family Papers*. Edited by Jean Fagan Yellin, Joseph M. Thomas, Kate Culkin, and Scott Korb. 2 vols. Chapel Hill: University of North Carolina Press, 2008.

IAPFP   Isaac and Amy Post Family Papers. Department of Rare Books, Manuscripts, and Preservation, University of Rochester Library.

JRL   John Rylands Research Institute and Library, University of Manchester (UK).

JRS   Journal of Rounseville Slocum. In *Account of Whaling Voyages in the Whalers By Chance, William Rotch, Liverpool, Royal William, Cora, Frances Henrietta, Newton, Dragon, Kutesoff, Russell 1828–1851*. Schuyler Otis Bland Memorial Library, United States Merchant Marine Academy. Kings Point, NY.

JWLD   Julia Wilbur Large Diary. Quaker & Special Collections, Haverford College Libraries, Haverford College, PA.

MSA   Massachusetts State Archives. Boston, MA.

NCSA   North Carolina State Archives. Raleigh, NC.

NBWM   New Bedford Whaling Museum. New Bedford, MA.

TT   "A True Tale of Slavery." In Harriet A. Jacobs, *Incidents in the Life of a Slave Girl, Written by Herself; with "A True Tale of Slavery" by John S. Jacobs*. Edited by Jean Fagan Yellin. Cambridge, MA: Belknap Press of Harvard University Press, 2009.

NOTES

Introduction

1. John Swanson Jacobs, *The United States Governed by Six Hundred Thousand Despots: A True Story of Slavery*, in this volume, 3 (hereafter referred to as *Despots*).

2. February 18, 1849, Julia Wilbur Large Diary, hereafter cited as JWLD (see abbreviations list for full source citation; reproduced in appendix 2); "The Walker Meetings," *National Anti-Slavery Standard*, January 6, 1848.

3. *Despots*, 3–4.

4. See Bonnie Honig, *A Feminist Theory of Refusal* (Cambridge, MA: Harvard University Press, 2021).

5. *Despots*, 60, 71, 69, 62.

6. Shklar makes this claim in her 1990 presidential address at the annual meeting of the American Political Science Association, arguing that a defining feature of American political experience was the "prevalence of chattel slavery long after it had disappeared from the rest of the world. Not racism—which is universal—but *slavery* in a modern constitutional state is truly unique. Until the Civil War amendments America was neither a liberal nor a democratic country, whatever its citizens might have believed. Yet it did have in place a set of institutions that were capable of becoming so and to an unequaled degree." Judith Shklar, "Redeeming American Political Theory," in *Redeeming American Political Thought*, ed. Stanley Hoffman and Dennis F. Thompson (Chicago: University of Chicago Press, 1998), 92.

7. John Sekora, "Black Message/White Envelope: Genre, Authenticity, and Authority in the Antebellum Slave Narrative," *Callaloo*, no. 32 (1987): 482–515; Amia Srinivasan, "The Aptness of Anger," *Journal of Political Philosophy* 26, no. 2 (2018): 135.

8. John S. Jacobs to Frederick Douglass, *North Star*, March 3, 1848 (reproduced in appendix 1).

9. Starling already argues in 1946 that Jacobs wrote *Incidents*, though her claim likely did not gain traction until her dissertation was published in 1981.

"Careful study of Mrs. Jacobs' text will show, however, remarkable consistency in the style of the whole book, and an integral relationship between that style and the contents . . . For this reason, it seems likely that what Mrs. Child has stated as truth, in the 'Editor's Introduction' to this narrative, is the truth." Marion Starling, "The Slave Narrative: Its Place in American Literary History" (PhD diss., New York University, 1946), 2, 300; Harriet A. Jacobs, *Incidents in the Life of a Slave Girl, Written by Herself; with "A True Tale of Slavery" by John S. Jacobs,* ed. Jean Fagan Yellin (Cambridge, MA: Belknap Press of Harvard University Press, 1987; hereafter referred to as *Incidents*).

10. A recent example is David Blight's *A Slave No More: Two Men Who Escaped to Freedom, Including Their Own Narratives of Emancipation* (New York: Amistad, 2009).

11. David Blight puts the number at 60 in *A Slave No More.* The University of North Carolina's North American Slave Narrative Corpus lists 94. Including post-1863 autobiographies, this number grows to around 300. If one includes the Works Progress Administration slave narrative field recordings, as well as short sketches found within abolitionist publications and elsewhere, the number swells to 6,006.

12. See Jean Fagan Yellin, "Texts and Contexts of Harriet Jacobs's *Incidents in the Life of a Slave Girl: Written by Herself,*" in *The Slave's Narrative,* ed. Charles T. Davis and Henry Louis Gates Jr. (New York: Oxford University Press, 1985), 262–82; Bruce Mills, "The Endings to Harriet Jacobs's *Incidents in the Life of a Slave Girl,*" in *Cultural Reformations: Lydia Maria Child and the Literature of Reform* (Athens: University of Georgia Press, 1994), 112–29; Albert H. Tricomi, "Harriet Jacobs's Autobiography and the Voice of Lydia Maria Child," *ESQ* 53, no. 3 (2007): 216–52; and Caleb Smith, "Harriet Jacobs among the Militants: Transformations in Abolition's Public Sphere, 1859–1861," *American Literature* 84, no. 4 (2012): 743–68.

13. In *Incidents,* when her daughter is about to head off to boarding school, Harriet/Linda tells her who her father is. This scene, which occurs just after they had moved to Rochester in 1849, represents the first moment when Harriet begins telling about how her "early sufferings in slavery . . . had driven [her] into a great sin"—and consequently the earliest known version of her autobiography (*Incidents,* 242). That same year, John Jacobs began telling the earliest versions of his autobiography on the upstate abolitionist circuit.

14. Numerous ex-slave authors were sailors, including Briton Hammon, Olaudah Equiano, John Jea, John Thompson, and Ashton Warner, but these narratives tend to put religion first and maritime protest second.

15. Paul Finkelman, "Frederick Douglass's Constitution: From Garrisonian Abolitionist to Lincoln Republican," *Missouri Law Review* 81, no. 1 (2016): 1–75. See also John Burt, "Political Violence and the Persuasive Engagement in Frederick Douglass," *Literary Imagination* 23, no. 2 (2021): 111–36.

16. John S. Jacobs, "A Colored American in England," *National Anti-Slavery Standard,* June 29, 1861 (reproduced in appendix 1).

17. See Peter Linebaugh and Marcus Rediker, *The Many-Headed Hydra: Sailors,*

Slaves, Commoners, and the Hidden History of the Revolutionary Atlantic (Boston: Beacon, 2013); and Julius S. Scott, *The Common Wind: Afro-American Currents in the Age of the Haitian Revolution* (London: Verso, 2018).

18. Harriet Jacobs to William Cooper Nell, June 27, 1851, Isaac and Amy Post Family Papers, hereafter cited as IAPFP (see abbreviations list for full source citation).

19. James Olney, "'I Was Born': Slave Narratives, Their Status as Autobiography and as Literature," *Callalloo*, no. 20 (1984): 47.

20. It may seem difficult to believe that he wrote his entire narrative in just two weeks. Consider, however, that abolitionist lecturers like Jacobs performed their life stories in hundreds of churches and schoolhouses, in the largest auditoriums of the biggest cities and on the most makeshift of stages in hamlets and fields, alone on a snowy evening or accompanied by hymns and instruments. Jacobs had so much practice that he probably carried around his life story the way a singer carries around a repertoire of songs, so it is unlikely that he needed to write his story from scratch.

21. "Interlineations are made either *before* or *after* the execution of an instrument. Those made before should be noted previously to its execution; those made after are made either by the party in whose favor they are, or by strangers." John Bouvier, *A Law Dictionary, Adapted to the Constitution and Laws of the United States of America*, vol. 1 (Philadelphia: Estate of John Bouvier, 1854), 659.

22. Olney, "'I Was Born,'" 49.

23. See Dwight McBride, *Impossible Witnesses: Truth, Abolitionism, and Slave Testimony* (New York: New York University Press, 2001); and Jeannine Marie DeLombard, *Slavery on Trial: Law, Abolitionism, and Print Culture* (Chapel Hill: University of North Carolina Press, 2007).

24. Lauren Berlant, *The Female Complaint: The Unfinished Business of Sentimentality in American Culture* (Durham, NC: Duke University Press, 2008), 54–55.

25. James Baldwin, "Everybody's Protest Novel," in *Within the Circle: An Anthology of African American Literary Criticism from the Harlem Renaissance to the Present*, ed. Angelyn Mitchell (Durham, NC: Duke University Press, 1994), 150.

26. *Despots*, 52.

27. Frederick Douglass, *Narrative of the Life of Frederick Douglass, an American Slave, Written by Himself*, ed. Robert Stepto (Cambridge, MA: Belknap Press of Harvard University Press, 2009), 19.

28. Walter Johnson, *Soul by Soul: Life inside the Antebellum Slave Market* (Cambridge, MA: Harvard University Press, 1999), especially 135–61; and Edward E. Baptist, *The Half Has Never Been Told: Slavery and the Making of American Capitalism* (New York: Basic Books, 2014); Berlant, *Female Complaint*, 35.

29. The "scourged back" image was first published as part of a triptych in *Harper's* in July 1863, all of which were said to be images of a man named Gordon. Drawing upon an extraordinary letter published pseudonymously in the *New York Tribune* in December 1863, David Silkenat persuasively argues that the "scourged back" image is actually of Peter, a Louisiana slave who escaped with Gordon, who is depicted in the left-hand image. See David Silkenat, "'A Typical Negro': Gordon, Peter, Vincent Colyer, and the Story Behind Slavery's

Most Famous Photograph," *American Nineteenth Century History* 15, no. 2 (2014): 169–86.

30. Emphasis mine. Karen Halttunen argues that nineteenth-century sentimentalism employed these kinds of rhetorical evasions—gesturing toward but not describing the actual infliction of pain—in order to avoid turning graphic scenes into pornographic ones; Jacobs's autobiography refuses to describe scenes of Black suffering for a reason that Halttunen fails to consider: the protection of the sufferer. This is one way that *Despots* rewrites the sentimental contract between narrator and reader. See Karen Halttunen, "Humanitarianism and the Pornography of Pain in Anglo-American Culture," *American Historical Review* 100, no. 2 (1995): 303–34.

31. Saidiya Hartman, *Scenes of Subjection: Terror, Slavery, and Self-Making in Nineteenth-Century America* (New York: Oxford University Press, 1997), 4.

32. See Lloyd Pratt, *The Strangers Book: The Human of African American Literature* (Philadelphia: University of Pennsylvania Press, 2015); and Sacvan Bercovitch, *The American Jeremiad* (Madison: University of Wisconsin Press, 1978).

33. Frederick Douglass, *My Bondage and My Freedom* (New York: Miller, Orton & Mulligan, 1855), 361–62. See also Nicholas Bromell, *The Powers of Dignity: The Black Political Philosophy of Frederick Douglass* (Durham, NC: Duke University Press, 2021), 60.

34. The quotation is from Robert Gooding-Williams, "Martin Delany's Two Principles, the Argument for Emigration, and Revolutionary Black Nationalism," in *African American Political Thought: A Collected History*, ed. Jack Turner and Melvin Rogers (Chicago: University of Chicago Press, 2020), 83.

35. Lauren Berlant, "The Theory of Infantile Citizenship," in *The Queen of America Goes to Washington City: Essays on Sex and Citizenship* (Durham, NC: Duke University Press, 1997), 52–53; Lauren Berlant, "The Queen of America Goes to Washington City," in *Queen of America*, 235.

36. Berlant, "Queen of America," 234, 226 (emphasis in original).

37. Honig, *Feminist Theory of Refusal*, 104.

38. Daphne A. Brooks, *Bodies in Dissent: Spectacular Performances of Race and Freedom, 1850–1910* (Durham, NC: Duke University Press, 2006), 67; see also Brooks's introduction to *The Great Escapes: Four Slave Narratives* (New York: Barnes and Nobles, 2005).

39. See R. J. M. Blackett, *The Captive's Quest for Freedom: Fugitive Slaves, the 1850 Fugitive Slave Law, and the Politics of Slavery* (Cambridge: Cambridge University Press, 2018).

No Longer Yours, *Chapter One*

1. Sylviane Diouf, *Slavery's Exiles: The Story of the American Maroons* (New York: New York University Press, 2014), 259.

2. This short, untitled newspaper item reports that a letter "written by one of the leaders" of the conspiracy was found on the body of a Black man in Halifax, NC. *Balance, and Columbian Repository*, March 23, 1802. Douglass writes that "[Patrick

Henry's] saying was a sublime one, even for a freeman; but, incomparably more sublime, is the same sentiment, when *practically* asserted by men accustomed to the lash and chain—men whose sensibilities must have become more or less deadened by their bondage." Frederick Douglass, *My Bondage and My Freedom*, ed. David Blight (New Haven, CT: Yale University Press, 2014), 226. Enoch Sawyer's nephew, Samuel, later fathered Harriet Jacobs's children. On Tom Copper's Rebellion, see Herbert Aptheker, *American Negro Slave Revolts* (New York: International Publishers, 1969), 228–34; and Diouf, *Slavery's Exiles*, 259–65. For Sawyer's letter, see "Insurrection Among Slaves 1802–1803 (Court Papers)," North Carolina State Archives, hereafter cited as NCSA (see abbreviations list for full source citation). On terror and the struggle over the significance of death, see Vincent Brown, *The Reaper's Garden: Death and Power in the World of Atlantic Slavery* (Cambridge, MA: Harvard University Press, 2008), and Terri Snyder, *The Power to Die: Slavery and Suicide in British North America* (Chicago: University of Chicago Press, 2015).

3. 1800 US Census, Pasquotank County, North Carolina, microfilm, Series M32, Roll 34, p. 634, Family History Library Film 337910.

4. "More about the Negroes," *New York Herald*, June 2, 1802.

5. "Seventeen Pounds Reward," *Virginia Gazette and General Advertiser*, May 2, 1792. For a plain-text version, see the digital collection of runaway slave advertisements, *The Geography of Slavery in Virginia* (Tom Costa and the Rector and Visitors of the University of Virginia, 2005), http://www2.vcdh.virginia.edu/gos/.

6. Ambrose Knox to David Leonard Barnes, November 13, 1792, Rhode Island Historical Society.

7. Deposition of Benjamin Clayton Lowry, November 22, 1793, Massachusetts State Archives, hereafter cited as MSA (see abbreviations list for full source citation).

8. "The Fugitive Slave Bill in This City," *Boston Atlas*, October 16, 1850.

9. William Rotch Jr. Petty Ledgers, 1790–1801, Series B: Financial Accounts, William Rotch Jr. Papers, 1789–1863, Rotch Family Papers, New Bedford Whaling Museum, hereafter cited as NBWM (see abbreviations list for full source citation).

10. Deposition of Andrew Stanton, MSA.

11. Elizabeth Buffum Chace, *Anti-Slavery Reminiscences* (Central Falls, RI: E. L. Freeman & Son, 1891), 8–9; Ancestry.com, *1790 United States Federal Census* online database, accessed May 9, 2023, https://www.ancestry.com/search/collections/5058/. 1790 US Census, Smithfield, Providence, Rhode Island, microfilm, Series M637, Roll 10, p. 209, Family History Library Film 0568150.

12. Yellin discarded the theory that the Jacobs's name came from a maternal grandfather and poor white farmer named Daniel Jacobs.

13. Ambrose Knox to David Leonard Barnes, December 17, 1793, NCSA.

14. Deposition of Elizabeth Harman; Deposition of Edward Penrice, MSA.

15. Amid hundreds of pages of Ambrose Knox's estate papers is one, dated November 15, 1798, from nephew Andrew Knox. Lucy, Theney, and Maria were

issued indictments by the state's attorney, referred to as slaves, and ordered to appear in Edenton court. Ambrose Knox Estate Papers, Pasquotank Wills and Estate Papers, 1663–1978, NCSA.

16. Stephanie Smallwood, *Saltwater Slavery: A Middle Passage from Africa to American Diaspora* (Cambridge, MA: Harvard University Press, 2007), 3.

17. It is also quite likely that they went through this process in the West Indies, which served as a transshipment point for many of the slave ships from West Africa (to the point that the triangular trade was often actually a square). Several ships that unloaded slaves on the Lower James River came from Barbados.

18. The 1720s is a best guess at when Tenea and Primus arrived. According to Ambrose Knox's fugitive slave ad, Athena/Theney was born in 1777; however, she was actually born around 1775, since she is also listed as a "negro girl" in a 1775 Perquimans tax list. In William Wyatt's will, "girl" Maria and "woman" Lucy were bequeathed to Mary Wyatt in 1762. As a "girl" Lucy had been bequeathed to William Wyatt in 1738. Assuming that a girl is defined as someone younger than eighteen, it follows that Maria was born after 1744, most likely in the 1750s, and Lucy was born after 1721, most likely in the 1730s. So Tenea and Primus probably arrived in the 1720s or early 1730s (the time span is vague because we don't know if they had other children and in what order, or how old they were when they were enslaved). "Seventeen Pounds Reward"; "Division of the Estate of William Wyatt," 1762, Perquimans Wills and Estate Papers, 1663–1978, NCSA; "Will of John Wiat," 1738, North Carolina Wills, 1663–1978, NCSA.

19. Marvin L. Michael Kay and Lorin Lee Cary, *Slavery in North Carolina, 1748– 1775* (Chapel Hill: University of North Carolina Press, 1995), 302–3.

20. Whitney R. Petrey, "Weapemeoc Shores: The Loss of Traditional Maritime Culture among the Weapemeoc Indians" (PhD diss., East Carolina University, 2014).

21. North Carolina Patent Books (Land Grant Record Books), 1693–1959, vol. 1, 7–8, NCSA.

22. White Southern naming practices tended to reuse grandparents' first names to name grandchildren.

23. Weynette Parks Haun, *Old Albemarle County, North Carolina: Perquimans Precinct Court Minutes, 1688–1738* (Durham, NC: Abstractor, 1980). In his will, John Wyatt left 86 cattle, 23 sheep, 18 sows and pigs, 5 oxen, 2 horses, 14 turkeys, 28 geese, and 11 ducks. "Will of John Wiat."

24. Elmer D. Johnson, "Knox, Andrew," in *NCpedia*, January 1, 1988, https:// ncpedia.org/print/6217; "A List of the Taxables given in to Andrew Knox for the year 1769, pursuant to order of Perquimans Inferior Court & held in July 1769"; "A List of Taxables, in the Districts of John Stafford & Andrew Collins Constables given in to Andrew Knox for the year 1775," both lists Perquimans County, North Carolina, Tax Records, List of Taxables, Tax Lists, Tax Records, NCSA.

25. This marriage was unlikely to bring a similar fortune back to the Wyatts.

26. "Will of Andrew Knox," 1776, Perquimans Wills and Estate Papers, 1663–1978, NCSA.

27. "Messrs. Andrew Knox & Co.'s Account of Interest with Samuel Johnston," Andrew Knox Estate Records 1772–1785, Edenton District, Estates Records, NCSA.

28. Caroline Randall Williams, "You Want a Confederate Monument? My Body Is a Confederate Monument," *New York Times*, June 26, 2020.

29. Kay and Cary, *Slavery in North Carolina*, 74.

30. Harriet A. Jacobs, *Incidents in the Life of a Slave Girl, Written by Herself; with 'A True Tale of Slavery" by John S. Jacobs*, ed. Jean Fagan Yellin (Cambridge, MA: Belknap Press of Harvard University Press, 2009).

31. Peter Force, *American Archives: Fifth Series, containing a Documentary History of the United States of America, from the Declaration of Independence, July 4, 1776, to the Definitive Treaty of Peace with Great Britain, September 3, 1783* (Washington, DC: M. St. Clair Clarke and Peter Force, 1848–53), 1383–84.

32. "John Horniblow," *State Gazette of North Carolina*, January 19, 1797.

33. Sharla Fett, *Working Cures: Healing, Health, and Power on Southern Slave Plantations* (Chapel Hill: University of North Carolina Press, 2002), 141.

34. Jeff Hampton, "N.C. House Weaves Tales from the 1700s," *Virginian-Pilot* (Norfolk, VA), August 30, 2015.

35. In his study of a New Orleans slave market, Walter Johnson found that "over nine tenths of those advertised by a skill that was nondomestic—coopers, carpenters, draymen—were male," and that "light-skinned men were three times more likely to be assigned those jobs than were dark-skinned men." Walter Johnson, *Soul by Soul: Life inside the Antebellum Slave Market* (Cambridge, MA: Harvard University Press, 1999), 150.

36. *Incidents*, 5.

37. Jean Fagan Yellin, *Harriet Jacobs: A Life* (New York: Civitas, 2004), 8 (hereafter cited as *HJAL*).

38. *Incidents*, 10.

39. *Incidents*, 7; *HJAL*, 7.

40. In keeping with Yellin, I assume that Harriet and John were born around 1813 and 1815, respectively, even though John could have been born as late as February 9, 1818 (the date listed on his death certificate). It is important to recognize—as virtually all ex-slave authors did in their autobiographies—that enslaved persons usually did not know their own birthdays.

41. "Edenton and Plymouth Steam-boat," *Edenton Gazette*, June 9, 1818; "Salt Works for Sale," *Edenton Gazette*, March 14, 1820; "In pursuance of a decree . . ." *Edenton Gazette*, April 9, 1821; "Notice," *Edenton Gazette*, January 21, 1822.

42. Jean Fagan Yellin, "Incidents Abroad: Harriet Jacobs and the Transatlantic Movement," in *Women's Rights and Transatlantic Antislavery in the Era of Emancipation*, ed. Kathryn Kish Sklar and James Stewart (New Haven, CT: Yale University Press, 2007), 158–72.

43. *HJAL*, 6.

44. *Incidents*, 7. "While the details of her illness are not known, its severity is clear," Yellin writes. "In a letter written the year before Jacobs's mother died, the doctor reports that Miss Margaret seemed somewhat better, 'gaining flesh and Strength' on a new regimen." *HJAL*, 11.

45. *HJAL*, 13; John Swanson Jacobs, *The United States Governed by Six Hundred Thousand Despots: A True Story of Slavery*, in this volume, 8 (hereafter referred to as *Despots*).

46. The Methodist church increased in size dramatically in two years, from 9 white and 9 Black members in 1809 to 39 white and 129 Black members in 1811. Edenton Methodist Episcopal Church record book, 1804–1863, Southern Historical Collection, University of North Carolina. Microfilm.

47. *Despots*, 7–8.

48. "*An Account of the Late Intended Insurrection among a portion of the Blacks of Charleston, South-Carolina* Concluded," *Weekly Raleigh Register*, September 27, 1822.

49. "African Colony," *Western Carolinian*, April 29, 1823.

50. *Incidents*, 5.

51. S. S. Satchwell, "A Memoir of the Life of Dr. James Norcom, of Edenton, North Carolina," *Nelson's Northern Lancet: An American Journal of Medical Jurisprudence* 4, no. 22 (1852): 173.

52. Satchwell, "Memoir of Norcom," 174.

53. Satchwell, "Memoir of Norcom," 179.

54. Will of Margaret Horniblow, 1825, Chowan County Wills and Estate Papers, 1663–1978, NCSA.

55. *HJAL*, 17.

56. *Despots*, 15, 12–13, 6; *Incidents*, 9.

57. *Despots*, 12–13.

58. *HJAL*, 21.

59. *Despots*, 13.

60. *Despots*, 13.

61. *Incidents*, 25.

62. *Incidents*, 29.

63. *Despots*, 14–15.

64. Sarah Hallowell Willis to Amy Post, October 20, 1850, Isaac and Amy Post Family Papers, hereafter cited as IAPFP (see abbreviations list for full source citation).

65. On ideal womanhood, see Hazel V. Carby, *Reconstructing Womanhood: The Emergence of the Afro-American Woman Novelist* (New York: Oxford University Press, 1989).

66. *HJAL*, 33; *Despots*, 15.

67. David Walker, *Walker's Appeal, in Four Articles, together with a Preamble, to the Coloured Citizens of the World* (Boston: David Walker, 1830), 85.

68. "Incendiary Publications," *Miners' and Farmers' Journal*, September 28, 1831.

69. *HJAL*, 35.

70. Henry Irving Tragle, *The Southampton Slave Revolt of 1831: A Compilation of Source Material* (Amherst, MA: University of Massachusetts Press, 1971); *Incidents*, 82.

71. "The Conspiracy," *Miners' and Farmers' Journal*, September 28, 1831.

72. *HJAL*, 38. See also "Nat Turner's Insurrection," 1831, in Chowan County

Criminal Actions Concerning Slaves, 1733–1869, Chowan County Slave records, NCSA; entry in the minutes of October 12, 1831, Chowan County Superior Court Minutes, Fall Term 1831, NCSA; Robert N. Elliott, "The Nat Turner Insurrection as Reported in the North Carolina Press," *North Carolina Historical Review* 38, no. 1 (1961): 17.

73. *Incidents*, 83; *HJAL*, 41; Norcom to Dr. John Norcom, January 29, 1833, Dr. James Norcom and Family Papers, NCSA; "A True Tale of Slavery," 267, hereafter cited as TT (see abbreviations list for full source citation).

74. Will of Mary Bissell, 1836, Chowan Wills and Estate Papers, 1663–1978, NCSA; Memory F. Mitchell, "Off to Africa—With Judicial Blessing," *North Carolina Historical Review* 53, no. 3 (1976): 269–71; *HJAL*, 52–53.

75. *Incidents*, 129–30.

76. *Despots*, 34.

77. *Despots*, 34.

78. *Despots*, 36.

79. *Incidents*, 136, 137.

80. Estate of Matthias E. Sawyer, 1835, Chowan Inventories, vol. A1, 1811–1868, NCSA.

81. *Despots*, 35.

82. Members of the 25th Congress were elected between August 1, 1836, and November 6–7, 1837. Sawyer was elected after the start of the March 4, 1837, session and before the September 4, 1837, session.

83. *Incidents*, 156.

84. James I. Robertson Jr., "Old Capitol: Eminence to Infamy," 91st Cong., 1st sess., *Congressional Record* 115 (October 9, 1969): 29360; *Congressional Directory of the Third Session of the Twenty-Fifth Congress of the United States of America* (Washington, DC: Thomas Allen, 1839), 36.

85. See Alice Elizabeth Malavasic, *The F Street Mess: How Southern Senators Rewrote the Kansas-Nebraska Act* (Chapel Hill: University of North Carolina Press, 2017).

86. Drew Gilpin Faust, *James Henry Hammond and the Old South: A Design for Mastery* (Baton Rouge: Louisiana State University Press, 1982), 166.

87. *Proceedings and Debates of the Convention of North Carolina, Called to Amend the Constitution of the State, which Assembled at Raleigh, June 4, 1835* (Raleigh: Joseph Gates, 1836), 80, 356.

88. *Despots*, 48.

89. *Incidents*, 173.

90. *Incidents*, 172, 173.

91. In Lydia Maria Child's recollection, John went to Boston first, where he was "much esteemed by a worthy Quaker's family." The identity of this Boston Quaker family remains a mystery. See *Harriet Jacobs Family Papers*, hereafter cited as *HJFP*), 1:288–89 (see abbreviations list for full source citation); and Lydia Maria Child to Sarah Sturgis Shaw, [January] 1861, Lydia Maria Child Correspondence, 1860–1880, Samuel J. May Anti-Slavery Manuscript Collection, Cornell University.

No Longer Yours, *Chapter Two*

1. Epigraph: *Despots*, 62; "Poetry," *Liberator*, November 17, 1843.
2. Kathryn Grover, *The Fugitive's Gibraltar: Escaping Slaves and Abolitionism in New Bedford, Massachusetts* (Amherst: University of Massachusetts Press, 2001), 12; Timothy Dale Walker, ed., *Sailing to Freedom: Maritime Dimensions of the Underground Railroad* (Amherst: University of Massachusetts Press, 2021).
3. *Despots*, 51. In the 1861 autobiography, the chiasmus chapter appears after the following sentence: "For the first week or so I could not realize the great transformation from a chattel slave to a man; it seemed to me like a dream; but I soon began to feel my responsibility, and the necessity of mental improvement" (TT, 282). On chiasmus in Douglass, see Bromell, *Powers of Dignity*, 63–66.
4. Frederick Douglass, "Frederick Douglass as a Preacher, and One of his Last Most Significant Letters," *Journal of Negro History* 66, no. 2 (1981): 140–43.
5. Douglass, "Douglass as Preacher," 142. On Douglass in New Bedford, see David Blight, *Frederick Douglass: Prophet of Freedom* (New York: Simon & Schuster, 2018), 87–101; and Gregory P. Lampe, *Frederick Douglass: Freedom's Voice, 1818–1845* (East Lansing: Michigan State University Press, 1998), 33–56.
6. Never having been in a position to manage his own finances, John had amassed some debts too; town recorder Henry Howland Crapo lists Jacobs as owing $1.50 in taxes for 1839 and 1840 (Henry Howland Crapo, "Memorandum of Tax Delinquents," 1837–1841, New Bedford Free Public Library).
7. *New Bedford Mercury*, August 7, 8, 1839.
8. Though whaling was more diverse than commercial shipping and about 2 percent of captains (52 of 2,500) were men of color, such opportunities were the exception, not the rule, and generally speaking, the officer class was white. See Nancy Shoemaker, *Native American Whalemen and the World: Indigenous Encounters and the Contingency of Race* (Chapel Hill: University of North Carolina Press, 2015), 43; Skip Finley, *Whaling Captains of Color: America's First Meritocracy* (Annapolis, MD: Naval Institute Press, 2020).
9. Michael Sokolow, *Charles Benson: Mariner of Color in the Age of Sail* (Amherst: University of Massachusetts Press, 2003), 63.
10. Between the 1790s and 1850s, it was not known that scurvy was caused by the absence of ascorbic acid. And although citrus juice was known to ward off the disease, the increasingly favored West Indian lime was later shown to contain a negligible amount of ascorbate. A good steward such as John also had to know whether to prepare and store the lime juice via the method of *inspissation* (a bain-marie reduction of the juice to a third of the volume) or a brisk boiling process, which reduced the effectiveness of the juice. See Jonathan Lamb, *Scurvy: The Voyage of Discovery* (Princeton, NJ: Princeton University Press, 2017), 35–36.
11. Sokolow, *Charles Benson*, 61–64.
12. William Comstock, *A Voyage to the Pacific, Descriptive of the Customs, Usages,*

and Sufferings on Board of Nantucket Whale-Ships (Boston: Oliver L. Perkins, 1836), 26.

. Frederick Douglass, "Oysters! Oysters!" *North Star*, November 2, 1849 (repro-duced in appendix 2).

. Journal of Rounseville S. Slocum, in *Account of Whaling Voyages in the Whalers By Chance, William Rotch, Liverpool, Royal William, Cora, Frances Henrietta, Newton, Dragon, Kutesoff, Russell 1828–1851*, October 15, 1839, hereafter cited as JRS (see abbreviations list for full source citation).

. JRS, November 13, 1839, November 19, 1839, and December 18, 1839.

. James Higgins, *Lima: A Cultural History* (Oxford: Signal Books, 2005), 86.

. JRS, June 5, 1840,

. JRS, September 1, 1840.

. JRS, December 11, 1840.

. JRS, January 14–24, 1841.

. JRS, October 8, 1841.

. JRS, March 20–30, 1842.

. Christopher Kindell, "'Brothel of the Pacific': Syphilis and the Urban Regu-lation of *Laikini Wahine* in Honolulu, 1855–1875," *Journal of Pacific History* 55, no. 1 (2020): 18–36.

. "Refuge of Oppression," *Liberator*, August 18, 1848.

. JRS, March 20–30, 1842.

. For cargo, see "Account of Ship Fr. Henrietta's Cargo," Charles W. Mor-gan Papers, Manuscripts Collection 27, vol. 26, G. W. Blunt Library, Mys-tic Seaport Museum, Mystic, CT; for Jacobs's wages, see "Sundry Accounts Dr to Whaling Voyages . . . of *Frances Henrietta*," Morgan Papers, Manu-scripts Collection 27, vol. 24. As Grover writes regarding the casks of oil, "it is unclear whether this was part of or a supplement to his stated wage" (*Fugi-tive's Gibraltar*, 316). For John's realization that his money was truly his own, see *Despots*, 52.

. *Incidents*, 218.

. Lydia Maria Child to Sarah Sturgis Shaw, [October] 1861, Lydia Maria Child Antislavery Correspondence (Box 5), Samuel J. May Anti-Slavery Manuscript Collection, Cornell University.

. James O. and Lois E. Horton, *Black Bostonians: Family Life and Community Struggle in the Antebellum North* (New York: Holmes and Meier, 2000).

. "Appendixes," in *Courage and Conscious: Black & White Abolitionists in Bos-ton*, ed. Donald M. Jacobs (Bloomington: Indiana University Press, 1993), 225–28.

. *HJAL*, 72.

. The "John Jacobs" who donated thirty-six cents to the New England Anti-Slavery Society is probably John S. See "New-England A. S. Convention," *Liberator*, June 23, 1843.

. "The New England Anti-Slavery Convention," *Emancipator and Republican*, June 8, 1843.

. "New-England Anti-Slavery Convention," *Liberator*, June 2, 1843. Marcy

NOTES TO PAGES 119–126   273

Dinius and Derrick Spires both read this speech as leaning upon Walker. See Marcy Dinius, *The Textual Effects of David Walker's "Appeal": Print-Based Activism against Slavery, Racism, and Discrimination, 1829–1851* (Philadelphia: University of Pennsylvania Press, 2022), 173–74; and Derrick Spires, *The Practice of Citizenship: Black Politics and Print Culture in the Early United States* (Philadelphia: University of Pennsylvania Press, 2019), 5.

35. "New-England Anti-Slavery Convention," *Liberator*, June 16, 1843.

36. "Anti-Slavery Meetings," *Liberator*, May 12, 1843.

37. "Adelphic Union Library Association," *Emancipator and Free American*, October 20, 1842; Peter Wirzbicki, "Black Transcendentalism: William Cooper Nell, the Adelphic Union, and the Black Abolitionist Intellectual Tradition," *Journal of the Civil War Era* 8, no. 2 (2018): 269–90; and Peter Wirzbicki, *Fighting for the Higher Law: Black and White Transcendentalists against Slavery* (Philadelphia: University of Pennsylvania Press, 2021).

38. William Cooper Nell to Wendell Phillips, December 14, 1860, Wendell Phillips Papers, Houghton Library, Harvard University.

39. See Carol Buchalter Stapp, *Afro-Americans in Antebellum Boston: An Analysis of Probate Records*, vol. 2 (New York: Garland, 1993), 350–51.

40. "Adelphic Union Library Association," *Liberator*, January 12, 1844 (see appendix 2). Though no extant document proves that John attended elocution classes, the odds are overwhelming that he did. For if he was appointed to the lecture committee of the Adelphic in 1845 and began to give antislavery speeches soon after, he must have (1) participated extensively in Adelphic events and demonstrated enough talent to merit promotion, and (2) been trained or at least practiced public speaking and demonstrated enough ability to be given a chance to speak as a representative of the Adelphic and other Black abolitionist organizations in Boston. The only obvious way to accomplish both these things at once was to enroll in the Adelphic's oratory and elocution courses and attend and perform at its lectures.

41. "Adelphic Union Library Association," *Liberator*, September 29, 1843.

42. H. I. Bowditch, "Important Correspondence," *Pittsfield (MA) Sun*, October 26, 1843.

43. "Adelphic Union Library Association," *Liberator*, November 10, 1843; Williams, "Poetry."

44. "Adelphic Union Library Association," *Liberator*, February 2, 1844; "Adelphic Union Library Association," *Liberator*, March 22, 1844.

45. *HJAL*, 74.

46. Benjamin Quarles, *Black Abolitionists* (New York: Oxford University Press, 1969), 102.

47. "Declaration of Sentiment, while under Slavery and Oppression," *Liberator*, December 23, 1842; "New-England Freedom Association," *Liberator*, March 31, 1843. This was actually the second such committee in Boston, which succeeded Charles T. Torrey's failed vigilance committee of 1841.

48. "British Emancipation," *Liberator*, July 28, 1843.

49. "New-England Freedom Association," *Liberator*, December 12, 1845.

50. "Meeting of the Colored Citizens of Boston for the relief of Charles T. Torrey," *Liberator*, August 9, 1844.

51. "Letter from Charles T. Torrey," *Liberator*, September 13, 1844.

52. John S. Jacobs to Sydney Howard Gay, September 7, 1845 (reproduced in appendix 1).

53. "Help the Fugitive," *Liberator*, January 16, 1846.

54. "Crowded Meeting of the Colored Population of Boston," *Liberator*, July 24, 1846.

55. "Torrey's Monument," *Maine Cultivator and Hallowell Gazette*, December 18, 1847.

56. William Cooper Nell, "Jonathan Walker and John S. Jacobs," *North Star*, March 31, 1848 (reproduced in appendix 2).

57. "The Rural Fair and Celebration of the Fourth of July at Dedham," *Liberator*, July 17, 1846. The quotation is from a letter from an unnamed fugitive that Garrison read out loud at the fair.

58. Jonathan Walker, *Trial and Imprisonment of Jonathan Walker, at Pensacola, Florida, for Aiding Slaves to Escape from Bondage, with an Appendix, Containing a Sketch of His Life* (Boston: Anti-Slavery Office, 1845), 32.

59. John Greenleaf Whittier and James Russell Lowell, "The Branded Hand" (Salem, OH: *The Anti-Slavery Bugle*, 1845), 33–34.

60. "The Walker Meetings," *National Anti-Slavery Standard*, January 6, 1848.

61. "Frederick Douglass," *Cayuga Chief* (Weedsport, NY), April 12, 1849.

62. Jonathan Walker, "Anti-Slavery in Western New York," *Liberator*, February 11, 1848.

63. "The Branded Hand," *Christian Contributor*, January 26, 1848 (see appendix 2, where a portion of this article is reproduced).

64. Nell, "Jonathan Walker and John S. Jacobs."

65. "The Branded Hand," *Christian Contributor* (emphasis in original).

66. John S. Jacobs to William Lloyd Garrison, *Liberator*, March 31 (letter dated February 27), 1848 (reproduced in appendix 1).

67. Jacobs to Garrison.

68. John S. Jacobs to Frederick Douglass, *North Star*, March 3, 1848 (reproduced in appendix 1).

69. Renato Rosaldo, *Culture & Truth: The Remaking of Social Analysis* (Boston: Beacon Press, 1989), 68–87.

70. Jacobs to Douglass, *North Star*, March 3, 1848.

71. Julia Wilbur Large Diary, March 26, 1848, hereafter cited as JWLD (see abbreviations list for full source; reproduced in appendix 2).

72. Nell, "Jonathan Walker and John S. Jacobs."

73. "The Branded Hand," *Liberator*, April 14, 1848.

74. John Stauffer, *The Black Hearts of Men: Radical Abolitionists and the Transformation of Race* (Cambridge, MA: Harvard University Press, 2002).

75. *Annual Report Presented to the Massachusetts Anti-Slavery Society, by Its Board of Managers, January 24, 1849, with an Appendix* (Boston: Printed by Andrews & Prentiss, 1849), 57.

76. Abby H. Price, "Anti-Slavery Convention at Milford," *Non-Resistant and Practical Christian*, August 5, 1848 (see appendix 2 for an excerpt). See also "S. W. Wheeler to William Lloyd Garrison," *Liberator*, August 11, 1848.

77. Price, "Anti-Slavery Convention at Milford."

78. *Incidents*, 243.

79. "Antislavery Office and Reading Room," *North Star*, April 20, 1849.

80. William Cooper Nell, "Antislavery Lectures at Minerva Hall," *North Star*, February 16, 1849.

81. Frederick Douglass, "The Address of Southern Delegates in Congress to Their Constituents; or, The Address of John C. Calhoun and Forty Other Thieves," *North Star*, February 9, 1849.

82. Frederick Douglass, "Editorial Correspondence," *North Star*, March 9, 1849 (reproduced in appendix 2).

83. Douglass, "Editorial Correspondence." Note: throughout the volume I choose to mask the *n*-word rather than reproduce it in full, for reasons like those that Koritha Mitchell lays out concerning what to do about the word in a classroom setting. See Koritha Mitchell, "Teaching & the N-Word: Questions to Consider," Koritha Mitchell (website), March 23, 2018, https://www.koritha mitchell.com/teaching-and-the-n-word/.

84. JWLD, February 18, 1849 (reproduced in appendix 2).

85. JWLD, February 18, 1849.

86. See Nancy Hewitt, *Radical Friend: Amy Kirby Post and Her Activist Worlds* (Chapel Hill: University of North Carolina Press, 2018).

87. John S. Jacobs, "Anti-Slavery Office and Reading Room," *North Star*, March 3, 1849 (reproduced in appendix 1).

88. John S. Jacobs to Frederick Douglass, *North Star*, May 4, 1849 (reproduced in appendix 1).

89. Frederick Douglass to Isaac and Amy Post, April 22, 1849, IAPFP.

90. Hilary J. Moss, *Schooling Citizens: The Struggle for African American Education in Antebellum America* (Chicago: University of Chicago Press, 2009).

91. "Fifteenth Annual Meeting of the American Anti-Slavery Society," *Liberator*, May 18, 1849.

92. "Fifteenth Annual Meeting."

93. "The Anniversaries: American Anti-Slavery Society; Third Day," *New York Herald*, May 11, 1849 (see appendix 2 for an excerpt).

94. John S. Jacobs to Zenas Brockett, [September 6, 1849] (reproduced in appendix 1).

95. "Oysters! Oysters!!" *North Star*, November 2, 1849 (reproduced in appendix 2).

96. "More Signs than True," *Rochester (NY) Daily Democrat*, December 28, 1850.

97. "Men Will Lie, but Oysters Cannot," *Rochester (NY) Daily Democrat*, January 9, 1850 (reproduced in appendix 1).

98. *The Fugitive Slave Bill: Its History and Unconstitutionality; with an Account of the Seizure and Enslavement of James Hamlet and His Subsequent Restoration to Liberty* (New York: William Harned, 1850), 31; Sarah Hallowell Willis to Amy Post, October 20, 1850, IAPFP.

99. "Meeting of Colored Citizens of New York," *North Star*, October 24, 1850 (reproduced in appendix 2).

100. See John Burt, "Political Violence and the Persuasive Engagement in Frederick Douglass," *Literary Imagination* 23, no. 2 (2021): 111–36, at 115.

101. Manisha Sinha, *The Slave's Cause: A History of Abolition* (New Haven, CT: Yale University Press, 2016), 504.

102. Sean Wilentz, "Crime, Poverty, and the Streets of New York City: The Diary of William H. Bell, 1850–51," *History Workshop* 7 (1979): 133.

103. *HJAL*, 109–10; *Incidents*, 245.

No Longer Yours, *Chapter Three*

1. R. J. M. Blackett, *The Captive's Quest for Freedom: Fugitive Slaves, the 1850 Fugitive Slave Law, and the Politics of Slavery* (Cambridge: Cambridge University Press, 2018); see also Fred Landon, "The Negro Migration to Canada after the Passing of the Fugitive Slave Act," *Journal of Negro History* 5, no. 1 (1920): 22–36.

2. The exception made in this part of the Constitution is of major importance for plantation-to-prison historiography. "Constitution of the State of California. 1849," Records of the Constitutional Convention of 1849, California State Archives, https://www.sos.ca.gov/archives/collections/constitutions/1849.

3. Even after 1852, California was characterized by a "laxity in upholding federal law." Janet Neary, "Mining the African American Literary Tradition: James Williams's *Fugitive Slave in the Gold Rush* and the Contours of a 'Black Pacific,'" *ESQ* 59, no. 2 (2013): 329–74. See also Carl Meyer, *Bound for Sacramento: Travel-Pictures of a Returned Wanderer*, trans. Ruth Frey Axe (Claremont, CA: Saunders Studio Press, 1938), 145.

4. Stephen Chapin David, *California Gold Rush Merchant: The Journal of Stephen Chapin David*, ed. Benjamin B. Richards (San Marino, CA: Huntington Library, 1956).

5. Harriet Jacobs to Amy Post, February 12, 1852, IAPFP.

6. Frank Soulé, John H. Gihon, and James Nisbet, *The Annals of San Francisco; Containing a Summary of the History of the First Discovery, Settlement, Progress and Present Condition of California* (New York: Appleton, 1855), 515.

7. George Payson, *Golden Dreams and Leaden Realities* (New York: Putnam, 1853), 92.

8. H. Jacobs to A. Post, February 12, 1852.

9. "The Mines," *Daily Evening Picayune* (San Francisco), October 1, 1851 (emphasis in original).

10. See Mae Ngai, *The Chinese Question: The Gold Rushes and Global Politics* (New York: W. W. Norton, 2022).

11. William Cooper Nell to Amy Post, January 6, 1853, IAPFP.

12. Harriet Jacobs to Amy Post, December 20, 1852, IAPFP.

13. William Cooper Nell to Amy Post, July 21, 1853, IAPFP.

14. Raffaello Carboni, *The Eureka Stockade: The Consequence of Some Pirates Wanting on Quarter-Deck a Rebellion* (Melbourne: J. P. Atkinson, 1855), 3.

15. See *Eurekapedia*, "John Jacobs," last modified March 5, 2021, http://www .eurekapedia.org/John_Jacobs.

16. Thomas Pierson, December 6, 1854, in 1853 Diaries, 2 vols., September 30, 1852– April 12, 1864, State Library of Victoria Manuscript Collection, MS 11646, 245.

17. Jeffrey Atkinson and David Andrew Roberts, "Men of Colour: John Joseph and the Eureka Treason Trials," *Journal of Australian Colonial History* 10, no. 1 (2008): 76, 81.

18. *Despots*, 58.

19. "Shall We Refuse to Admit the Chinese?" *Argus* (Melbourne, Australia), March 15, 1855.

20. "Shall We Refuse to Admit the Chinese?" *Sydney Morning Herald*, March 23, 1855.

21. Harriet Jacobs to Amy Post, after December 27, 1852, before February 14, 1853, IAPFP.

22. H. Jacobs to A. Post, December 20, 1852.

23. Harriet Jacobs to Amy Post, August 7, 1855, IAPFP.

24. On the disappearance of Joseph Jacobs, see Lydia Maria Child to John Fraser, November 20, 1866, in *The Collected Correspondence of Lydia Maria Child, 1817– 1880*, ed. Patricia G. Holland, Milton Meltzer, and Francine Krasno (Millwood, NY: Kraus Microform, 1980), 66/1746.

25. *HJAL*, 225. According to the stranger, Joseph was in Melbourne and had gone to the Goulburn diggings south of Sydney. Joseph was said to have lost the use of one of his arms after an illness and perhaps been the victim of foul play; when Harriet sent four hundred dollars in gold to a certain James Armstrong in Melbourne, the money was irretrievably lost. After enlisting Lydia Maria Child in the hunt, Child wrote John Fraser, an Anglican minister who had sailed for New Zealand from Boston in 1863 and was presumably in Australia by 1866. On Fraser, see "Our Colonies," *Evangelical Magazine and Missionary Chronicle*, January 1864, 27.

26. Joseph probably died of a fever around 1860. See October 31, 1905, entry in the Robert Apthorp Boit diaries, 1876–1918, 16 vols., Massachusetts Historical Society, Boston.

27. H. Jacobs to A. Post, February 12, 1852, IAPFP.

28. Joseph Conrad, *Notes on Life and Letters* (New York: Doubleday, Page, 1923), 262.

29. Harriet Jacobs to Amy Post, June 21, 1857, IAPFP.

30. George Thompson to Amelia Chesson, December 24, 1857, John Rylands Research Institute and Library, hereafter cited as JRL (see abbreviations list for full citation).

31. Diary of Frederick William Chesson, March 14, 1858, John Rylands Research Institute and Library, hereafter cited as DFWC (see abbreviations list for full citation); "The Horrors of the Coolie Trade," *Evening Star* (London), August 13, 1858.

32. Minutes of the London Emancipation Committee, JRL.

33. Thomas E. Sebrell II, *Persuading John Bull: Union and Confederate Propaganda in Britain, 1860–65* (New York: Lexington Books, 2014), 99.

34. William Cooper Nell to Amy Post, September 22, 1857, IAPFP.
35. William Cooper Nell to Amy Post, November 10, 1857, IAPFP.
36. See Nell to A. Post, September 22, 1857; Harriet Jacobs to Amy Post, March 1, 1858, IAPFP.
37. Harriet Jacobs to Amy Post, May 3, 1858, IAPFP.
38. Diaries of Amelia Chesson, July 23, 1858, hereafter cited as DAC (see abbreviations list for full citation).
39. Richard Davis Webb to Samuel May Jr., July 28, 1858, Boston Public Library, hereafter cited as BPL (see abbreviations list for full citation).
40. DAC, October 2, 1858.
41. Harriet Jacobs to Amy Post, October 8, 1860, IAPFP.
42. *HJAL*, 140; Lydia Maria Child to [Lucy Osgood], August 8, 1860, Lydia Maria Child Antislavery Correspondence (Box 5), Samuel J. May Anti-Slavery Manuscript Collection, Cornell University.
43. Lydia Maria Child to Lucy Searle, February 4, 1861, Lydia Maria Child Antislavery Correspondence, Samuel J. May Anti-Slavery Manuscript Collection, Cornell University; H. Jacobs to A. Post, June 21, 1857, IAPFP; Lydia Maria Child to Harriet Jacobs, September 27, 1860, IAPFP.
44. Official Logbook of the *Pilot Fish*, December 17, 1860, National Maritime Museum, Greenwich, UK.
45. There is a possibility that he changed the text himself, either of his own volition or in response to external pressures from Chesson or the magazine. However, given that TT was published three months after Jacobs went to sea, and given how extreme the changes are, it seems more likely that his narrative was bowdlerized by someone else while he was away. "To be Sold by Auction," *Southern Reporter and Cork Commercial Courier*, May 25, 1861.
46. Harriet Jacobs to Amy Post, March 1857, IAPFP.
47. "Preface by the Author," *Incidents*, 1–2.
48. Harriet Jacobs to Amy Post, June 18, 186[1], IAPFP; *Incidents*, 36.
49. John S. Jacobs, "A Colored American in England," *National Anti-Slavery Standard*, June 29, 1861 (reproduced in appendix 1).
50. *HJFP*, 1:354; George Thompson to William Lloyd Garrison, June 7, 1861, BPL.
51. "Leeds Young Men's Anti-Slavery Society," *Leeds Times*, June 1, 1861.
52. "Official Inquiry into the Loss of the Steamer Queen Victoria, of Hull," *Hull Packet*, July 25, 1862.
53. "The Prince of Wales in Egypt," *Berkshire Chronicle*, March 29, 1862.
54. DFWC, March 31, 1862.
55. Current scholarship says that the ship was bound for Veracruz in Mexico, not Havana.
56. "Running the Blockade," *New York Independent*, July 28, 1862 (reproduced in appendix 2).
57. Michael Craton and Gail Saunders, *Islanders in the Stream: A History of the Bahamian People*, vol. 2, *From the Ending of Slavery to the Twenty-First Century* (Athens: University of Georgia Press, 1998), 77.
58. "Running the Blockade," *New York Independent*, July 28, 1862 (reproduced in appendix 2).

59. "Running the Blockade."
60. Harriet Jacobs to Amy Post, December 8, 1862, IAPFP.
61. "The Charleston Blockade," *Connecticut Courant*, October 3, 1862.
62. "The Northern States and the Emancipation of the Slaves," *Morning Advertiser*, April 3, 1862.
63. 1861 England Census, microfilm, Class Rg 9, Piece 273, Folio 120, p. 22, GSU roll: 542604.
64. H. Jacobs to A. Post, December 8, 1862, IAPFP.
65. "Police Office—Saturday," *Cork Examiner*, April 23, 1866.
66. "The Society of Friends," *Christian World*, March 6, 1868.
67. DFWC, August 29, 1869.
68. "Foreign Intelligence," *Globe*, June 23, 1871.
69. DFWC, August 29, 1869.

No Longer Yours, *Epilogue*

1. Superintendent Scorgie to Louisa M. Jacobs, September 1, 1911, and September 14, 1914; work order to reset "Brother" as lawn stone, November 26, 1957, Mount Auburn Cemetery Historical Collections & Archives, Boston.
2. Nell, "Jonathan Walker and John S. Jacobs."
3. Louisa M. Jacobs to William Lloyd Garrison, December 20, 1873, BPL; *HJAL*, 226.
4. "Remarks of William Lloyd Garrison," in *In Memory, Angelina Grimké Weld* (Boston: Press of George H. Ellis, 1880), 77.
5. *Greenough, Jones & Co's Cambridge Directory for 1874* (Cambridge, MA: Greenough, Jones & Co., 1874), 215. The address listed on his death certificate is 11 Brewer Street.
6. Thanks to Syd Nathans for this information.
7. "Not Yet Out of Danger: Recorder Trotter Still in a Precarious Condition," *Cleveland Leader and Morning Herald*, April 9, 1887.
8. Friends of Mount Auburn, "Harriet Jacobs (1813–1897): Author, Abolitionist, and Freedom Seeker," Mount Auburn Cemetery, November 22, 2011, https://www.mountauburn.org/harriet-jacobs-1813-1897/. By coincidence, Mary Walker's family had bought a new lot in Mount Auburn three weeks prior, disinterred Walker from the adjoining Cambridge Cemetery, and reburied her in the new plot.
9. 1900 US Census, Somerville Ward 2, Middlesex, Massachusetts, Roll 665, p. 15, Family History Library Microfilm 1240665.
10. "William Jacob Knox, Jr," MIT Black History Project, Massachusetts Institute of Technology, accessed June 14, 2023, https://www.blackhistory.mit.edu/archive/william-j-knox-jr-ca-1925; "CCB Spotlight: William Knox, A.B. '23 & Lawrence Knox, Ph.D. '40," Harvard University Department of Chemistry and Chemical Biology, February 25, 2022, https://chemistry.harvard.edu/news/ccb-spotlight-brothers-william-and-lawrence-knox.

11. Arthur Jafa, "Keep Smiling, Virgil," *Daedalus*, January 8, 2022 https://www
.daedalusmagazine.it/keep-smiling-virgil/
(first published on Instagram, December 7, 2021; post now deleted).

John Jacobs at First Sight

An earlier version of "John Jacobs at First Sight" appeared in *Vistas* 1, no. 1 (2022),
published by the New Bedford Whaling Museum.

1. The daguerreotype that Frederick Douglass's sister-in-law, Charlotte Murray,
once possessed is lost, and Harriet Jacobs never published her proposed illustrated edition of her autobiography. Harriet Jacobs to Amy Post, January 11,
1854, Isaac and Amy Post Family Papers (see abbreviations list for full source
citation of IAPFP).
2. Historical Society of Pennsylvania, with the Balch Institute Institutional
Records.
3. As announced in the *Liberator*, Brown lectured in Plympton on April 1 and 2,
and in Pawtucket, Worcester, Franklin, Bellingham, Dedham, Uxbridge, and
Millbury between April 12 and 25. "Old Colony Anti-Slavery Society," *Liberator*, April 21, 1848; "William W. Brown," *Liberator*, April 7, 14, and 21, 1848.
4. Series II: Correspondence, 1976–1987, Box 1, Folder 5, Juliette Tomlinson
Research Files on Joseph Whiting Stock, circa 1970s–1987, Frick Museum
Art Reference Library.
5. "In May of 1847 Stock was in New Bedford, where he painted Captain Stephen Christian in May of that year, a work he signed and dated. Because there
is no listing for him in the 1848 Springfield Directory, it may be assumed that
he extended his stay in New Bedford." Juliette Tomlinson, "A Biographical
Note," in *The Paintings and Journal of Joseph Whiting Stock* (Middletown, CT:
Wesleyan University Press, 1976), xi.
6. Marcus Wood, "Slave Narratives and Visual Culture," in *The Oxford Handbook
of the African American Slave Narrative*, ed. John Ernest (New York: Oxford
University Press, 2014), 198–99.
7. See William W. Cook and James Tatum, *African American Literature and Classical Tradition* (Chicago: University of Chicago Press, 2010).
8. Frederick Douglass, "Negro Portraits," *Liberator*, April 20, 1849.

INDEX

AAMP. *See* African American Museum in Philadelphia (AAMP)

abolitionism: in Australia, 158–61; in Boston, 123–26, 129–33; Christianity and, 19n*; Douglass and, xix, xxvii, 1n, 6in*, 143–44, 194, 197, 218n, 236, 238–51; the *Empire* and, 3n; Garrison and, xviii–xix, 1n, 52–53, 53n*, 58n†; gradual approach to, 147; Hildreth and, 4n*; Harriet Jacobs and, 125, 162, 164, 177, 183; John Jacobs and, xviii–xix, 1n, 53n*, 125–26, 130–40, 143–44, 147–48, 161, 164–66, 169, 181–83, 197, 210–17, 221, 230, 236, 238–54; mottos of, xviii, 58n†, 103, 132, 150, 161, 235; Quakers and, 116, 144, 202n*; radical, xviii–xix; and slave narratives, xxi, xxiv, xxvii, 168–71, 197–98; slaveowners and, 96; sundry manifestations of, 169, 218n, 228, 233, 233n, 239; Jonathan Walker and, 133–37, 139–40. *See also* American Anti-Slavery Society; Boston Vigilance Committee; New England Anti-Slavery Society; New England Freedom Association; Torrey Monument Association

Adams, Charles Francis, 185

Adams, Henry, 184–85

Adams, John Quincy, 46, 46n, 209, 231, 231n*

Adams, Samuel, 81

Adelphic Union Library Association, 124, 126–29, 131, 137, 142, 184–85, 224–25, 274n41

Admiral Kanaris (ship), 167

African American Museum in Philadelphia (AAMP), 192, 195

African Methodist Episcopal Zion Church (New Bedford, MA), 115–16, 194

Agnes, xxv, 29–31, 29n†, 31n

Allen, William Gustavus, 158

Almy, William, 84

American Anti-Slavery Society, xxvii, 2n, 133, 137, 147, 202n*, 245, 252–54

American Board of Commissioners for Foreign Missions, 8n, 253n

American Colonization Society, 19n†, 21n†, 55n, 96, 104–5

antislavery activism. *See* abolitionism

Anti-Slavery Advocate (newspaper), 167

Anti-Slavery Bugle (newspaper), 233n

Anti-Slavery Collection, Boston Public Library, 182

Anti-Slavery Office in Boston, 170

283

Post, Amy Kirby, 144, 150, 151, 162, 166, 168, 171, 176
Post, Isaac, 144, 162, 171, 221
Potter, Lydia, 124
Powell, William P., 115
Price, Abby Hills, 140, 233–35, 233n
Prigg v. Pennsylvania (1842), 123
Primus (grandfather of Maria Knox), 85–88, 268n18
Primus (son of Maria Knox), 85, 88
Pritchard, Hannah, 12n, 99
Prosser, Gabriel, 80, 92
Putnam, Joseph Hall, 158

Quakers, 62, 81, 83, 96, 113, 116, 123, 124, 139, 144, 177, 202n*
Quarles, Benjamin, 129, 192
Queen Victoria (ship), 172, 174
Quincy, Josiah, 83

racism: in California gold rush, 157; faced by Jacobs and Douglass on lecture tours, 137–38, 143, 145; and immigration laws, 160, 161; in justifications of slavery, 136; on sailing vessels, 118; and skin color, 92
Rambler (newspaper), 202, 202n†
Ramsey, Mark (uncle of John and Harriet Jacobs), 5n†, 12n, 13–14, 40n, 42–43, 43n, 93, 98–100, 106, 107, 109, 110, 124, 176
Ram's Horn (newspaper), 144
Randolph, John, 69n
rape, 90, 101
Raymond, Patrick H. and John T., 185
Regent (ship), 178
religion. *See* Christianity
Religious Tract Society, 169
Remond, Charles Lenox, 126, 134, 193
Remond, Sarah Parker, xvi, 165
Revolutionary War, 91
RMS *Cuba*, 177
Rochester (New York), xviii, 4n*, 116, 134, 139–40, 142, 144, 149–50, 228–31, 229n*

Rodman, William Rotch, 5n*, 115
Rosaldo, Renato, 138
Rotch, William, Jr., 81–84, 114–15
Royal African Company, 86

Sailors' Home (London), 163–64, 168
Salisbury, Candace, 218n
Sanderson, Jeremiah Burke, 124, 191, 195, 196
Sargent, John T., 224
Sawyer, Enoch, 79
Sawyer, Lavinia Peyton, 47, 47n*, 111
Sawyer, Lemuel, 39n
Sawyer, Matthias E., 25–26, 25n†, 40–41, 44–45, 45n*, 50, 110
Sawyer, Samuel Tredwell: children of, with Harriet Jacobs, xxvi, 5n†, 90, 101, 111; as congressman, xxvi, xxviii–xxix, 5n†, 44n, 47n*, 103, 109–11; Harriet Jacobs as mistress of, xxv, xxvi, 90, 101; John Jacobs as slave of, xxvi, 5n†, 37–42, 40n, 44–45, 47–50, 108–13, 115; marriage of, 47, 111; purchase of Harriet's children by, 105–6, 108; slaves owned by, 42n; uncle of, 39n
Sawyer, William, 39n
Sayres, Edward, 234n
Schomburg Center, 192
scurvy, 87, 118, 119, 165, 272n10
sentimentalism, xx, xxiv–xxv, 5n†, 77, 99, 266n30
Sewall, Samuel, 132
Shaw, Lemuel, 123
Shklar, Judith, xiv, 263n6
Sims, Thomas, 32n
skin color, 71, 90, 92
Skinner, Joseph Blount, 14, 14n, 39, 39n, 100, 108
slave hunters, 23–27, 32, 46n, 55, 59, 81–82, 84
slave narratives: abolitionist framing of, xxi, xxiv, xxvii, 168–71, 197–98; autobiographical elements of, xxi, xxiv; conventions of, xx, xxi,